# THE WICKED AMONG US

# THE WICKED AMONG US

JAMES OWEN

A POST HILL PRESS BOOK
ISBN: 979-8-89565-210-7
ISBN (eBook): 979-8-89565-211-4

The Wicked Among Us:
Murder, Blackmail, and Book Collecting in the Ozarks


Cover design by Cody Corcoran

Post Hill Press
New York • Nashville
posthillpress.com

Published in the United States of America
2 3 4 5 6 7 8 9 10

To my dad, whose spirit urged me to live life and to get this book done.

To those portrayed in this book who can no longer speak their truths for themselves.

# TABLE OF CONTENTS

# CAST OF CHARACTERS

**David Adair**—Civil attorney for Alberta Comstock. Sought to withdraw from her case the day of the murder.

**Carol Aiken**—Greene County probate commissioner overseeing the Velma Brown Estate.

**Jose Alvarez**[1]—Paramour of Rolland's. Canceled trip to Springfield the weekend before the murder due to an argument.

**E. L. Anderson**—Mayor of Springfield in the 1960s. Political foe of Rolland's.

**Jim Arnott**—Deputy with the Greene County Sheriff's Office at the time of the murder. Elected sheriff during the investigation.

**Michael and Shaun Baumer**—Owners of a gas station outside of Springfield where Alberta allegedly left her truck the night of the murder.

**Alan Bayer**—Deputy with the Greene County Sheriff's Office. Drove Becky home from her interrogation.

**Hon. Don Bonaker**—Former officemate of Rolland's when they were both lawyers in the 1960s. Presiding judge over the Velma Brown will contest.

1 Denotes the actual name was changed

**Cliff Brown**—Attorney appointed to handle the Velma Brown Estate during will contest.

**Velma Brown**—Client of Rolland's. Benefactor of the Comstock family.

**Butch the Bulldog**—Client of Rolland's. Beneficiary of the owner's estate.

**Hon. Don Burrell**—Probate judge. Personal friend of the Comstocks. Gifted a gun to Alberta.

**Shane Cantin**—Criminal defense lawyer who represented Alberta in the *Stocker v. Comstock* civil case. Law partners with Tom Carver.

**Ray Juan Carlos**—Client of Rolland's in a high-profile criminal case in the 1960s.

**Tom Carver**—Criminal defense lawyer who represented Alberta in the *Stocker v. Comstock* civil case. Law partners with Shane Cantin.

**Alberta Comstock**—Rolland's ex-wife. Defendant in *Stocker v. Comstock* civil case. Murder suspect.

**Ashley Comstock**—Michael's daughter and beneficiary of Rolland's estate.

**Howard and Minnie Comstock**—Rolland's parents.

**Lois and Betty Comstock**—Rolland's sisters. Much older and almost out of the house by the time Rolland was born.

**Max Comstock**—Rolland's younger brother. Derisively nicknamed "Precious" by Rolland.

**Michael Comstock**—Son of Rolland and Alberta.

**Rodman Comstock**—Son of Rolland and Alberta.

**Rolland Comstock**—Lawyer, world-renowned book collector, politician, and decedent.

**Stephen Comstock**—Son of Rolland and Alberta.

**Sue Ann Comstock**—Rodman's ex-wife who derailed the Velma Brown will contest for the Comstock family.

**Hon. Michael Cordonnier**—Judge presiding over *Stocker v. Comstock* civil case.

**Robert Dante**—Deputy with the Greene County Sheriff's Office assigned to locate Michael Comstock the day after the murder.

**Irene Dixon**—Client of Rolland's. Potentially last person to talk to Rolland other than the murderer.

**Terrance Dotson**—Associate of Michael's. Told law enforcement Michael boasted of "killing and would kill again."

**Frank Duren**—Greene County detective initially in charge of the murder investigation.

**James Farrell**—Greene County sheriff's sergeant on call during Alberta Comstock's interrogation. Warned detectives to Mirandize the potential suspect.

**Becky Frakes**—Paralegal for Rolland Comstock. Executor of his estate. "Like a daughter" to Rolland.

**Jack Frakes**—Becky's husband.

**Mike Friend**—Owner of Oklahoma gun shop the Firing Range. Sold Alberta the "cheap .38."

**Dana Gray**—Greene County probate clerk. Had the misfortune of staffing the office when Alberta Comstock came in with her blackmail photos.

**"Doc" Groves**—Republican who beat Rolland for state representative in 1966.

**Jerry Hall**—Associate of Michael's. Claims to have seen Michael the night of Rolland's murder.

**Vicki Hayward[2]**—Velma Brown's niece. Filed will contest against Rolland and the Comstock family.

**Hon. John Holstein**—Mediator appointed to resolve disputes between Rolland and Alberta.

**Craig Hosmer**—One of Stuart King's law partners.

**Joyce Hull**—Stuart King's paralegal.

**Curtis Hunt**—Deputy with the Greene County Sheriff's Office whom Michael Comstock requested for his interrogation.

**Sammie Johnson**—Associate of Michael's. Told law enforcement Michael "fucked his dad up."

**Crystal Jones**—Stephen Comstock's girlfriend.

**Glenda Joplin**—Housecleaner for Rolland Comstock who testified she did not see the black briefcase the last time she was in the house.

---

2 Denotes the actual name was changed

**Ruby Keen**—Caregiver for Butch the Bulldog.

**Ron Killingsworth**—Greene County investigator who interviewed the Baumers.

**Stuart King**—Attorney for Faith Stocker in *Stocker v. Comstock* civil case.

**Carolyn Little**—Client of Rolland's. Greene County public administrator from 1980 to 2008.

**Billy Lowell**[3]—Neighbor of Velma Brown.

**Angela Maholy**—Deputy with the Greene County Sheriff's Office. First responding law enforcement officer to the crime scene.

**Evelyn Mangan**—Probate and estate planning attorney. Defense lawyer for Alberta Comstock in *Stocker v. Comstock* civil case.

**Debbie and Mac Mathis**—Neighbors of Stephen. Mac heard the gunshots on the night of the murder.

**Darrell Moore**—Greene County prosecutor.

**Todd Myers**—Prosecuting attorney assigned to the Comstock case.

**Rev. C. M. Newton**—Client of Rolland's. Pentecostal preacher charged with a noise ordinance violation.

**Shawn Pool**—Associate of Michael's. Was driving car titled in Rolland's name.

**Dean Price**—Lawyer submitted by Alberta's defense as an expert witness on the Fifth Amendment.

**Roy Quick**—Alberta's brother. She suggested to law enforcement he stole her gun.

**Carmel Rhoten**—Sister of Alberta Comstock. Provider of alibis.

**Johnnie Rhoten**—Son of Carmel Rhoten and nephew of Alberta Comstock. Was identified by the Baumers as one of the men who picked up Alberta's truck the day after the murder.

**Tim Richardson**—Civil attorney for Alberta Comstock. Initially represented Alberta on the *Stocker v. Comstock* civil case.

**Allen "Al" Rose**—Son-in-law of Rolland. Former associate of Rolland's.

**Sherry Rose**—Daughter of Alberta and Rolland. Wife of Allen Rose.

---

[3] Denotes the actual name was changed

**Mary Shearholt**—Deputy public administrator. Confronted Alberta when she tried to show off her blackmail photos.

**Judith Shepherd**—Rolland's first wife. Testified in the Pentecostal noise ordinance trial.

**Bob Stillings**—Personal lawyer to the Comstock family. Former associate and friend of Rolland's.

**Faith Stocker**—Daughter of Rolland and Alberta. Business partner with Rolland. Trustee of the Comstock trust. Plaintiff in *Stocker v. Comstock* civil case.

**Robin Stokes**—Roommates with Michael at the time of the murder and told authorities she threw away the clothes he was wearing on July 2.

**Tom Strong**—Rolland's lawyer in Velma Brown will contest.

**Hon. Miles Sweeney**—Judge who ruled on property dispute between Rolland and Alberta.

**Kevin Thomure**—Alberta's nephew. Only person listed on Alberta's phone records on the day of the murder.

**Rodman VanSant**—Alberta's first husband. Natural father of Michael, Faith, Rodman, and Sherry.

**Deborah Wade**—Greene County detective who conducted interviews of Alberta Comstock and Allen Rose.

**Ken Weatherford**—Greene County detective who took over the murder investigation after Frank Duren was promoted.

**Steve Westbrook**—Deputy with the Greene County Sheriff's Office assigned to locate Michael Comstock the day after the murder.

**Hon. Bob Wiley**—Divorce lawyer for Alberta Comstock.

**Dale Wiley**—Son of Bob Wiley. Represented Alberta Comstock on various lawsuits after the divorce.

**Tina Williams**—Attendant at a Walmart gas station who testified she saw Alberta's truck the night of the murder.

**John Zongker**—Baptist who called the police on the Pentecostal tent revival.

# PROLOGUE

The life of a lawyer is that of quiet, almost anonymous, desperation. You try your cases, or you settle them. You draft documents, and your client signs them. In most instances, the lawyer is merely swept into the conflicts of others. Their official role is to be an advocate for their client, but the important job is to be a cool head in a torrent of emotions and hostility.

Yet every town has lawyers who rise to the regional zeitgeist. Those are the ones with personalities that capture the intrigue, imagination, or infuriation of the public. In modern times, the lawyers with the most visibility are the personal injury figureheads who settle their clients' cases fast and cheap. By merit of this business model, these lawyers must work on volume to eke out a small fortune. Hence, they go on television talking about "your" rights and the entitlements being kept from "you." The bad things happening in your life aren't your fault; that's someone else's problem. Let me, the well-dressed professional, fix it for you. Their faces and slogans pollute the landscape on bright, tacky billboards.

While those types of lawyers are recognizable, they aren't particularly interesting. There are also legal personalities that fit their particular place in the world. Springfield, Missouri, sits near the top of the Ozarks, a former mountain range beaten down and eroded by time and forces of nature. In the buckle of the Bible Belt, some 350,000 souls reside in the metropolitan area. In that area, nearly seven hundred lawyers are members of the bar. That's one lawyer for every five hundred people, which is a lot.

At first glance, it is puzzling how a lawyer like Rolland Comstock was unable to get the same attention from his fellow Springfieldians. Rolland was a good lawyer. He practiced law on the town's working-class north side for well over forty years. He knew the ins and outs of the probate code and IRS regulations dealing with estates as well as any lawyer in Missouri. Rolland served in elected office, albeit briefly. When the local paper did a series on how estate planning and probate law work, they spent a week of coverage exclusively on Rolland's practice. Rolland was assigned a case to represent a dog who was going to receive a six-figure inheritance that caught the attention of the public, as well as national tabloids and even made it into a Johnny Carson monologue.

Rolland was colorful. Scratch that. Eccentric. Rolland was best known in town and around the world, really, as a book collector. He obsessed over having authors sign first-edition copies of their work. He built a three-story library in his palatial estate north of town. This is the same house where his family kept a pack of wolves as pets. They were hybrid wolves, but that was hard to tell by the way they looked and the way they howled. The neighborhood pets—those smart enough to stay away—feared them. The neighbors themselves just found it another impossibly odd thing about the family down the road who was much richer than they were.

As a result of this book-collecting hobby, Rolland was the subject of profiles in national and international newspapers. His legal writings were littered with literary references other lawyers could barely penetrate.

Yet Rolland occupied a part of Springfield the town was reluctant to discuss. While the other lawyers had civic club memberships and dined at places like the Metropolitan Grill or Steak & Ale, Rolland could be found at the Oz on Commercial Street. That was the gay bar on skid row, just a stone's throw from the homeless shelter known just as "the

Hotel." Rolland would peruse the aisles of the Old Highway 13 Book Store, an adults-only sort of place for people of all sorts of inclinations. These were the places Springfield knew existed but chose not to discuss. It was improper. Those spots were the underbelly Springfield preferred you not see. That's where Rolland spent his time.

Rolland was gay, although he denied that even when proof otherwise was presented to him. Hiding such things and repressing such feelings matched where and when he was born. In a town like Springfield before Ellen DeGeneres or *Will & Grace*, being openly gay wasn't even an option. You simply accepted the role as "confirmed bachelor" and didn't talk about it. If you opted for a public-facing job like that of a lawyer, you got married and had kids. You played the part of someone "normal."

Rolland did the latter. His first marriage didn't take. He married a woman. Alberta. She had four kids from another marriage. They had a son together. From all accounts, they got along well for nearly forty years. Stories vary about when Alberta knew, or should have known, about her husband. But everyone agrees it became impossible for her to ignore the truth in late 2004 when she filed for divorce. The couple's marriage was dissolved in about eight months' time. But the conflict and the fighting just kept going. It became ugly, as contentious as some lawyers had seen in their entire careers.

Rolland was found dead on July 3, 2007. Like Rolland's life, his death was complicated. Dysfunction is hard to kill, after all. Rolland's fights were inherited by his closest loved ones. He was murdered, that is conclusive. But there have been no arrests and no charges. Several people will point to the circumstances of the crime that seemingly left little to no evidence. Others will point to an investigation fraught with errors and omissions.

Even others will say law enforcement never made the investigation a priority. In death, Rolland belonged where he lived—in the shadows, away from public view. Rolland represented something shameful and sinful. Something that should remain forgotten. It was not "Springfield" as they saw it. Besides, whoever killed him wasn't going on a spree.

There was no harm posed to anyone else. Just another dead gay guy no one would worry about.

With the typical avenues of justice blocked off or otherwise unavailable, Rolland's daughter Faith Stocker took another route. That's when this story becomes about another lawyer, a lawyer who was able to process the chaos and turmoil of litigation with a steady hand and a steely gaze. Stuart King was no one's idea of a lawyer seeking justice for justice's sake. He liked the money that came along with the profession and developed a reputation as a guy who would take on any case as long as it offered a challenge. The case of Rolland Comstock became a case unlike any other he had ever taken, and its outcome proved to offer one surprise after the next. He would later say it was the defining case of his career.

This was too good of a story not to tell, not simply because of Rolland's death but also of his life. When I first met Rolland, I was a young lawyer looking for a job in the private sector. There was a posting for his firm, so I sent in a résumé. He called me and noticed I lived in Lawrence, Kansas, because of my law school and my first job after graduating.

"Tell me this," his gravelly voice hummed into the phone. "Who's the most famous author to live in Lawrence?"

I paused and wondered if this guy was for real. But I also thought this might be a trick question. "Well, I know Langston Hughes was raised there and graduated. He was a poet, so I am not sure he counts. So, I am going to say William Burroughs."

There was a silence on the other end, then, "Yes, yes. That's very good." I am almost certain I got the job then and there. Rolland was funny and interesting. The more I talked to him, the more I was shocked I never heard of him despite having lived in the Springfield area for almost my entire life. Even though probate law didn't seem very interesting to me, working for Rolland did seem interesting, and I took the job. I hoped that, as someone who only worked in the government prior, I could become a protégé to this person who was truly like no one I ever met. I could learn from the best.

Of course, I had no idea he was going through so much ugliness. There was not just the divorce, which was over by then. There were other lawsuits that stemmed from the divorce. His ex-wife was blackmailing him. She was showing compromising photos of Rolland around town. I didn't know any of this when I took the job. All these distractions left little time for Rolland to practice law, let alone mentor a young lawyer. Money was short. The tension in the office was palpable.

The bright side of the period countering the crippling stress I faced, was meeting the other people in the office. Becky was Rolland's paralegal and right-hand woman. I learned more from her than any other lawyer I've met. I also met Faith, Rolland's daughter, who became a good friend.

But I knew that I was the last one hired, and I would be the first one cut if things totally dried up. I had next to no clout to draw in clients. People who came to the firm were annoyed that they had to deal with me and not the big man himself. So, I fled to another firm. It's the other firm in this book, where Stuart was a partner. I became the probate/estate planning lawyer for Hosmer King & Royce. A few months later Rolland was killed, and Becky needed a place to work. I staked the entirety of my reputation at the new firm on her being hired to help spruce up my fledgling practice. It worked.

That's also how Faith found our firm: because Becky and I were there. The story told in this book comes from personal experience. Whenever I reference something involving me, I often just refer to myself as "the associate." I did my best to keep those references to a minimum. I am the least interesting person in this story.

I was also given a trove of information from Rolland's trust and his estate. Old newspaper clippings, personal files, and notes from his practice, from his book collecting, from his time in politics, and even his fights with the State of Missouri whether he could keep wolves as pets.

For a lot of his older cases, I had to rely on the courtroom staff from throughout Southwest Missouri. Dedicated public servants had to dig through dusty old banker boxes to find some random case from 1968, as an example. There's no way this book could have been written without those people helping me. But I also had to get help from the Springfield Public Library, the Missouri Historical Society, and the archival library at the University of Missouri–Kansas City.

I also received access to personal essays Rolland wrote. Sometimes, these resembled fictionalized versions of cases he worked on. These are lifted and quoted for this book as well, and I've done my best to identify them as such. Other times, he offered personal observations I quoted that help offer additional details about his life and experiences.

In terms of Rolland's observations from his personal and professional dealings, the estate provided me with many letters and memos he wrote. Sometimes, I offer a direct quote from his writing. Other times I have presented his observations from these writings as a thought. All of it is hemmed to make it as authentic to Rolland's frame of mind as possible.

There are passages in the book where dialogue and thoughts from living individuals have been recreated from my research in order to make the narrative more coherent. In some cases, the names of living persons were changed to protect their identities. I've noted that in the "Cast of Characters" section at the beginning of the book.

Having direct interviews with Becky Frakes, Faith Stocker, Stephen Comstock, Stuart King, and others who would not go on the record was also invaluable for telling the story of a lawyer whose death, and life, should not be forgotten and—at times—seems too fantastic to be real. Rolland Comstock was one of a kind and more than simply a crime victim. While the murder itself is interesting in a ghoulish way all true-crime stories are, I think you will like reading about Rolland and the time and place of his life even more.

# THE BUSY SIGNAL

The phone was busy. Becky Frakes assumed it meant her boss was dead.

Such was the routine every morning. The loyal paralegal called Rolland Comstock to see what was on tap for the day. The chat also put Becky's mind at rest that he was okay. If Rolland didn't answer or she got that busy signal, her mind always went to the worst place. But the safe assumption was he'd been working in his library late into the night. Maybe a few too many drinks. He probably clumsily left the phone off the cradle after talking to a book dealer.

On the morning of July 3, 2007, Becky did what she always did when Rolland didn't answer: She grabbed all the documents he needed to sign and got into her comically large truck to drive north of town to handle everything in person. Becky struggled to hoist her short, wiry frame into the cab. Her red hair and sharp features barely could be seen over the wheel.

It was a ten-minute drive through Springfield's depressed north side into the bucolic valley of the Little Sac River. The Comstock Estate was surrounded by eight feet of iron rod fence. What you couldn't see was the three feet of fence buried in the ground. This fence was not designed to keep people out, but rather to keep the wolves in.

Complaints were made to authorities by neighbors who were losing beloved pooches who ambled into the wolves' territory. Rolland built the massive fence as a compromise in order to keep his pets from being impounded. Yet problems persisted. Cats, succumbing to whatever pheromones drew them to the property, would climb atop the fence as the wolves waited patiently below. After the jump, the cats wouldn't even hit the ground.

Becky pulled up to the gate. It was closed. There used to be a code. But the automated system hadn't worked in years, so there was just a chain she had to slide over the latch.

Her truck crawled along the horseshoe driveway. She didn't want to hit one of the wolves but didn't see any signs they were out. Perhaps Rolland had the good sense to let them inside to escape the oppressive Ozark heat. The only evidence of the wolves were all the oversize chew toys in the driveway, and the frayed top of Rolland's Cadillac where the "puppies" pawed and chewed on the vinyl roof.

She pulled up to the house. The paint was chipped, and there were shingles dangling in the overgrown shrubbery after blowing off the roof. The columns looked to be on the verge of collapse. Becky remembered when Rolland and Alberta built this monstrosity. Rolland saw it not only as a monument to his money-making abilities as a lawyer, but also a place worthy of his book collection. Now, the house was just like its owner: a crumbling vestige of its former self.

The mansion was on the market because of the Comstocks' divorce settlement. There was no surprise that a run-down estate in the middle of the country with a cavernous room designed solely to hold thousands of books would receive little interest from the home-buying public. This was built with only one person in mind, and now a court was forcing him to sell it.

There'd been no showing in months. The real estate agent was cautious with giving tours to avoid catering to people simply curious about the book collection they had read about. Serious calls were sparse. The house was disgusting. In addition to Rolland letting it fall apart—and to be fair he had given much of his money to Alberta to settle other issues in the divorce—it smelled like wolf piss. The tile floors were splattered with dead ticks Rolland picked off the wolves and smashed with his shoe.

Of course, Becky remembered it was no longer on the market. The real estate listing expired the day before. Rolland's concern about his ex-wife's displeasure with the topic of the house was becoming more intense.

Alberta, the Mrs. Comstock of nearly forty years, had little to be happy about. Despite their advanced ages, she was confronted with a fact about her husband she could no longer accept. In the legal proceedings of the divorce, she called herself "humiliated" and "ruined."

It wasn't surprising to Becky. Or to anyone else. But the divorce, or at least the fighting that continued once the divorce was finalized, took its toll on Rolland nonetheless.

It wasn't as though his body could handle much stress. Rolland was diabetic. Had emphysema. Polyps in his lungs. High blood pressure. None of this kept him from smoking or drinking. He would often forget to eat. Becky could just imagine him slumped over his chair, having succumbed to any number of ailments. Or he could have drunkenly stumbled down the stairs. His demise could come in many forms. None of them would be a shock.

When she thought of Rolland lying there, she wondered what his pack of wolf-German shepherd hybrids would do. Protect him? Chew on him like one of those squeaky toys in the yard?

Stephen, Rolland's only biological child who lived in an apartment around the corner, left for court-mandated rehab days before. He wasn't around to check in on Dad, which Becky knew he was good to do. While Rolland and his daughter Faith had a good relationship, she only came by once a week or so. The other kids had fallen out of favor. Becky only worried about Michael, as he had been making noise lately about being out of money. Michael had a history with meth. Using it, making it, selling it. Threats against the family. Forging signatures. Stealing a gun from Alberta and Rolland. Bad news.

Rolland was fine, Becky told herself. She couldn't imagine her life otherwise. If something happened, there would be no more law practice, no more work. Becky worried about that every time she heard the busy signal. She would be cast out from the only job she knew, a life with plenty of stress but years of stability, money, and friendship.

Becky honked her horn. She wasn't going to get out alone unless she had to. Even after years of coming out to the property, the wolves did not trust her. She did not trust them. The pack would circle her while one would go up to nip at her fingers.

No one came out. Becky listened to country music and drummed the steering wheel. She didn't even see the dogs stirring around through the window.

Becky unmounted from her truck with her workbag in hand. Rolland never locked the back sliding door that led to the kitchen. Everyone who knew the house knew this.

She walked around, did a courtesy knock, and opened with a bellowing "Rolland!" There was no answer. She heard scurrying wolves farther into the house. There was a howling. A mournful howl caused the hair on her neck to rise. She opened the sliding door. The house reeked of stale cigarette smoke competing with a slight rotting smell from trash Rolland neglected to take out. "Rolland," she yelled again.

Becky saw him once she stepped into the kitchen. Rolland was lying on the ground. She saw his feet first. Then his face. Still. No movement. Not a twitch. The eyes still open to the last thing they ever saw.

Her hand went to her face. Becky's instinct told her not to touch him. Not to move anything. Just call 911. Cell phone reception in the house was terrible. She ran outside to find a signal.

Everything was a blur. Becky didn't see the two bullet holes in the wall behind the body. She did not hear the television blaring from the bar area. Becky didn't register the blood. She did not see the signed first-edition copy of *Lord of the Flies*—Rolland's most prized and valuable artifact—sitting out on the kitchen table next to where he lay.

Becky did not notice the trail of crimson wolf tracks all over the house, their paws reddened from their master's blood as they circled his body on the floor in order to protect him one last time.

# THE FILTHY LUCRE

Rolland was born to Howard and Minnie Comstock on November 9, 1936. He grew up at 2230 North Rodgers in Springfield, Missouri, just north of the bustling Commercial Street railroad area. The neighborhood was well-off compared to the rest of the country still toiling in the Great Depression. The Comstock home was modest-sized with two bedrooms, a kitchen, mudroom, and a living room with a bay window that jutted out over the porch. There was a white picket fence out front and an outhouse in the back.

Dad was a fireman. A tall and stout man, with a bull head and a thick tousle of hair cut "high and tight," he hauled heavy hoses and breathed in the soot and smoke of burning wood and smoldering brick. The job caused him a multitude of physical problems, from a bad back to a constant cough.

Minnie stayed home. She dressed frumpily and wore her long dark hair flat with a part in the middle. Rolland had two sisters, Lois and Betty. Both were significantly older and almost out of the house by the time he came around. They were never close, and Rolland had no contact with either of them throughout his life.

Rolland also had a younger brother named Max. Rolland hated the attention Max took away from him. Older brother referred to him as

"Precious" all the way up until little brother died and Rolland was heard to remark, "The world is a little better off without Precious in it."

Even at an early age, his parents were aware of Rolland's unusual intelligence. Unbothered by cousins who were ordered to play with him, Rolland would quietly deal himself cards or read a magazine.

His parents took him to the neighborhood St. John's Episcopalian Church. Later in life, Rolland would discuss faith in stark terms: "Episcopalians are mostly an upper-class set whose morality is to be viewed through a stained-glass prism in a church that permits most sins and nurses a fondness for the bottle and a huge vanity for its own physical attributes—an elite endorsed by the very hand of God. It is a good church to join especially as it offers a passport to an even brighter one at the end of the road."

While his family wasn't particularly religious, Rolland became intrigued by the power of the pulpit—the ability to sway the parishioners with verve and scripture. As someone who liked to read from an early age, Rolland found the symbolism used by the Episcopal church appealing. He would sit up and memorize stories from study books handed out in Sunday school.

His voice always boomed, eventually grated by smoking and alcohol, and this made Rolland predestined for oration. On the Friday nights before Mass, Rolland would stand on the corner near the church regurgitating his Bible lessons and imploring any passersby to save their souls the following day. While he never considered the ministry, young Rolland noticed his street preaching got the neighbor's attention. People would listen to him.

As he got older, Rolland consumed books voraciously. Since he liked reading them over and over, Rolland chose to buy them rather than rely on the local library. He turned this into a vocation, "renting" comic books out of the garage for a nickel a day. If the comic book was never returned, he would serve as collector and demand the full price.

Around the same time, he started helping neighbors with their taxes. Rolland was good with numbers and details in school. Someone remarked he might be able to do that sort of work when he was older.

Not willing to wait, he checked out some IRS guidance documents from the library and figured anyone could do it, including a preteen.

Later in life, he said his motivation for working at a young age was to avoid being poor. Rolland would say—as a child—that all his family could afford to eat was chicken. "I hated the taste of that bird, and I don't want to ever feel like I have to eat it ever again."

By the time he turned sixteen years old and attended Central High School, Rolland opened his own bookshop on Commercial Street. He named it Addison's, after the seventeenth-century English poet and essayist who founded *Spectator* magazine. He rented the second floor of a shoe store for fifteen dollars a month. Rolland's reason for renting the space had nothing to do with wanting to become a book proprietor. His collection had simply grown so it would no longer fit in the family house.

Rolland soon realized, as he spent weekends categorizing and labeling the books, it wasn't so much his interest in reading but in obtaining them; for trying to find books considered so rare and unique he could call them his own. He wanted a good story to tell—where he got it, what the person traded in exchange, trying to piece together the imperfections of the copy, and how it affected the value and quality. He would share his stories and opinions on the book with his fellow Commercial Street merchants, who found the young man odd but rather beguiling.

A reporter for the *Springfield News & Leader* detailed Rolland's struggle to run a business as a high schooler. The article's accompanying photo offers a glimpse of fifteen-year-old Rolland: awkward and tall, in between the baby fat of his youth and the alcoholic bloat he later obtained. He's fitted with a seersucker suit draped over his frame and a bow tie adorning his neck. His black hair is slicked back in a pompadour atop a narrow face, his eyes bespectacled with horn-rimmed glasses right above his pointed nose and a toothy smile.

After high school, Rolland took the money he'd saved up from preparing taxes and traveled to France. In the fall, he enrolled at Drury University, just a few blocks away from Commercial Street and across from his high school. "I was the only person on the campus in the late

1950s who had a copy of *Howl* and was one of the two members of the Young Democrats Club," Rolland later wrote.

After graduation and a stint teaching French at a nearby country school, Rolland began pursuing a master's degree in British history at the University of Kansas City (now the University of Missouri–Kansas City). He was always drawn to history and more so to England, with its formality and pomp. Rolland was an Anglophile, making a point to wear orange on St. Patrick's Day signifying his allegiance to England.

Rolland returned to Springfield frequently, primarily because he found it easier to focus on his writing when he was home. Plus, there was the matter of Addison's and his neighbors' tax returns.

Rolland's professors gave his work high marks, particularly for his gruesome thesis on corporal punishment in fourteenth-century Britain. He began with a passage from the 1951 Daphne du Maurier novel, *My Cousin Rachel*, describing an unrefined and violent past. Rolland used this to emphasize how the British viewed reform at the time:

> *They used to hang men…in the old days. Not any more, though. Now, when murderers pay the penalty for his crime, he does so (in private), after a fair trial at the Assizes. It is better so. Like a surgical operation. And the body has a decent burial, though a nameless grave. I can remember as a little lad seeing a fellow hang in chains where the four roads met. The rain had rotted his breeches, if not his body, and strips of worsted drooped from his swollen limbs like paper.*

But there was something nagging him about the pursuit of a career in academics. Specifically, the money. Even during his master's studies, Rolland would seek out new books for his collection. The tax preparation business didn't work as well in a town like Kansas City where he was not established, and no one knew him as "Howard's boy." There would be no way to make enough money teaching to afford his efforts to locate the perfect book. One night over dinner, Howard suggested

Rolland would be a good lawyer. "You like to talk and read." The comment caught Rolland's attention.

In an interview about his book collection, Rolland laid out his quandary. "I was at a crossroads. What was I going to do? Chase a PhD in history or practice law? I opted to practice law for the money it would bring."

Rolland would call it his desire for the "filthy lucre."

# CIRCLING WOLVES

The operator said deputies would come out and do a "wellness check." Becky nodded at the phrase. They would find nothing well about the situation.

Becky called Faith and told her what she saw. Faith heaved a sigh. She, too, had been expecting this day for what seemed like ages.

"I am heading to the house. I will be there in a few minutes. Just stay put." Faith had to center herself. Find her purse. Get her glasses. Make sure she had enough cigarettes to get her through a long day.

Rolland and Faith had the most traditional relationship of any of the kids. Faith was a bookkeeper and accountant, following partially in Rolland's footsteps. Starting at age twelve, she served as the office receptionist during tax season, presiding as people brought in their receipts and pay stubs.

They worked in the same office and referred their clients to each other. Business-wise, estate planning and probate was intertwined with taxes. Faith could take care of the numbers and Rolland could take care of drafting documents. Their personalities suited one another.

Faith and Rolland just talked Sunday night, two days before. Rolland seemed relieved Stephen was off to rehab. Rolland told her he signed the contract on a house just a few blocks from Faith. Much smaller than his estate but a nice place with room for most of his books.

The rest of the collection—as well as the wolves—would be a topic for another day. Faith sensed a peace from her dad she hadn't heard in three years at least. Perhaps the battle between her mother and father would end once Rolland relinquished possession of the home. Faith worried Rolland would never see the end of the fight.

Of the five kids, only the girls survived childhood with any functionality and without addiction. Faith certainly was the only one who could be described as independently successful thanks to her pairing with Rolland. While she remained neutral during the divorce, she sympathized with her mother. After the divorce was over and things became acrimonious, Faith began to abhor Alberta's desire to ruin her adoptive father's life.

Faith did what she could to help. She would check on Rolland from time to time and make him meals. She offered to have Rolland move in with her, but there was certainly no room in her house for the books. Nor had Faith ever gained the trust of the wolves. It was the primary reason she limited her time with her dad. They would try to take a bite out of her every time she went there.

As she drove, Faith thought about their last conversation. Rolland talked about how the listing for the estate was expiring the next day. Even though he found a house, Rolland knew his ex-wife would be angry when she realized the deadline had come and gone with no sale. No hope for a sale.

Faith's mind turned to what would happen next. She was the trustee of his estate. Death meant planning a funeral, searching through bank statements, notifying creditors, dealing with real estate agents, and winding down the firm. There were no other lawyers working with Dad, so the place would close. Bad news for Faith's business, too.

Alberta's lawsuits would continue, and Faith would have to step in for her father.

At least now there would be a grave Alberta could spit on.

Faith's gripped hands were quaking, her lips quivering. She wanted to call Stephen, but she wasn't even sure of the name of the facility.

Rolland and Alberta had high hopes for him, but Steve had too many problems, first and foremost Michael's influence on him.

Her car pulled up to the gate to see Becky pacing along the end of the driveway. There were two Greene County Sheriff's Office cars at the top of the hill by the house. Another by the road. Faith pulled into the driveway.

Becky's eyes were welled up and swollen. All she could do was shake her head. Faith tried to process while giving Becky a hug.

"I know he's dead. I know."

The words bounced around Faith's head, trying to find a place to land.

"Beck, did they say what happened?"

Becky used her shirt to dab her eyes. "No, they haven't said anything. I kept asking. They took my phone. They took my truck. I don't know what they are doing."

Faith walked over to the patrol car parked in the ditch. The deputy was reading into a radio. She announced she was a daughter and asked what they knew.

"Nothing," the authority mumbled. "Still being investigated, ma'am."

"Can I go in?"

The deputy shook his head as the radio blared behind him. "No one is being allowed in right now. It's an active scene." Faith just stood there uncertain what to do with herself.

An ambulance with flashing lights pulled up to the gate, and the driver talked to Becky. She lifted the chain on the gate. When they got to the house, a deputy walked up to the driver. Something was said, the lights were turned off, and everyone disappeared inside.

For an hour, Faith and Becky stood at the end of the driveway. Faith smoked. Becky paced. Becky, who never had a cigarette in her life, thought about taking up the habit. The two talked, but nothing registered for either of them. They waited for something, anything that would let them know what happened. They watched as other patrol cars pulled in and drove up to the house. Becky would lift the chain every time and warn them about the wolves. Each time, the deputies would look up with confusion and concern. "Wolves?"

Deputy Angela Maholy was the first in the house. The pool of blood was massive. She saw the bullet holes in the wall behind him. Backup was called; Maholy knew now she was going to need to call in every available unit on the day before a holiday. The wellness check was now the site of "unknown and suspicious" circumstances, and assistance was required.

"Homicide likely," Maholy noted to the deputy on the other end of the line.

She pulled out latex gloves and felt for a pulse on the neck. Not a trace. Maholy tried to lift the body to see the injuries, but the blood and Rolland's girth made that too challenging for one person.

The deputy heard scuffling and scurrying. She did a search, making her best attempt to scan the cavernous rooms. Maholy kept seeing dog-like shadows darting here and there. *That must be the wolves the woman outside warned about.*

Maholy looked for signs of a break-in. While the patio door entering the kitchen was opened—Becky didn't stop to close it as she left—there were no signs that any entry had been forced. No broken windows or kicked-in doors. There did not appear to be any kind of alarm system. Maybe the owner thought the gate and the wolves was enough security.

The house was unkempt but didn't look ransacked. This wasn't a break-in.

The blood around Rolland coalesced, but there was no way of knowing how long he'd been there without forensic review.

There was also something Maholy didn't see: a gun.

***

"Ma'am. Are you Faith Stocker?"

"Yes, yes. I am the daughter."

"Of course." He looked at his notes. "I'm Corporal Johnson of Greene County. Deputy Maholy is securing the home, and I'm working on checking out the outer perimeter. Outside the house." Faith hadn't noticed him walking down from the house, as her mind was far away.

Faith nodded. The deputy continued to eye the road as he talked. "Ms. Stocker, I am going to walk the ditches. We also need to look for evidence. Standard procedure. But Detective Wade will want to ask you questions when other officers arrive. Will that be all right with you?"

Faith wiped her brow. "Can you just tell me what happened to Dad?"

"We don't know. The victim is unresponsive with no pulse. We are securing him for transport. We're securing the location. It appears suspicious. But that's all we know."

Becky started to cry. Faith went into another daze. "Suspicious." "Victim." Cold terms lacerating the unforgiving humidity.

Johnson muttered into his radio that the animals were wolves and animal control needed to come out immediately. He offered some assurances to the women and walked away as he stared down at the ditch. Becky and Faith watched, wrecked with disbelief.

Eventually, Detective Deborah Wade arrived and asked Faith to come with her to the sheriff's office to take a statement. Faith could take her car as long as she followed the detective, Wade assured. She agreed right away. Detective Wade said they would come and get Becky "when they were ready." Faith nodded. Becky sighed.

After Faith left, another law enforcement officer walked up and asked, "Do you know anything about these dogs? We've got the one we've got collared. The other one is proving to be a real problem. It's taken a bite at one of our men."

Becky developed a puzzled look on her face as she tried to process talking about these wolves on top of everything else. "Other one? Sir, there should be one more. Rolland had three dogs."

A pause. "We've only seen the two." A longer pause. "It could be hiding. But we've looked everywhere already."

Becky looked out toward the woods across the road. It'd probably gotten loose when the gate was opened.

*That poor dog*, Becky thought as her eyes welled up again. *He'll never make it on its own.*

***

The Greene County Judicial Courts Facility was a gray bureaucratic box a few blocks south of Rolland's office. Faith was ushered by Detective Wade through the security as they walked to a windowless, sterile room with a camera and audio equipment away from the public area.

Wade explained to her, finally, what happened. It was a homicide. Faith's stomach dropped at the word. The sheriff's office needed to know who to look at. The detective told Faith they would not Mirandize her because they were only trying to get information and didn't consider her a suspect. Faith understood. At least, she was nodding to the words. None of it was landing.

The camera light clicked on. Wade marked the time as 10:53 a.m.

"When was the last time you talked to your father?" Wade started.

"Sunday. A few days ago."

"Other than you, who's Mr. Comstock's immediate family?"

"Rodman, Stephen, and Michael are my brothers. Sherry Rose is my sister. Stephen is Rolland's only blood child. The rest of us were Alberta's by a previous marriage, but Rolland officially adopted all of us."

Wade had to take her time to identify the names. "Alberta. Wife?"

"Oh, no," Faith declared. "Divorce started in '04. It's done, but there's still a couple of lawsuits between the two of them."

"Tell me about that," Wade implored.

Faith told her all about it.

"Where does she live now? When was the last time you talked to her?"

"Fairland, Oklahoma. I don't talk to her. Not since the divorce. She thinks I took Dad's side. Which I did. Eventually.

"I don't blame Mom for divorcing him, but she took it too far. She's bitter. She's vengeful. You should look at her."

"Being bitter is no reason to kill someone. Why would she kill her ex-husband?"

"The only thing left between them was to sell the house and split the proceeds. She thought Rolland was dragging his feet because he didn't want to move out. She needed the money. Alberta was convinced Dad was trying to keep her away from her money."

Money as a motive made more sense to Wade. "What about his other kids? How are they with your father?"

"Stephen and I are the only two who talk with him."

"Do you know how we can get ahold of Stephen?"

"Right now? He's been at a rehab clinic since Sunday. My dad mentioned that on our phone call."

"What kind of rehab is it?"

"Drugs, mainly. He tested positive for drugs while being on probation."

"Why was he on probation?" Wade asked.

"Oh, drugs, mainly."

Wade made a note of this. Son has a criminal background. "What about the other kids? You said they weren't close with…"

"Oh yeah. Michael was stealing money from Dad. He's been barred from the house. Barred from the office. But he also calls around for money. I won't give him anything. He's scary. I want nothing to do with him."

"Why is he scary to you?"

"He's violent. He's on drugs, too. He's threatened to kill me. Threatened to kill Dad."

Faith recalled a memory from when she was sixteen and her parents bought her a car. She walked up to Michael, who initially appeared to be tooling with the engine under the hood. When she asked him if he saw anything that needed fixing, Michael turned around and put a screwdriver to her throat.

"You tell Mom and Dad you saw me doing this, I will fucking kill you." Michael's eyes locked with hers in a frenzy. She had no idea what was happening, so she just nodded. Faith was able to squeak out a "yes, yes" as Michael moved the screwdriver away, and proceeded to remove the battery from under the car's bonnet and carry it off into the night.

When Faith was unable to drive her vehicle, she had to explain to Rolland and Alberta what happened. They confronted Michael about it, who said he just needed some spare cash to catch a movie. They sent him off, and Rolland had to call his mechanic to see how much it would cost to replace the battery. He got off the phone and handed Faith a wad of bills.

"Sorry, I can't help you, honey. I don't know a goddamned thing about cars." That was the last time Rolland or Alberta mentioned the situation to Faith.

"When did Michael threaten to kill your dad?" Wade asked, regaining Faith's attention.

"I don't remember. Might have been a few years now. I haven't heard Dad mention that for a while."

Wade looked at her notes and asked about Rodman.

"Not been in the picture for a while. I mean, like well over a decade. Strange guy. He just hasn't had much contact with Dad. Drinks all day, as far as I have heard."

"Also, Sherry. What's her relationship with your dad?"

"She married Dad's old partner Al Rose. They hate Dad. Dad asked Al about some missing money. They broke up around ten years ago. Al is sort of dangerous, too."

"Dangerous how?"

"Hangs out with a rough crowd. Runs guns. Trains with survivalists. He always frightened me. He would break into my office and mess with my computer. But that was a long time ago, I guess."

"Would he have any reason to harm Rolland?"

"Maybe some time ago. Al wants to make money no matter what he has to do. He's got nothing to gain from anything happening to Dad. So, I doubt it."

"Who do you think might have done it?"

Faith didn't hesitate.

"I would look at Mom or Michael. I would look in the kitchen drawer. If there's no cash in there, Michael took it after he killed him. No question."

***

As Faith's interrogation began, Becky peered through the fence watching the activity around the grounds. More deputies were searching the ditches. One watched the road and took notes of license plates of cars driving by. There were others combing the yard.

The deputies were watching her right back.

Becky needed to call her kids, Chris and Ashley, to tell them she was all right before they heard this from someone else. Would the police go to her house looking for clues? They wouldn't, and this became a big point for defense lawyers later on.

Becky was approached by Detective Alan Bayer, who asked if she would submit to a gunshot residue test.

"A what? What are you talking about?"

"Ma'am, it is a test where I swab down your hand for gunpowder residue."

"Yes, I can do it. Wait!" She stopped. He listened. "I was firing off fireworks with my kids last night. Is that going to do something to the result?" *That sounded like something a guilty person would say*, she thought the moment she said it.

Bayer assured her the fireworks wouldn't, although the deputy could have no certainty of that. When a gun is fired, the muzzle projects residue containing burnt and unburnt gunpowder. This can travel as far as five feet away from the gun and can last on someone's hand anywhere from four to eight hours after the gun is shot, which is what the test is supposed to indicate.

But results are never conclusive whether someone even used a gun. A clean sample can simply be the result of someone who thoroughly used the right combination of soap and hand sanitizer. Additionally, someone can test positive if they were standing near someone who shot a gun or were near any kind of gunpowder, like fireworks. But when a crime involves a gun, everyone at the scene gets tested.

They took the swab of Becky's hands and asked if she would get in a deputy's car and go down to the Judicial Courts Facility for some questions. Becky agreed, still distressed about events over the past few hours.

At the sheriff's department, in the room next to Faith's as she was finishing up and taking her own gunshot residue test, Becky gave mainly the same answers to the same questions. But she had some details Faith did not have.

"Rolland was supposed to have a visitor this weekend. But they got into a fight, and he didn't end up coming."

"A visitor? Do you mean a friend or a relative?"

Becky hated talking about this, but she knew it might be important. So, she spilled her guts about the men Rolland met online. About the Mexican condo. About the photos she printed off for her boss because he didn't know how to use a computer.

This led her to explaining about the man Rolland met online a year ago. His name was Jose, and he was from Texas. He was a college student who'd been up to Springfield several times. All trips paid for by the law firm. Becky even met him on one occasion. Seemed all right. Becky remembered earlier in the year when Rolland confessed that this new love interest could be "angry" and "violent."

Certainly, not all right.

"Did Mr. Comstock say what the fight was about? With this Jose fella."

Becky shrugged. "Didn't seem like my business. I just wanted to cancel it so we could get the money refunded." The law firm could use the money.

"You don't know if it had anything to do with Jose being 'angry' and 'violent'?"

"I don't know. If I were to guess, I would say it was over money. Rolland was running out of it, and I am sure that's the only reason Jose was, you know, interested in him."

Seems anytime anyone fought with Rolland it was over money, Becky thought. That's all anyone cared about with him. That's how he tried to get his kids to love him. Alberta loved him so long as she got a good allowance.

"Do you think it's possible he came up here this weekend anyway?"

"If he had been at the house, Rolland would have mentioned it yesterday. Plus, Rolland always needed me to help with things like travel arrangements."

After the interview was over, another deputy met Becky outside the interview room and gave her cell phone back. Its history included phone calls to Rolland at the times Becky said she called him every day. Some texts to her husband and kids. Normal stuff.

Becky asked about her truck, and Bayer said it might be much later before the department could release it, so he offered to drive her home.

Becky's phone was inundated with missed calls and messages, from her kids and also from clients and friends. *What's going on?* she wondered. How did anyone know what was happening? Becky barely knew what happened.

As Deputy Bayer drove her home, Becky called the office and spoke to the stricken receptionist Micaela, who heard about the murder on the local news. The phones were jammed with clients calling. Micaela said one call stuck out. Irene Dixon, who was having some estate planning updated, mentioned talking to Rolland the night before.

Even in the haze of everything, Becky knew this might be crucial. "Did she say when she talked to Rolland?"

About 6:30 or 7:00 p.m., as detectives later found out. Dixon said Rolland called to give her an update on her paperwork. During the conversation, Irene asked how he was doing. Rolland said things were great even if his legs were hurting. Just a hot night playing with the dogs, he said.

Becky looked at Bayer, who was on his phone. He'd also been listening to Becky and moved his mouth from the phone.

"This is good," he said. "Make sure we get everything like this."

Becky nodded. She was now knee-deep in a murder investigation.

***

Late in the morning, Frank Duren reported to the scene. Though he would become the chief investigator on the case, Deputy Sheriff Jim Arnott had simply put him in charge of the crime scene for the time being. Duren was a slender, bald man with a slight dusting of facial hair. He got a quick brief from Maholy about the decedent's location, the bullet wounds, the wolves, and the two women who were now downtown being questioned.

Duren regrettably got used to seeing bodies in his career, but there was always a shock when you first see a person splayed out on the ground. Someone's loved one. Someone's friend. Also, almost always, knowing it was more likely than not that someone close to them was responsible.

His eyes scanned over details of the scene. Looking for signs of what might have been going on when this murder happened. Or something that was out of place. The television was on. The phone off its hook. Had someone done that before the murder?

Duren saw the book on the table. *Lord of the Flies.* It would be out of place in Duren's kitchen. This was a book he had to read in high school. But this guy was different. Clearly a bit of a book nut.

Duren peeked his head into the library. He'd remember something about a quirky lawyer living north of the city limits who had this massive book collection. Seemed strange at the time he heard it; something someone does with too much time and too much money on their hands. Looking at it in person, it was amazing. The woodwork itself looked elaborately handcrafted. The rolling ladders seemed like something you'd see in a mansion in a movie.

*How many books are in here?* Tens of thousands, perhaps. Why was that one book out?

Duren went back into the kitchen and stepped over the body to look at the bullet holes in the wall. Without measuring, it was hard to tell Rolland's precise height. But these holes looked like they were over his head if he had been standing up when the bullets were fired.

Hovering above, Duren could see a gaping hole in the back of the departed's head. That looked like an entry wound. If the bullet exited Rolland's body from the front, and there were wounds on his face suggesting the possibility, nothing suggested any bullet exited the back of the head and hit the wall. But could someone have shot so many times and just missed? Were they that bad of a shot? Or was it just someone nervous about using a gun on another person?

Duren ordered the dusting of the entire premises for fingerprints. On the doors. On the walls. Even on the gates in front of the house. They also needed to check for footprints both indoors and outdoors.

Someone passed by, and Duren told them to get an imprint of Rolland's shoe before the coroner arrived. That way they would know what shoe prints the victim left, and those could be distinguished from any other prints.

Duren looked down at the ground around the body. The initial report was that no weapon had been located. He asked if anyone picked up casings.

"No casings," someone yelled back.

That meant one of two things. It could have meant someone picked them up. But it did not appear anyone tampered with the scene.

Or it meant the gun used was a revolver. If it had been a revolver, the spent casings would stay in the cylinder and not be discharged to the floor. With a semi-automatic gun, the spent casings are ejected.

Duren looked at the bullet holes in the wall. "Let's bore these out, please." Deputies hustled back to their vehicles to find tools needed for the task.

Duren kneeled down. He saw an entry wound in the abdomen as well as the wound on Rolland's face. Upon closer inspection, it was a grazing mark on his chin. Sloppy shots, too. But a shot taken from the front. The bullets in the back of the head suggested the killer wanted to make sure the job got done.

Duren walked back to the library, about to ask someone dusting there to make sure they went through every level to see if anything looked disheveled or missing.

There, he noticed a black vinyl Coach briefcase. He snapped on a pair of latex gloves and began to look through the contents.

Legal documents. Real estate documents. A health-care power of attorney for Alberta Comstock. Was this the old guy's briefcase? Lawyers are usually a pretty organized bunch. This looked as though someone just crammed a bunch of paperwork into a bag. One investigator walked by and noticed a wolf pendant pinned toward the top of the case.

Duren bagged up the documents and ordered another deputy to fingerprint each piece of paper as well. As the documents were being arranged, the briefcase was placed back on the couch.

***

After Faith and Becky were interrogated, the sheriff's office had to contact other family members. They started with Stephen because records indicated he lived in an apartment nearby. Though Becky and Faith told detectives Stephen was a few hours away, nobody at the scene was aware of this fact.

When Rolland and Alberta bought the property in 1976, Rolland purchased stone cottages just around the corner that had once been a motor lodge next to McDaniel Lake. The lake wasn't much of an attraction; it was just a municipally owned reservoir for Springfield's water supply that permitted neither boating nor swimming. You could fish, but the lake was so far away from the highway many locals didn't even know it was there.

Rolland never had luck finding decent tenants—most people desiring to hide in the country did so because they could drink, smoke pot, or cook meth in relative peace—but at least Michael or Stephen could live there when they had no other place to go.

Deputy Steven Westbrook and Detective Robert Dante were directed to the unit with "Comstock, S." on the mailbox. This house was bigger than the other cottages, with a big, airy porch. They knocked on the door and a woman answered.

Her name was Debbie Mathis, and she said a "Crystal Jones" asked her to secure the apartment because Crystal was going to go pick Stephen up from rehab. Crystal was Stephen's girlfriend, Debbie explained. The detectives laid out the situation with Rolland in basic terms and asked if they could look around the apartment. Debbie stepped aside and let them in.

The apartment was roomy but run-down. As they checked the upstairs and the basement, Mathis followed, explaining she was a neighbor and knew Stephen and Crystal well. She said there was no way it was Stephen because he went to do a rehab stint and hadn't been home since Sunday.

"You've not seen him in the past few days?"

Mathis shook her head.

"What about Michael Comstock? Is he ever around?"

Before she could answer, Debbie's husband Mac pulled up. While he was still in his idling vehicle, Westbrook approached and asked if they had seen or heard anything unusual the night before.

Mac said he was working on his van and heard seven or eight "booms" between 8:00 and 8:20 p.m. that sounded like gunshots coming from the direction of the Comstock house.

Dante asked the obvious question given the timing of the holiday. "How did you know they weren't fireworks?"

"Out in the country," Mathis said matter-of-factly, "you're used to what a gunshot sounds like."

They asked Mac about Michael. He confirmed Rolland kicked Michael out of the fishing cottages "maybe over a year ago" but he would still come around. "Yelling and screaming at people, usually."

The detective asked Mathis if he knew where Michael might be living now or if he could identify his vehicle. Mac did not know but was certain he worked at a place called Jerry's Appliance and Repair on Commercial Street and usually drove around in a company truck.

***

During their interview, Detective Wade asked Faith for phone numbers for her other siblings. She confessed to having no contact with any of them.

"Each and every one of them hated Rolland and hated me for staying close to him."

Michael, Faith noted, had been cut off entirely in the spring of 2005. She remembered that specifically because Rolland wrote all the kids a letter about it. Titled "My Present Attitude Towards Michael," Rolland accused Michael of stealing a brand-new riding lawn mower from Rolland's garage after scaling the fence. Further, Rolland alleged, Michael tried—but failed—to cash a $1,000 check by forging Alberta's signature.

"I just found out today he succeeded in forging a check with my name on it." Rolland assured the family he would not demand a refund for the money because then they would turn it over to the police and Michael "would probably get an additional five years for that" given his previous run-ins with the law.

"Never again will I do anything for him or allow him to come on my property. He is the prime example of a sociopath." Rolland ended the letter by telling the family he intended to take care of Michael's daughter, Ashley, no matter what happened.

***

Faith shared Crystal's number with Detective Wade. Crystal answered and said Stephen already left the rehab clinic by the time she got there. Wade asked who picked him up. "The place thinks it was his brother."

Crystal also told the detective she talked to Rolland Sunday night to let him know Stephen had made it to the rehab clinic and was settling in. She said Rolland sounded upbeat. He was going to the grocery store to get dog food for the wolves. She asked if she could get that for him, as she promised Stephen to help the old man with odds and ends.

Rolland told her he needed to get out of the house but appreciated the offer. That was all Crystal knew.

Wade asked if Crystal would let her know when she was back so they could set up a meeting. Crystal said that would be no problem.

"Do you have any way of reaching Sherry or Michael or Rodman?"

"No one knows how to get ahold of Rodman. Steve only mentioned him once or twice." Michael, Crystal said, would normally come by when he needed something and generally had no working number.

As far as Sherry went, Crystal talked to her that morning. "Sherry called me this morning and told me about Rolland. That he died."

Based on what Crystal said, Wade could assume, Sherry knew about Rolland's death before Becky discovered him.

"Where does she work?"

"She's a receptionist for her husband. He's a lawyer, too."

Wade asked for Sherry's number, but Crystal said Al and Sherry were skittish about giving it out.

Wade implored her. Crystal relented and provided the number for the Law Offices of Al Rose. Wade thanked her and they hung up, then dialed the number.

"Law offices."

"Yes, this is Detective Wade from the Greene County Sheriff's Office. I am looking for a Sherry Comstock. I meant Rose. Sherry Rose."

"This is a professional answering service. There is no one at that office today. I can forward a message."

Wade explained it was urgent and asked for a direct number.

"Well, I will let them know," the voice said curtly. "Thank you." Click. Wade called Crystal back to ask if there was other contact information, like an address. All Crystal knew was Sherry and Al were staying at a place owned by a doctor in an older subdivision on the south side of town, but she didn't have a specific address.

Wade got the doctor's full name and could figure out the rest. She called dispatch to look up the address. About that time, her cell phone lit up with an undisclosed number. She answered.

"Who is this?" a deep baritone voice boomed before Wade could say anything.

"This is Detective Deborah Wade from the Greene County Sheriff's Office. Is this Mr. Rose?"

"Yes, that's me. Is this about Rolland?" The man's tone didn't change.

"Yes, it is. I need to talk to your wife, Sherry."

"I put her in bed. She's beyond upset about this. I heard about Rolland this morning in court. I went back out to the truck and told Sherry. She wanted to talk to Michael. So we closed the office to go find him."

"You talked to Michael?"

"We both went to Michael's place of work, where he completely freaked out. We tried to calm him down. Said we would take him out for coffee. He declined and took off."

"Can you get your wife? This is important."

The calm in his voice broke a bit. "She's upset. Can I have her call you when she's up?"

Wade sighed. "No problem at all. Thanks for your time."

There were a few things about the phone call with Rose that didn't add up. How did he know that Rolland was dead? So early in fact that Rose found out in court, went to talk to Michael, and allowed Michael enough time to drive to Clinton to pick up his brother?

Dispatch buzzed. Someone was able to confirm an address where the Roses were staying.

***

There was the main house with a long driveway. While there was a security gate, it was wide open. Wade got out and rang the call box. No one responded. Wade drove up to the main house and could hear music around the corner. A fence opening led her to a guest quarters, where she knocked on the door.

Al Rose came to the door. He was a heavyset man in his forties with a flowing mange of gray hair going all the way down his back and a beard. Though his eyes were quiet, they were darkly penetrating.

"How did you find us?" he said.

"Mr. Rose," Wade said, "I need to talk to your wife."

Rose adjusted his approach. "You need to understand I do a lot of work with mental-health detentions, and I get appointed to a lot of matters where very unstable people can get very upset at me. I don't give my address out to anyone. It's just concerning."

"I understand. Is she awake yet?"

"Yeah. She's out back."

They went into an adjoining kitchen area with a patio door leading to a pool area. A heavyset woman with braided blonde and gray hair was sitting up in a stiff beach chair. She was unsuccessfully hiding a beer can. There was a half-drained mixed drink on a side table next to an empty chair. Right next to that was another beer can. This was a celebration, she later noted.

"Ma'am, I am Detective Wade with the sheriff's department. I've been trying to reach you this morning."

"Please," she slurred. "Can you talk to my husband? I would prefer that right now. I am very upset."

Resigned, she turned back to Al. "Do you mind answering a few questions."

Rose became even more cordial. "Anything I can do to help."

According to Rose, Sherry hadn't talked to Rolland since Christmas of the past year and they "were no longer close."

Al said he would see him in court from time to time. They often had cases against one another. While always professionally combative, there was nothing personally antagonistic. They had differences in the past but could always look past that in a courtroom setting.

"Why did the two of you split up as business partners?" Wade asked.

"I thought he was stealing money from clients. I mean, that was years ago."

Wade asked if they talked to Michael earlier in the day. Al nodded.

"But you don't know where he is?"

"He didn't say where he was going, no. If I knew I would tell you. He's upset, and no telling what he would do."

Wade was taking notes, and there was a lull in the questioning from the detective.

"What do you think happened to him? To Rolland."

"You mean you don't know? I thought you said…"

"I know he's dead. That's what they said at the courthouse this morning. That he got shotgunned. That's all I know. I wondered if you knew who might have done it."

He seemed to know quite a bit.

Wade told them what the sheriff's department knew. She asked if he could think of anyone who wanted Rolland dead.

"Well, I don't know where he was, but I would look at Stephen if this were suspicious. He knows that house better than anyone else. You might look at Faith or Becky, too. They would have everything to gain from Rolland dying."

Wade was curious as to why that was.

"My understanding is they are beneficiaries of his trust. Them, and my niece. Michael's daughter. I mean, Sherry was cut out of the estate some time ago. If Rolland dies, Faith and Becky would get most of his money.

"I hate to say this because I know it's a stereotype with gays," Rose continued unprompted. "But I'd always heard there were parents upset because they thought Rolland molested their kids. I know Rodman, Sherry's brother, said Rolland touched him inappropriately when he was a kid."

Wade stared back. Stopped writing for a bit. Al didn't sound like someone who had "nothing against" Rolland.

"But those are just rumors," Al said. "I don't know if any of that is true or not. Rodman isn't very reliable."

Wade didn't really know how to follow up with this information. But Al seemed fine to keep talking. Best to let him do so.

"You know, I wouldn't put it past the old man to set up a murder just to make his death a better story. Like he would want someone to write a book about it."

# THE INSIDERS' OUTSIDER

When Rolland decided to go to law school, he didn't have to take a test to be admitted. In the 1960s, all you needed was sixty to ninety hours of undergraduate credit with a C average in order to qualify. He also didn't need any money, as the University of Missouri–Kansas City allowed Rolland to teach European history to undergrads in lieu of the $200 yearly tuition.

During spring break of 1962, Rolland signed up to run for state representative in North Springfield. If there was a question as to how he would serve as an elected official in Jefferson City while attending law school in Kansas City, it didn't matter because winning was never the desired outcome. "Being active in the community through politics helped lawyers get business," according to Comstock contemporary Andrew Dalton.

Rolland drew John Newberry—another lawyer—as his opponent. Newberry beat Rolland in the August primary by eighty votes. In the November general election, Newberry lost to Loren "Racy" Davidson. Even with this outcome, Rolland accomplished his primary mission. Besides, he could run again in two years when he moved back.

Rolland graduated in the spring of 1963. Nowadays, recent law school graduates must immediately take the bar exam and wait a month (or longer) to get the results back before they can begin practicing.

When Rolland graduated, there was no such requirement. You just needed to sign a pledge before a judge that you would sit for the bar within a year. After taking that oath, any potential lawyer could start taking clients and representing them in court. Rolland didn't pass the bar until 1971, almost seven years after signing that oath.

One way Rolland learned the trade was through court-appointed work for indigent clients. Many saw it as the legal profession giving back to a community that enriched them; others saw servitude. Young lawyers would voluntarily place themselves on the court's list for assignment. Older lawyers got stuck with assignments as punishment when they showed up late for court.

Even though he went the route of a lawyer for the money, these appointments appealed to Rolland's interest in social justice. It was also a good way to learn how the courtroom worked. Paying clients demanded results, not to pay for on-the-job training. Law school only trains you to think like a lawyer; there are not many practical skills offered. Plus, no one really expected a lawyer to win one of these cases.

Rolland's first assignment tested his abilities as well as the limits of fairness afforded by the American justice system. An African American deaf-mute, Ray Juan Carlos, was accused of the attempted rape of a churchgoing woman walking to the home of her preacher so "they could pray together" at 10:00 p.m.

Rolland got the case and went down to the jail, unaware of the difficult task ahead. He offered paper to write, but Ray refused. This man wanted to talk; he did not want to write things down like an invalid. The jail informed Rolland they reached out to some interpreters, but no one called back.

An interpreter was finally found, and Rolland learned Ray didn't fully understand what the police were saying, didn't want to answer any of their questions, and thought he was signing not a confession but something that was going to let him leave. He was simply being "polite." Ray's confusion was furthered by the fact he had been drinking all day. Ray claimed he loaned his car to a friend that night and had been at home the entire time.

Armed with information, Rolland got to work. He filed a motion to throw out the confession, where he reached back to Lord Coke's *Institutes of the Lawes of England* that said the "crown would not charge a Defendant with a commission of a serious crime unless the evidence was 'clear and manifest.'"

Rolland cited authority from 1836, when King William IV required all criminal defendants be granted representation by the courts. The brief concluded that, if the court did not see fit to fund the defense of an indigent, "the pews in the courtroom might as well be chopped up and used as firewood."

Despite the historical heft of Rolland's arguments, all were denied.

Now being deprived of any resources and stuck with a bogus confession, Rolland had to prepare for trial. A confession alone was not enough to convict. There would need to be other evidence. But a confession would be a big deal to a jury. He needed to find some morsel of reasonable doubt to plant in the minds of those sitting in Ray's judgment.

Rolland worked on discrediting this written confession. While Ray had trouble understanding people when they talked to him—a common problem for deaf-mutes—he had just as much trouble when it came to reading. He could not have understood what he was signing. More importantly, Rolland concluded Ray was possibly mentally ill or at the very least emotionally disturbed. If something upset him, Ray would grind his teeth. He would refuse to communicate for days at a time. Perhaps this was the sign of a bigger issue.

Rolland filed another batch of motions seeking to suppress the confession on grounds of Ray's mental state. The court punted on this motion until the time of trial. Rolland also asked for a psychiatric evaluation, which the magistrate granted. The psychiatric report concluded Ray was of a "feeble mind" with "borderline intelligence." While the confession was ultimately allowed as evidence, Rolland would be able to bring up Ray's mental condition to say he couldn't completely understand what he was signing.

The all-white jury deliberated for four hours and came down 8–4 for an acquittal. Criminal juries must be unanimous, so the jury was hung. The prosecutor asked for a retrial. The court granted the request and appointed a triumphant Mr. Comstock a second time.

The facts and the law would still be the same, but he wasn't completely doomed to repeat the experience. He filed motions seeking a different judge and a new venue. The court granted him a new judge, but the case would stay in Greene County. Likewise, everything else—the prosecutor and the witnesses—would be the same. Even with a new judge, the rulings were the same. At this trial, the jury came back with a unanimous verdict: guilty for attempted assault with the intent to rape.

Rolland, in his mind, knew he had done all he could. But he also knew history—in a town where innocent men had been lynched on the square in 1906, and their body parts handed out as souvenirs to a ravenously racist crowd, a black defendant would never get a fair shake. Even if they won, the legal system would do everything it could to get Ray eventually. Try and retry. Had the legal system not gotten Ray, someone in the town would have seen to it themselves. That's how it worked. "They used to hang men…in the old days."

When Rolland ran for election again in 1964, he made criminal justice reform a tenet of his campaign based on this experience. He presented an address to the parishioners of St. John's Episcopal Church entitled "Is There Justice for the Poor," where Rolland argued simply appointing a lawyer for someone accused of a crime was a "hollow act" without funds expended not necessarily for the lawyer's fee, but for expenses incurred in researching and investigating matters of defense. This policy position was clearly influenced by his experience representing defendants like Ray.

In the middle of all this, Rolland did what any proper politician needed to do in order to appeal to voters: He got married. He and his first wife, Judith Shepherd, tied the knot at St. John's, and the couple moved into a starter home on North Fremont Avenue.

There's little known about Judith. Rolland rarely talked about her. Married once before Rolland and married two other times afterward, she still lives in Springfield and has little interest in talking about this time in her life. She does make a prominent appearance in another notorious legal case Rolland took on, where the City of Springfield was pitted against a traveling Pentecostal preacher who set up a revival tent in the middle of town.

In the heat of the election cycle, the Reverend C. M. Newton, an Assemblies of God minister from Memphis, was cited for violating the city's noise ordinance. A neighbor complained the tongue-speaking went late into the night and his sleeplessness was heightened by the cries of the revival's attendees.

The Comstocks lived across from the empty lot where Newton Family Ministries pitched tent. Rolland spied police cars rolling up, and he crossed the street to see what was going on. Newton was not only cited for being too loud but ordered by law enforcement to take down the tent and cease all ministry activities.

Rolland spoke up and volunteered to offer his legal representation free of charge. Newton, knowing a sign from God when he saw one, gladly accepted.

Rolland asked the officers about who filed the complaint. They said it was lodged by another neighbor, John R. Zongker, who taught at one of the local Bible colleges. Comstock smelled religious motivations.

Reverend John Warren of the Church of God, the local sponsor of the revival, asked parishioners to pack the courtroom for support during Newton's first appearance. Over one hundred people showed. When they filled the courtroom pews, the faithful assembled outside the municipal court to pray. Protestors raised their hands to the sky, spoke as the spirits compelled them, and cheered on Newton and his lawyer as they walked into chambers. The local paper provided plenty of free press to Comstock the candidate.

After the preacher pled not guilty, Rolland made his request for a jury trial. Even though a bunch of citizens would have to be wrangled, the court set the proceedings for the following week.

Newton addressed the crowd outside with Rolland by his side. "God will work everything out to His honor and glory. I remember how Jesus was led to an illegal trial at night. The mob came for Him with spears, staves, and torches." Newton asked for everyone there to pray for him and his family and to come to the trial. Then, a hat was passed to collect tithing and Rolland's attorney fee. The crowd emptied their pockets. A miracle, indeed.

When the day of the trial arrived, five hundred people congregated at the courthouse in the middle of a sunny afternoon. The chambers were packed. The hallway full. Those who couldn't get in held a vigil outside hoping for divine justice.

After a jury was whittled down and sworn in just over a few hours, the prosecutor called Zongker, who testified the noise kept him awake late into the night. He testified to hearing noises. What kind of noises, the prosecutor asked. The witness tallied he heard "glory-glory-glory" five or six times, he endured "hallelujahs" for seven minutes, and "praise the Lord" for "several" minutes after that.

On cross-examination, Comstock got the witness to confess he did not like the revival in the neighborhood, and had attended the first night carrying a club and looking to cause a disturbance. Zongker said he was ushered out after starting an argument and left his weapon behind.

Comstock brandished the club and asked Zongker if that was indeed his weapon. It was, Zongker admitted. The jury was astonished the mild-mannered man before them could be so full of violent rage.

Rolland called Judith to attest the noise hadn't bothered her. She testified to attending the revival every night, not because she sought conversion but to be friendly. The noise was appropriate given the amount of people, Judith added.

In his closing argument, Rolland spoke of the freedom of religion won from "King John by the *Magna Carta* and the terror of the Bastille in France, as well as the atrocities of Hitler's Germany." This caused the prosecutor to remind the jury that this is not a problem for "Europe, but for northeast Springfield."

The matter was then turned over to the jury. After a few hours, they told the judge they were hopelessly deadlocked. The judge declared a mistrial and released Reverend Newton. Just in time to deliver his sermon that night, he told the excited crowd outside according to news reports. The revival went on for another week before heading off to the next town.

The episode became a pamphlet—"Pentecost on Trial"—Newton handed out at revivals for years to come. He hoped to "reveal a small portion of the trials of some of the men of the field. My life is fully surrendered to the Lord. I pray someone will shine the light of Christ in my life. While some stand back finding fault, crying, that man has an easy life, I press on that I may be counted worthy to bear in my body the marks of our Lord Jesus Christ." Certainly, Springfield left an impression.

The trial got Rolland lots of attention. In the end, a wave crashed on Election Day of 1964. President Lyndon Johnson walloped Senator Barry Goldwater, and this helped Democrats everywhere. Though Rolland was running in the generally Democratic part of town, he still had to beat an incumbent and did so handily.

On November 27, only weeks after the election, Rolland failed to stop in a left turn lane before rear-ending another driver. When the other driver began to approach the car, Rolland drove off. The cops were called, and Rolland was pursued. It was his second hit-and-run in so many months. Although Rolland unsuccessfully tried to argue for legislative immunity, despite the fact he wasn't even sworn in yet, the judge revoked his license. Rolland would have to fly a local airline to the state capitol until he could drive again.

During the 1965 legislative session, Springfield was concerned with two issues: how they would collect taxes and how their city-owned utility would operate. Rolland would find himself, at various points during the session, at odds with city leaders on both topics.

In the 1960s, almost all city governments were funded by property taxes collected by the county. People who owned property, rich people who had quite a bit of sway with local politicians, did not like how county assessors overvalued property as a means of getting more money for government coffers.

Mayor E. L. Anderson wanted to see lower property taxes with an alternative option to raise money. He and the city council liked a bill that would allow Springfield to collect an earnings tax, placing a levy on people who worked within city limits but lived elsewhere.

Anderson told a reporter he wanted a lawmaker from the Springfield area to carry the issue. Rolland read about Anderson's desires in the paper. Rolland did not like the idea. He believed in a "progressive income tax," one that applied a tax on everyone—rich or poor—and increased as the person's income got bigger.

Rolland called the reporter. When asked whether Springfield should impose an earnings tax, Rolland declared he "personally had no intention of filing an earnings tax bill."

The reporter called the mayor for comment, who replied, "Nobody asked him to." The editorial board, entrenched with the efforts to run the city, signed off on a column titled "Advice from Our Freshman 'Expert'" deriding Comstock as a "self-constituted authority on municipal government" and claiming Comstock was trying to create "intentional confusion" in the minds of the public. "[A progressive income tax] is a thoroughly unpopular proposal and we welcome the furor the idea would cause" if Rolland succeeded in getting a bill filed on the matter. The article concluded by saying Comstock simply did not understand the needs of Springfield.

The term "Freshman Expert" stuck to Comstock throughout the opinion page's coverage. The paper would include a caricature of Rolland—wearing high shorts and a beanie—every time they ran a column about him.

The image would end up defining the young politician's career. Rolland ended up keeping the depiction hanging in the bar area of his house late into his life.

Despite the bad press, Rolland made a laundry list of topics he wanted to tackle. But the lawmaking process is slow. There was a seniority process. Recently elected reps got lousy committee assignments. Passing a bill took a lot of work: talking to your colleagues, working out deals, overcoming opposition. No one lawmaker could do that with more than one bill at a time. Even for a guy naturally as smart as Rolland, the legislative process could be so muddy it would take several terms just to figure out how to effectively maneuver it.

All of that ignores the constituency work that must be done. Helping neighbors with their frustration with the state government. Connecting them to the right agencies. That took time as well.

There was also the business of running Missouri to take care of the poor and affirmed, the state-built hospitals and clinics that would house "insane adults" and "mentally retarded children." A committee recommended expanding the program and listed Springfield as a potential site for one of the new facilities.

Rolland, having campaigned on the issue, sought to secure funding for this Springfield location. However, the mayor was in no mood.

With the funding for a mental health clinic pending, the city would have to provide the land and utility hookups. Seeing a chance to let Comstock squirm, Anderson announced Springfield would seek financial assistance from surrounding counties to foot the initial expenses, as these rural areas would be sending their residents to the clinic.

Comstock knew there was no way the city could force surrounding counties to help cover these costs. To try and earn some goodwill back from Springfield leaders, Comstock used his position on the House Municipal Corporations Committee to shepherd along Senate Bill 10, which would help consolidate Springfield's municipal utility services.

Yet Rolland had initially been a roadblock and helped slow down the legislation. At the urging of Democratic party bosses, Comstock bottled up the bill in the committee "for study" in order to help with negotiations on another piece of legislation that would help the unions in their efforts to obtain collective bargaining.

Comstock's about-face on this municipal utility issue only made matters worse. The Springfield Chamber of Commerce wrote Comstock a letter saying Senate Bill 10 was "dead" but "although belated, your enthusiasm and support for the measure may be helpful."

Comstock shot back in a letter to the newspaper that also included the private correspondence from the chamber. "I was truly amazed at the tone of your letter," Comstock opened. "The letter's arrogance and misinformation does not, I sincerely hope, typify the attitude of the Chamber of Commerce or the City Administration."

Senate Bill 10 indeed died in committee despite Rolland's "belated" efforts. The newspaper attributed its demise to "conniving, jealousy, or legislative tomfoolery which is quite common in the House of Representatives." The editorial went on to warn Greene County voters—in a column titled "City Sacrificed to Ignorance and Prejudice"—to be more "careful" with who they elect to represent them. "For many years, we have enjoyed capable, dedicated Representation in the Senate; not so much in the House. It will do us little good if we do not improve the quality of our choice."

In 1966 election, Republicans urged local businessman "Doc" Groves to run. Rolland looked dismissively at his opponent, referring to him as nothing but a "god-dammed auto mechanic."

Rolland would lose to Groves in the fall, making his political career very short. He had made a significant mistake during his time in the legislature. No matter how big Springfield became, its small-town ways never changed all that much. People inherited not only their businesses and livelihoods from their families but also positions of power. Rolland's family was not of importance to city leaders or captains of business. He was strange and a smarty-pants. Because the only thing you had to know to get by in a town like Springfield was who was really in charge and to make sure you were in their good graces.

Plus, those two hit-and-runs suggested a disregard for the law and possibly even a drinking problem. The newspaper went out of its way to cover these dalliances.

Grease monkey or not, Groves could be controlled. He would vote the way those in charge wanted him to vote. It didn't matter if he wasn't educated or experienced—the guy would toe the line.

The mental-health hospital Rolland championed would get built, but not until much later. Rolland would be forgotten politically by the time ground was broken.

Rolland ran again for the seat in 1968 but lost the primary. Now he would just have to go back to practicing law and playing house. But things changed, and Rolland would enter a new relationship, one that had things in store he could never possibly imagine.

# ROADS TO OKLAHOMA

Deputies Dante and Westbrook made their way to Jerry's Appliances and Repairs on Commercial Street. It was only a few blocks away from the building that housed Rolland's bookstore he ran as a teenager. A few more blocks more from his law firm.

"Not at the moment," owner Jerry Abbey said when asked if Michael was there. "He was here earlier and got a call about his dad. Got pretty upset and got in one of my trucks and took off. He was supposed to do a job, but I bet he didn't do it."

Dante and Westbrook could not have known Al Rose volunteered to Detective Wade that he and his wife told Michael about his father's death. While Jerry didn't know who called Michael, Al specifically said he and Sherry talked to Michael in person. This was the first inconsistency in the story of how Michael learned of his dad's death.

For the time being, Westbrook pressed. "You don't know where he went?"

Jerry shrugged. "I know sometimes he stays at an apartment with a gal over on the north side of town."

"Know the address?"

"Over there across the fairgrounds. I think it used to be a motel or something."

The cops looked at each other. Interstate Inn. Notorious with law enforcement for being the den of drug pushers and hookers taking advantage of traffic off Interstate 44.

They headed over and searched the parking lot. No sign of Jerry's truck. None of the other license plates they ran indicated they were owned by any Comstock or any known associates.

As Dante started calling some of Michael's associates to find a location, they got word that both Stephen and Michael arrived at their dad's house.

***

Crystal broke the news to Stephen that Rolland died, and she would drive the three-hour round trip to pick him up. Michael called his brother shortly thereafter. By the second phone call, Stephen was inconsolable. When Michael said he, too, would drive to the rehab center to pick him up, Stephen said yes, so distressed he forgot Crystal said she was already coming to get him.

Michael picked up Stephen shortly after 11:00 a.m. Crystal barely missed them.

Michael talked about things Stephen couldn't quite recall. It was a blur. But there were a few things Stephen remembered later when he talked to law enforcement. First, Michael knew their dad had been murdered. As Stephen later put the timeline of the morning together, it seemed unlikely Michael could have known by the time they talked.

Michael also made a point to say he talked to Mac Mathis at around "seven p.m." the night before but otherwise "had no alibi" for the time when Rolland would be murdered. Why would Michael make a point to say that, Stephen would wonder aloud during his interrogation with the sheriff's deputies.

Mac made no reference to Michael when he talked to law enforcement that morning. Even though Stephen told investigators about Michael's interaction with the neighbor, no follow-up interview with the witness—the one person primarily responsible for helping Greene County pinpoint Rolland's time of death—was ever conducted.

As Stephen thought about the murder while Michael nervously talked away, something became clear: Whoever did this knew Stephen wouldn't be around. That Stephen was over at Rolland's most of the time. Any other night, Stephen would have stopped by to feed the wolves or do some yard work. Or just be there to make sure his dad had some company. The fact he was out of town when Rolland was killed seemed like too much of a coincidence.

"I want to go by there," Stephen said.

"Go by where?" Michael asked.

"Dad's place. I want to go by there."

"I can't take you there. Cops are looking for me."

Stephen said nothing. Michael lit up a cigarette. "I'll drop you off at your place, and you can go over there in the cart." Rolland bought a golf cart that would make it easier to get from the old fishing shacks up to the property. It wasn't legal to drive on the highway, but that wasn't really a rule that was followed in the county. As long as you didn't annoy the neighbors, you could get away with anything.

Stephen agreed. They turned off the highway, and Michael took the back way to the fishing cottages. Stephen got out. Michael stayed behind the wheel while the truck continued to run. Stephen assumed Michael might wait for him.

"Where you going?"

"Gotta take the truck back. Jerry is probably pissed that I took off with it." Stephen nodded and Michael drove off. Stephen stood there, a tear streaming down his face.

He started thinking about what Michael said. All of those suspicious things. Stephen headed to the house. Someone needed to tell him what was going on and not whatever Michael was spouting off.

***

Deputies found a number of cigarette butts in the ashtray in the kitchen that could indicate more than one smoker used it lately. These butts would be a good source of DNA material.

There was also a computer in the library. You could learn a lot by looking at someone's browser history or their emails. It was the day before the holiday, but there would be at least one judge "on duty" to review and sign off on a warrant at any given time.

Radios crackled. There was a disturbance outside the house. It was Stephen, screaming to be let in. Talking about money in the kitchen. Deputies, who were monitoring the road, surrounded him and asked him to calm down. He was crying. "He doesn't have a weapon," they shouted into their wireless radios.

About the same time, Michael drove around the corner up the farm road followed by a sheriff's car. Of course, the roads were swarming with cops, and they spotted him in the missing work truck immediately. Deputies pulled him over and asked if he would cooperate. Michael said he would but wanted to talk to his brother first. They agreed to follow him back to the crime scene.

Michael pulled into the ditch, got out, and started walking toward his brother. Every law enforcement official watched with anticipation, hands hovering over their holstered weapons. Michael walked up and asked Stephen if he would agree they could be interviewed together. Stephen processed the request.

"No, no. I'll go and be interviewed. But I want to be interviewed by myself."

Stephen got in the car with a deputy. In addition to talking about the odd things his brother said on the drive, Stephen mentioned talking to his dad the night before around 6:00 p.m. when he called to let him know he'd checked into the rehab clinic and things were going well. Detectives asked about Rolland's "enemies." Stephen said the only person who would wish Rolland harm was Alberta.

Michael and Alberta talked a lot, Stephen added. He then thought for a moment and repeated what his brother said about not having an alibi the night before.

Stephen submitted to a gunshot residue test and was released. He never thought about going back to the rehab clinic.

Michael was in a nearby room and had another request: Could Curtis Hunt do the questioning? Michael knew Deputy Hunt from previous dealings and trusted him. He would be more comfortable if Hunt could be there at the very least, even if he wasn't doing the questioning. Authorities agreed.

Hunt showed up, and Deputy Dante asked Michael if they could record the interview. Michael said he changed his mind and didn't want to talk. The detectives gave Michael looks of annoyance, explaining they went to a lot of effort to accommodate him. Michael shrugged and said nothing further.

***

All the parties who talked agreed son Rodman was so far out of the picture there was no way he could be involved with the murder. But all family members, estranged or not, would be interviewed.

Rodman was asked about his estrangement with his father. He told them. They listened and took notes. They asked about the last time Rodman talked to Rolland. The son slowly got up to retrieve a letter he received from his dad in 2005, two years before.

Rodman explained that, after he was cut off, Rolland and Alberta bought him a house. A problem arose with the sewer line and became so expensive Rolland agreed to sell the house and keep the money for Rodman's future use. Rodman agreed and moved out.

Unknown to Rolland, Alberta was giving Rodman money from the trust to the tune of $2,000 a month. When that money ran out, Rodman wrote his father asking for money. Rolland, of course, was apoplectic. "There is no money, nor do I have any for retirement because of you. I would have never agreed to sell your house if I had known the money would not have been kept for your future security. Mom giving you money is not the proper use. I blame her for wasting it, not you. You should remember her 'doorstep,' not mine, when you need money several years from now."

He ended the letter with "Love, Rolland."

Rodman's wife and stepson were in the house and could verify he was home all day on the second. "I never leave the house." Rodman was cleared but would have run-ins with the law later. In 2013, he was convicted of stabbing his stepson, the same one who provided him an alibi for the night of Rolland's murder. Upon his release in 2020, Rodman moved in with Sherry and Al—who now moved to the country north of Springfield—where he continued drinking. His mind deteriorating from alcoholism, he would wander off and stagger along the graveled back roads. His sister and brother-in-law would rely on neighbors to call when Rodman passed out in the ditch.

One morning, when he didn't come down, Sherry went to check on him. He died in his sleep. Cirrhosis of the liver. Rolland suffered from that as well, the autopsy would reveal. As though he were the subject of an Irish poem, Rodman died alone, surrounded by family. Just another casualty of his father's neglect. Al and Sherry would bury him on their property, right next to Alberta.

***

After breaking up Sherry and Al's pool party, Wade was assigned with Detective Kenny Weatherford to interview Alberta Comstock at her home in Fairland, Oklahoma. Weatherford was scheduled to be on vacation for the week, but the murder investigation required someone with extensive experience to be in charge. Duren made him number two on the case.

Wade contacted the local police for assistance; it was common courtesy when a police investigation traipsed into another jurisdiction.

Fairland, where Alberta lived, was an hour and forty-five minutes away from Springfield. Just south of Miami and its Native American–owned casinos, Fairland was a town time had passed by. After the tire plant closed in the 1980s, anyone who lived in Fairland worked for the casinos or otherwise spent all their time there. Alberta fell into the latter category.

After the divorce proceedings began, Alberta moved in with her sister, Carmel Rhoten. They were from the area, and both liked the bingo tables. When Alberta finally got money out of the divorce settlement, she bought the house across the street.

Wade and Weatherford arrived at Alberta's house at around 10:30 p.m. Alberta came to the door in a bathrobe and pajamas. She was a hunched, small woman with long silver hair, and her face made a permanent sneer with crow's-feet and other wrinkled tracks. Alberta's look suggested she'd surveyed the world and did not like what she had seen.

They asked to come in. She declined and stepped onto the porch.

Wade asked what she heard about her ex-husband.

"Well, I heard he was killed. So, I take it that's why you are here."

"Actually, my daughter called and said they found him. I assumed he died of a heart attack. He was in terrible health. But she called back later and said he'd been shot in the head." The daughter was Sherry, not Faith, Alberta clarified.

Alberta scanned the detectives up and down. "You know he was gay, don't you?"

The detectives asked if Rolland being gay ended the marriage. Alberta nodded. "I asked him to leave and he would not. So, I moved out."

"When was the last time you were in Springfield?" Wade asked.

Alberta thought for a moment. "It was on June 25."

"What year?"

"This year. Last week. I was told by the real estate agent the house was falling apart and so I wanted to see for myself. I drove there, and she was right. It looked terrible."

"Did you talk to Rolland?"

"I didn't see his car in the driveway, so I assumed he wasn't home. I did talk to him on the phone later."

"How did that go?"

"It was fine. I told him he needed to fix up the house if we had any hope of selling it. He said he would."

"Did anyone see you while you were in town?"

"No, I went to see our son Stephen around the corner, but he wasn't home, either. So, I drove back."

"When was the last time you saw Rolland, ma'am?"

"Oh, that would have been about six months ago. We were in court over the Velma Brown case." Weatherford wrote this name down. Alberta explained she was owed money from an estate, and Rolland was keeping that money away from her.

"Do you have any guns?"

She had a gun, Alberta said. A short, black Colt Cobra .38 that had been given to her by Judge Don Burrell, the old probate judge, as a gift about twenty years ago.

"I carry it everywhere."

"You worried about someone threatening you?"

"I am an old woman and scared of people. My husband has been terrible to me. Who knows who he would send after me?"

"Can we see the gun?"

"You could, but it isn't here." Alberta explained that, in May of 2007, she suffered a heart attack and had a stroke. After a lengthy hospital stay, she returned home to find the gun was gone.

"Were there signs of a break-in?"

"No," Alberta sighed. "This is a small town. No one locks their doors. I guess I was too trusting."

It seemed odd that Alberta was so scared she had to carry a gun with her everywhere she went but then didn't lock the doors to her house. Then, she went a couple of months without a gun.

"I did buy another gun," Alberta offered. "Yesterday."

"You bought a gun yesterday?"

"Yes. I went to the Firing Line and bought a new .38."

She admitted to buying a gun on the day before her hated ex-husband was murdered. "Can we see that gun?"

Now, Alberta felt like she had to let them in. She stepped aside, and they all went into the bedroom where the gun was sitting on the bed-stand. Wade snapped a picture. The detectives got her permission to look through the house as well as Alberta's red 2001 Dodge pickup.

In the floorboard of the truck there were a number of items. Five .22 caliber rounds that suggested she lied about not having any guns other than the .38. There was also a cleaning rod and two price tags—one of which read "S&W $279."

Alberta explained the tag was from the gun and the bullets were from the Firing Line, a local gun shop. The rounds, the tags, and the rod were left in the truck. They were never taken for evidence or examined further. There was no attempt to sweep the floor mats, check the seats, or look in the ashtray of the truck for evidence.

The group went back into the house, and Weatherford did another sweep but found no other guns. He asked who might have taken the gun while Alberta had been in the hospital. She speculated it might have been her brother, Roy Quick, who just got out of prison and had a fascination with guns.

"Did you report the gun as stolen?"

Alberta paused. "If it was my brother, I didn't want him to get in trouble and go to jail. So no, I didn't report it." Quick was later questioned and said he never broke into Alberta's house and never took any gun from her. He had plenty of guns already.

He, too, asked the detectives about whether they knew Rolland was gay.

"We'd like to get that new gun tested," Weatherford said.

"Would I get it back?" Alberta asked.

"Eventually, yes."

"Then that's fine."

"Mind if we check your hands for gun residue?"

"No problem," she said. "But I will let you know I had to fire my new gun when I bought it. To make sure it worked."

Later, this would be used by Alberta's lawyers to explain why her gunshot residue test proved positive.

The Greene County detectives went out to grab the testing kit and discussed what they found. Weatherford showed Wade a photo he snapped: a FedEx envelope sent from Springfield to Alberta early in the morning on the third. It was from an "A. Rose."

"That's the son-in-law I talked to today," Wade noted. "The lawyer. Al Rose. The one that was partying by the pool. He already knew Rolland had been killed with a gun."

"Was there anything inside the envelope?" Wade asked.

"Looked like a set of keys."

While a theory emerged over the first week of the investigation as to why Rose would have mailed keys to Alberta, neither Alberta, Rose, nor anyone was ever asked about the package.

After a couple of minutes, the Fairland chief of police—who'd stayed in the living room—came out and said he heard Alberta on the phone with what sounded like a son saying she believed the police were planting evidence to make her look guilty.

By the time Wade and Weatherford got back in the house, Alberta was off the phone. They swabbed her hands and wished her a good night. On the way out of town, Wade called Sergeant James Farrell—on duty after hours that day—and told him about what they learned. All these details sounded significant to Farrell, especially the part about her gun being stolen. Had she been read her rights and offered a formal statement? he asked.

"No," Wade had to admit.

"You need to go back and Mirandize her and talk about this missing gun!"

They went back to the house before midnight. The day Rolland had been found dead was about to end.

Alberta asked them what they wanted now. Weatherford said they needed to talk to her about this missing gun. She understood. They presented her with the Miranda form. She read it, pondered it for a moment. She knew the words. Everyone heard them on television or in the movies. Signing a form was much less dramatic but was standard protocol. Alberta signed it.

"Okay," Weatherford said. "We'll be candid with you, Mrs. Comstock. We're concerned about this gun, and about what Chief Sly said you and your son were talking about while we were outside."

Alberta scowled. "You have to understand, Michael is very sweet when he is not on that stuff," she volunteered. "When he is," she continued, "he gets paranoid and worried. He has called me all day. He thinks the police are out to get him. He thinks you all are going to blame him for this murder and send him to prison."

"Do you think he might have taken the gun?" Wade asked. "Did he know you had a gun?"

"He did. I doubt he took it. But..." Alberta trailed off. "Michael stole that gun in 2001. It was back when Rolland was mad at him and wouldn't loan him any money. Wouldn't let me loan him any money. He planned to pawn it off. But he started feeling bad about it because he knew I kept it for protection, and he brought it back."

Alberta stopped again. "Well, no, I take that back. We called the police, and they had to chase him down. That's right. That's how they got the gun back."

"To be clear, you don't think Michael stole your gun back in May of this year?"

"Michael? No. If he had taken it, I would have told you. I want him to be safe. I wouldn't want him out there to hurt anyone else if he did have that gun."

If the detectives asked her about why she thought Michael would be dangerous, there's no record of it. But, as the detectives would say in depositions later, they were very aware of Michael Comstock's reputation.

"Bob Stillings is Rolland's lawyer," Alberta said. "You should know that. Rolland was supposed to sell our house, and he wouldn't do it because he doesn't want me to have any money. I know what he was going to do. He was going to sell it to Bob, and then they would freeze me out of it. Bob would have made a lot of money off of Rolland dying. Had a lot to gain."

"We'll look into it."

"I wanted to buy that house. That house wouldn't be there if I hadn't been home to take care of those kids. Rolland never cared about us. He cared about his books. He cared about his money. But he never cared about me or my kids. I told you he was gay, didn't I?"

Alberta's tone was angry, bitter. The rage she felt for her dead ex-husband hung in the air.

"He would go to Mexico every year. He said he went down there because of a book conference. But that was a lie. He went down there because it was a gay resort. He would go down there and hang out with his 'sissies.' That's what he called them. I found papers where he said that. He was talking to the people who owned the resort, and he was requesting sissies. I also…" Alberta stopped as she choked up a bit. She bit her lip and looked right at Weatherford.

"I found photos of him and one of his boys. Rolland just left that photo around our house. In our bedroom. What kind of man does that?"

"What kind of man do you think he is?"

Alberta pulled out a thin, brown cigarette out of the top pocket of her nightdress. "I don't know," she murmured as she lit. "I guess someone I don't have to be married to anymore."

"It's late, Mrs. Comstock. We will be in touch."

She blew out her smoke and nodded. That was all they were going to get.

Though they had gone to Alberta's home twice that evening, not once did the detectives attempt to take clothes or shoes or try to extract any evidence from the house. They never asked to. It would be several weeks before the Greene County Sheriff's Office went back looking for that kind of evidence. That evidence would have been tossed or washed well before then. During this first interview, they never asked Alberta where she had been the night before.

***

Back north of Springfield, before Detectives Wade and Weatherford made it to Alberta's porch, Rolland's body was removed by the county coroner and an autopsy ordered to confirm the precise nature of the death to help with the investigation and, inevitably, the prosecution.

Over the course of the rest of the week, the medical examiner would confirm Rolland had been shot four times: once through the chin, once in the stomach, and twice in the back of the head. While there could be no deduction of where he was shot first, the coroner concluded Rolland died from bleeding out of his abdomen.

The sheriff's department found no other fingerprints or shoe prints in the house other than Rolland's. What was also never located was any envelope or coffee can, or anything with the cash Rolland kept on hand to pay various people doing odd jobs around the house. Rolland's cleaning lady, Glenda Joplin, would testify she saw it the week before. The library assistants would later tell investigators they worked for Rolland the Friday before the murder and had been paid from cash in an envelope. They would report that, as they watched the old man take twenties out of the bundle, more cash was inside.

The search warrants for the computers, from his home and from his law firm, were signed, and detectives got access to Rolland's email and files. Deputies arrived on July 4 to pick them up from the house and office to haul them back to the sheriff's department for forensic investigation.

When the computers were checked, the deputies found what they would describe as "gay stuff." Pictures, mainly of unclothed young men. Porn clips. Rolland was also prolific on a website called Silver Haired Daddies for older gay men to meet younger gay men. There were multiple chats with a man named Jose Alvarez. According to the chats, Rolland met up with him at a condo in Mexico. Jose asked for money—$1,200 here, $600 there. Rolland indicated his "assistant" would take care of the transfer.

There was also evidence in Rolland's emails that an airline ticket had been purchased for Jose to travel from Dallas to Springfield on Saturday, June 30. This was the same person Becky said was supposed to be coming to visit.

Springfield has an airport that only offers flight to and from certain hubs. If you were in McAllen, Texas—as Jose was—you would have to fly from McAllen to Dallas–Fort Worth and then to Springfield. Lengthy and costly, this wasn't going to be a weekend getaway.

The return ticket was for the sixth of July. While Becky said the trip was called off after Rolland and Jose got into an argument, that only raised the sheriff's department's interest in learning more. Investigators traveled to McAllen, and Jose sat for an interview so he could prove his whereabouts for the entire week. To be sure, deputies checked with the airport and the Greyhound bus station. Nothing indicated Jose bought any tickets to Springfield.

He was cleared even though no investigator, after nearly traveling to Texas to talk with him, asked Alvarez what he and Rolland fought about that caused the trip to be canceled.

Then there were the wolves, which were handed over to animal control. Eventually they would be turned over to a wolf sanctuary in Colorado. No one else wanted them or, frankly, knew what to do with them. The wolves started the day protecting their master's body. Now, they were cast away and had to start over far away from the Ozarks.

The escaped wolf, the one that got out while deputies were securing the crime scene, was never found, nor was a body recovered. It is almost certainly gone now, spending the last years alone in the woods around its old estate.

***

As Becky was the executor of Rolland's estate under the will, she was asked to drop by the house so the sheriff's office could relinquish control to her now that it was no longer an active crime scene. Despite the July 4 date, the house was still a flurry of activity as deputies were removing possible evidence and clearing out their equipment.

It was still blazing hot outside. Even in the heat and daylight, fireworks blasted off the hills and hollers all around the estate. Usually Becky would drown it out; it was just a noise you heard out in the country for a week around the holiday. Now, she cringed every time there was a "POP!"

Becky brought her husband, Jack, to help. The house had now been closed off for a day with the air conditioner off. Becky could still smell the moldiness of the house and the wolf pee that seeped into the floor. But now there was something different. It now smelled like dried blood. It smelled like death.

Since Becky was in charge of the house, she would also be in charge of cleaning it up, securing it, and working with Faith to make sure the place could be sold, something Rolland couldn't even get done.

Even in death, Becky would have to clean up Rolland's messes.

"Can we just scrub it up without protection?" she asked about the blood.

The deputies agreed to find a hazmat suit that would fit her.

"Make it a little bigger since it's going to have to fit him," she said while pointing to her husband. Jack was used to Rolland's messes as well.

After briefing the couple on taking over a crime scene, Detective Duren asked Becky if she would walk through the house to see if anything seemed out of place. Becky explained Rolland was so disheveled it would be difficult to figure out what was, in fact, in place.

"Just give it a try," Duren urged. Becky nodded. They walked into the library. Becky nearly welled up looking at the ornate shelves and the chandelier knowing how much Rolland loved this room, a refuge from the chaos of his life.

Her gaze moved to the couch, to the Coach briefcase that had been searched the day before.

"The briefcase. I don't recognize that."

Duren remembered ordering all the documents removed from the briefcase. It was doubtful anyone looked at them closely yet. "That's not Rolland's briefcase?"

"His is leather and brown and sort of beat-up. I'm sure it's at the office."

Duren eyed it again and went right for the pendant. "We saw the wolf on it and thought it might be Mr. Comstock's."

Becky shook her head at the assumption. "They were Alberta's idea at first. The wolves. She loved them."

Duren asked a deputy wandering around the foyer to take the Coach bag into evidence.

They moved into the kitchen. Becky couldn't help but look at the dried puddle of blood and the blot where Rolland had been. She maintained her composure as she tried to look around the room. Anything but looking at the floor again. That's when she saw the book.

She pointed. "That right there. That's Rolland's prized book." *Lord of the Flies*. Duren remembered seeing it the day before.

"What do you mean 'prized'?" Duren asked. "Valuable?"

"He talked about this book all the time," Becky exclaimed while lighting up at the thought of her old boss's enthusiasm. "Signed by the author. Rolland said it was so valuable he wasn't even sure what it was worth."

Duren stroked his chin and pulled out his latex gloves and picked up the book. He flipped through the pages. They were old but had been cared for. Other than its age, Duren wouldn't know why this was considered valuable. Clearly, Rolland did. What was of little consequence yesterday now seemed important.

Duren began to secure the book in a bag. "Would there be any reason for this book to be in the kitchen?"

Becky had to think for a minute. Best to let the detective know all her thoughts in case it would help. "Rolland was having money trouble. He might have been trying to sell it. I don't..."

She trailed off for a minute. "I mean, maybe he thought whoever was in the house would take the book. Maybe they demanded money, and he offered it to them."

Duren picked up on her thought. Maybe Rolland was using his most "prized" book to bargain for his life.

***

On July 4, after staying in Fairland at a hotel cheap enough to be covered by the sheriff department's travel budget (for two rooms, no less), Wade and Weatherford contacted the owner of the Firing Range, the place where Alberta bought her gun. Mike Friend was the proprietor.

He recalled two nights ago with detail. Alberta came in at 6:00 p.m.; it was so close to closing, Friend already locked the door, and she knocked on the glass loudly enough to get his attention since he was in the back. Friend remembered Alberta didn't look nervous as much as frazzled. She reminded him she had taken classes there for her Oklahoma gun permit.

Alberta told Friend she needed a "cheap .38" for "target practice" since her gun had been stolen. The first gun Friend had her try out in the acreage behind the store had a firing pin that didn't work. Alberta emphasized, a second time, that she did not care what kind of gun she bought. She grabbed another gun—he couldn't remember what kind—and went out and shot that. It worked. She seemed satisfied. As she was buying the gun, Alberta mentioned to Friend she had a gun that needed repair. She asked how long it would take for him to work on it.

"Depends," he drawled. "I am a little backed up. Maybe a week."

"You can't do it today?"

He shook his head. Alberta looked put out but continued with the sale.

"So, where you doing your target practice? You may notice I've got a nice setup out back, and I charge pretty cheap rates."

"I've got to go over there," she answered as she pointed east. Toward Missouri. Toward Rolland.

Friend explained she needed to try out the gun before she left just to make sure it worked and there were no problems. She looked at her watch and said fine. Alberta and Friend went to the back patch of grass where he watched her clumsily shoot off a few rounds into a paper target. She could barely hit the broad side of a barn, he thought. But the gun worked.

Good thing she was going to do some target practice, he figured. He took her money. In cash, he pointed out when the detectives asked if she used a credit card. As Friend locked the door again, he watched through the glass door as she drove off on US Highway 60 toward Missouri.

# DEATH, TAXES, AND INSANITY

Rolland and Judith were divorced in March of 1967. She filed the paperwork. According to the blurb in the newspaper that noted a recently defeated state representative was seeing his marriage fall apart, Judith claimed she wanted to end things because Rolland was "quarrelsome and abusive." The petition went on to say he refused to "discuss various problems, including financial conditions" and said he told her to leave the house. As there were no kids to fight over, Judith simply asked for $10,000 in alimony plus monthly payments of $250 to keep up her lifestyle. Rolland responded he didn't really make enough money to pay her anything. The matter went to a hearing. She got a divorce but no money.

Shortly after Rolland became a bachelor again by court decree, he met Alberta. The exact time and location of their meeting is lost to time. Faith suggested it was "somewhere that surely sold alcohol."

The courtship was quiet and quick. This was not Alberta's first marriage, either. She and her first husband, Rodman VanSant, had four children.

Faith recalled she didn't meet Rolland until the night she learned her mother would be getting married again and they would be moving into his house. Rolland and Alberta tied the knot in Fairland on February 21, 1968. Stephen was born shortly after, which helped explain why the wedding felt so rushed to the other children.

There was some question as to whether Alberta knew Rolland was gay when they married. Rumors circulated she was warned by her friends not to marry someone everyone knew was "funny." There was also talk at the time of the murder that Alberta found out about Rolland's secret early in their relationship and blackmailed him, and the marriage was part of this scheme.

Such stories contradict Alberta's own testimony in the divorce proceeding, as well as in countless conversations she had after the marriage collapsed. Alberta said under oath the marriage was happy until the immediate end.

That, and the photos she found. Her wish for Rolland to leave the house immediately. These reactions did not sound like a woman who was hatching a decades-long scheme or someone warned by her friends years before.

Rolland and Alberta discussed adopting the four children from her previous marriage. Her former husband consented, signed away his parental rights, and Rolland was able to proceed without issue.

After getting married, and after he decided there was no serious chance he would become a state representative for north-side Springfield again, Rolland purchased a ranch-style residence in an east-side subdivision well outside his natural constituency. It was modest construction but pricey due to its location and the need to house the entire family. His books took up an entire room, forcing all four children to share a single bedroom.

Though he moved away from his childhood neighborhood, Rolland still wanted to keep his business there even as the southward shift of the city saw Commercial Street slide into decline. Though storefronts shuttered and homeless people started appearing on the sidewalk, Rolland's reputation was that of a north-side lawyer, and moving the firm made little sense. He suspected his clients would prefer someone who practiced closer to where they lived.

He purchased the Addison's building and expanded the law firm to every floor. Owning a bookstore simply to store a collection was a money loser. Plus, he didn't want to share an office anymore. If Rolland wanted to make real money, that "filthy lucre," he needed his own space and needed other lawyers to work under him.

After a few years, the Addison's building fell into a state of decline. Making costly repairs to a historic building was something Rolland was willing to do, particularly for a place that meant so much to him. But the decreasing value of the Commercial Street district made moving a better proposition. It was at this time the Comstock Law Firm moved to the Court Street location, where Rolland would spend the rest of his life practicing law.

The books being stored in the Addison's building came home. In 1975, knowing his children could no longer sleep in the same room without causing serious psychological damage, and the fact he needed yet another room for his books, Rolland moved the family to a newer subdivision with enough rooms for every kid to have a room of their own and enough space for his full collection.

By this point, in his thirties, Rolland acquired thousands of books. Most of them—at first—were out of general interest for the subject. Lots of tomes on British history. But by this point, Rolland understood the mechanics of a valuable book collection. First-edition books were the most prized and most elusive, thus coveted most by collectors. Having those first-edition copies signed by the authors themselves was even more important.

After he got home from the office (or from frequent happy hours), Rolland would quiz his children about current events and their schooling. Afterward, he would leave Alberta to clean and tend to the children's bath and bedtimes while he holed up in the makeshift library down in the basement. His main task was color-coding. Rolland explained in a profile that "the books are wrapped in acetate with color-coded stickers. Red stickers are for signed or inscribed authors, blue are for unsigned US editions, and green is for unsigned English editions."

Rolland did not simply collect books. He sought broadsides, passages from unpublished books, autographs, and magazine articles. Whatever could be signed. When he was profiled in *The New Yorker* in the early aughts, he was described as a "Missouri lawyer who for decades has been collecting and warehousing modern first editions, plus ephemera, arcana, curiosa, and marginalia on an obsessive, industrial scale not for profit but all for passion."

Rolland wrote an essay attempting to capture the nuances of his book collecting. He was aware of a writer's tendency to recycle work in progress repeatedly. "I'm told that those in the author business have a thing called the 'First Law of Freelancing' which requires everything to be repackaged three times. Publication in parts is a bane for the collector. It's collector lore that the devotion of a collector to an author is measured by the degree of aggressiveness with which the collector searches for periodical appearances."

"I am very aggressive," Rolland emphasized.

Rolland did his best to maintain a sense of domesticity, but he was never very good at it. "Dad was born in a suit," Faith remembered. "He did nothing to learn about basic handiwork around the house. He ended up burning every meat he tried to grill. When we went camping, he packed Bermuda shorts and a bottle of bourbon as his gear."

Rolland ultimately focused on probate and estate planning, or "death, taxes, and insanity" as he called it. Despite the self-deprecating nature of this description, he found helping people through the myriads of paperwork and tax codes during a time of grief was a useful service rather than just chasing money. It seemed more noble to Rolland compared to personal injury claims or divorces.

Make no mistake, the money was good. Everyone died, and everyone needed to have documents in place to take care of their affairs. You could charge a lot for a trust. Boilerplate documents like a last will and testament or a power of attorney were still good for the minimal work required to modify them for each client.

The real source of money was in representing people who had to administer the estates of the deceased or of people who were no longer able to do so themselves because of illness or infirmity.

When you die or when you are declared incapacitated, your stuff—real estate, bank accounts, and whatever else—must be handled legally. Under Missouri law, if no other arrangements were made, a probate estate must be established. That means a judge oversees how your assets are disposed and makes sure those entitled to your estate—either someone named in a will or by the court if there is no will—receive their proper share. In the case of incapacity, the judge simply has to make sure your bills are paid and your funds safeguarded. The process is invasive, slow, and expensive. It's good for lawyers, bad for everyone else.

No person handled more of these cases than the Greene County public administrator, an elected official who handled estates when the court determined no one else was qualified to do so. Rolland represented the office for nearly forty years and covered officials who were both Republican and Democrat. This client alone was worth several hundreds of thousands of dollars a year in attorney fees.

Then, there's a trust. Trusts have been around since ancient Rome. If you have a lawyer like Rolland draft a trust, you then have to retitle everything you own into the trust's name. When you die, the person named as trustee takes over and continues handling things until everything can be wound up and assets distributed to the beneficiaries of the trust.

The administration of a trust means everything can be done outside of probate court. It's private and costs less money. The court will not get involved unless there's something tricky afoot, like a trustee with sticky fingers. Or when someone wants to leave their earthly belongings to a dog.

Butch the Bulldog to be exact. His owners died and, under the terms of their trust, Butch was to live in the house until doggy death as well as have full use of his owner's Ford van. Plus, the trust directed trustee and family friend Ruby Keen to live with Butch, tend to his needs, and serve as his driver. With a salary for doing so. Butch also was provided an allowance for food—KFC fried chicken was his meal of choice—and whatever else a pooch could want.

The nieces and nephews of Butch's dearly departed owner would get the house and the van, but only after Butch got to use them first. They would get the money if any was left. In fact, the trust contained a provision that, upon Butch's death, his body was to be examined to make sure the dog had not met his end through nefarious means.

None of this sat well with the relatives who had to wait in line behind Butch. They hired a lawyer who urged the court to ignore the provisions of the trust regarding Butch's right to live in the house and to have use of the van because this would cause "unnecessary depreciation" to the assets. The house and the van should be sold, the lawsuit said. The heirs' lawyer argued there was no problem with providing for this eighty-pound dog, but letting the property languish until Butch expired was unfair to the relatives. Doing so, the lawyer argued, "would border on the ludicrous."

Ms. Keen also had a lawyer, who said the court had to follow the provisions of the trust "with the strictest of compliance." It was a real dispute, but the party who had the most to lose—Butch himself—had no ability to hire his own lawyer.

Judge Burrell, the same Judge Burrell who gifted Alberta her Colt Cobra .38 handgun, decided Butch needed his rights protected. Therefore, the dog required a guardian *ad litem*. Usually reserved for minor children or adults who could not make decisions due to a mental incapacity, Burrell believed Butch needed someone to watch out for his interests. A lawyer who could appreciate that, no matter how absurd, justice should be served.

Rolland was just such a lawyer.

The local media, upon hearing of the controversy, were thrilled. Butch's lawyer, never one to skip free publicity, reciprocated. Rolland brought Butch to every court hearing and held press conferences afterward. Snippets in the Springfield paper got carried over the wires and ended up as a joke in a *Tonight Show* monologue. The military newspaper *Stars and Stripes* ran one of those "Can You Believe This?" columns about Butch and his lawyer.

Rolland knew it was good advertising for his law firm but confessed to Becky he hated the dog. "His breath stinks and his farts are nonstop," Rolland complained. "That goddamn mutt is disgusting."

By the conclusion of his investigation, Rolland determined there was nothing unusual about granting the use of a home or a vehicle to Butch. Three experts—all retained by Rolland at the trust's expense—testified Butch should be allowed to continue with his luxurious lifestyle. Dogs get used to the things in their life, the experts maintained, and if those trappings were taken away the dog would not be as happy as he had been, and it could limit his lifespan. The judge agreed and denied the heirs' request.

Butch spent the rest of his days sticking his head out the window of his van as he and Ms. Keen cruised Kearney Street. He ate his buckets of chicken for dinner. Butch watched television from his own chair and slept in a baby crib. Keen was awarded $9,100 for previous care to the dog with $300 a month in salary going forward.

When Butch finally passed away in 1992, he was buried next to his owner. His death was marked by a brief mention in the *National Enquirer*. The house and van were sold and the proceeds split up between the contingent beneficiaries.

The autopsy revealed no foul play.

# THE FIRST 48

The first forty-eight hours after a murder is a critical period in an investigation. If a crime is not solved in that time, evidence can get lost, misplaced, or moved. Memories of events begin fading immediately. It is easy to see how Rolland's murder being discovered right before the Fourth of July factored into the frustrations of the sheriff department's work.

Detectives were investigating; law enforcement never sleeps and in fact might be busier on holidays. But businesses were closed, and people were out of town. Those witnesses could not be interviewed. Mike Friend was an exception to that rule.

Any effort to do substantive work by an investigator might be hampered by any number of things. Moreover, any gunshot residue tests or forensic work on computers seized from the home would not be conducted until the following workday. For almost all state workers were off on the Fourth and wouldn't have any conclusive results until later in the week, or maybe the week after that.

There were questions in Becky's mind about how closely the sheriff's office searched the kitchen for clues. As she and Jack cleaned up the crime scene, Becky discovered Rolland's eyeglasses underneath a table. She called a deputy and asked what she should do with them. The deputy said there was no value to collecting the glasses as evidence.

"What about smudges or fingerprints?"

The deputy said that was unlikely. Exasperated, Becky just put the glasses in a storage box.

Other than the glasses, the *Lord of the Flies,* and the briefcase, there was little physical evidence at the scene. When a person is killed with a gun, there's usually less movement. There's no physical struggle, so it's less likely that a hair follicle or a dead skin cell will drop to the ground.

The lack of evidence from any altercation also was very telling in regard to the fact that the wolves did not attack whoever did this. If the perpetrator had been a stranger—rumors were already circulating about Rolland's love life, and he'd invited the wrong person over for a rendezvous—the wolves likely would have attacked them. That attack would have resulted in blood drops, ripped cloth, or any number of small clues to help identify the perpetrator.

Whoever killed him had been careful, but anyone who knew the house was aware of how easy it was to slip in and out. The unlocked sliding kitchen door wasn't an obstacle. The chain to the massive gate out front could be slipped off.

This led to an initial conclusion that the killer had not broken in, but Rolland invited him or her in, or it was someone who knew you could get into the house without much effort. It also had to be someone who would not have scared the wolves. The wolves remained the biggest impediment to implicating anyone other than a close family member.

Becky was asked to review the remains and perform a formal identification. She noted Rolland's right ring finger. She asked whether a ring was retrieved. The deputies weren't sure. They called the evidence locker, and there was no ring. Rolland had a three-carat gold ring he never took off. If it wasn't found on his body, Becky knew that someone removed it. The deputies took note of this, but there is no indication any search of pawnshops in the area focused on finding a valuable ring that disappeared from the crime scene.

Compare this with an anonymous tipster who said Rolland would frequent an adult bookstore not very far from his house on Highway 13. Even though that particular store closed years ago, two detectives took several days going to every adult-themed bookstore in the Springfield area with a picture of Rolland to see whether any clerks recognized him. There's no indication from the report detailing these efforts or why such efforts were undertaken. Nearly ten local businesses were interviewed.

Perhaps there was a good reason—detectives should follow their leads and instincts. Since they didn't find anyone who knew Rolland, the record is unclear about what they thought they might find.

It could have been in line with the searches made of local bookstores—of the nonadult variety—to see if any of Rolland's books had been traded in for cash. None of them had been or, at least, nothing looked like it belonged in Rolland's collection. No stickers or signatures.

Or maybe law enforcement used this search to confirm preconceived notions about the murder victim.

***

Approximately ten days after Rolland's body was discovered, two deputies were assigned with checking every convenience store between Fairland and Springfield. The law enforcement officers were given a recent photo of Alberta as well as pictures of Michael and Stephen. They also had a photo of Alberta's small maroon truck.

Tina Williams worked at Murphy Oil in Monett, Missouri. Murphy Oil is the formal name of all the gas stations located at Walmart parking lots. Williams worked both on July 2 and July 3 and couldn't identify Alberta, but did remember seeing the truck because she recognized the smiley face decal on the front license plate holder. Williams was absolutely certain of the identification but could not recall what day it was.

"What about the *time* of day?" deputies pressed. "When was that?"

"Oh, that's easy," Williams said. "I don't really keep track of time in here, but I seem to remember it was when the sun is right over the Burger King." She pointed toward the fast-food joint nearby to the west as the best way of keeping track of things at her job.

It was a little after 6:30 p.m. when Alberta left the Firing Range with her new "cheap" .38. Monett was fifty miles away from the gun shop on a road with a sixty-five-mile-per-hour speed limit. If Alberta drove straight from the Firing Range to the Walmart gas station at the speed limit or a bit faster, she would have arrived at Tina Williams's gas pumps on or around 7:15 p.m. that night. Right as the sun would have been above the roof of the Burger King. Alberta was only forty-three minutes away from Rolland's house. You could be there around 8:00 p.m. if you were able to top off a gas tank in just a few minutes.

Shortly thereafter is when Mac Mathis heard booms that weren't fireworks.

Then, there was the matter of Baumer's Food Mart on Interstate 44, which also takes you back to Oklahoma. Greene County Sergeant Ron Killingsworth interviewed the owners on July 20—a week after the initial canvass of convenience stores was done on Highway 60. Michael and Shawn Baumer were shown pictures of Alberta and her truck. Shawn recognized both. She had been to the store "around the Fourth of July" and asked whether her truck could be left overnight because it had broken down. She was there with a man who resembled neither Stephen nor Michael. Michael Baumer had no recollection of what they looked like. After some thought, Shawn said it could have also been "really late on July 2" when he talked to Alberta.

Killingsworth noted a couple of monitors behind the counter.

"You have tape from that night?"

They shrugged. "Gets recorded over every three days."

Law enforcement came back with several other photos, including of Roy Quick and Johnnie Rhoten. Shawn recognized Rhoten as the man who picked up the truck on July 3. He was there with a trailer and another man, who Shawn didn't get a good look at. But neither of those men was the man Shawn had seen the night of the second.

Greene County investigators later contacted Johnnie Rhoten, who indicated he knew about Rolland's death but didn't know many details.

"Hadn't seen him in years," he'd recalled and said his stepmother Carmel—Alberta's sister—didn't mention him much. Detective Duren asked if Rhoten had been in the Springfield area to pick up Alberta's truck. He said his memory wasn't great "due to a couple of strokes" and couldn't recall whether he had been in Springfield. He did say he remembered Alberta and Carmel talking about leaving a truck there but couldn't remember when.

"Did you know he was gay?" Rhoten asked his interrogators. Seemed he had no problem remembering that point.

***

Though a forensic team removed all the cigarettes from the ashtray in the house, it would be several weeks before deputies collected butts from the driveway and the yard. This is where a sample of Michael's DNA was ultimately recovered. However, Stephen Comstock would later place doubt on whether this made Michael a suspect. He could remember mowing his dad's yard shortly after the murder and Michael stopping by the house. They talked. Michael stubbed out a few cigarettes during the conversation.

Others came forward to discuss whether Michael might be a suspect in his father's murder. But law enforcement had reason to doubt the motivation of these tipsters in almost every case. Sammie Johnson dated an employee of Jerry's Appliances and would get high with Michael on occasion. Michael told Sammie a story about how he'd asked his father for money a few weeks earlier and had been told no. Michael said that made him mad. He usually always went to his mom for money, but she said she didn't have any. She blamed Rolland for "screwing her" on some deal. "Go talk to him about money," Alberta said. "He has my money."

Johnson also said that, in his frustration, Michael got a .38 from his mother. While not confessing to anything directly, Michael admitted to "fucking my dad up."

But Johnson, at the time of this admission, was facing ten years in prison for possession and distribution of meth as a prior and persistent offender. Authorities would ask Johnson if he had any evidence to back up this conversation. He didn't, and he got sentenced.

Shawn Pool was pulled over for driving a car registered in Rolland's name, and police discovered material used to cook methamphetamine during the stop. Pool said he bought the car off Michael Comstock, who said he was going to leave town because he didn't want to get caught up in "his mother's deal."

Terrence C. Dotson said he was having a conversation with Michael about the problems Dotson had with kicking meth.

"I've got lots of problems," Michael said. "Bigger problems than that. I've been known to kill, and if something is ever said, I'll kill again."

Later, when investigators went to follow up with Dotson, he denied having said anything about Michael. The sheriff's department asked him to take a polygraph test and noted any cooperation might help him with the pending charges he was facing for theft. He agreed, but the test revealed Dotson was lying. So much for cooperating. The next morning Dotson fled the state, and an arrest warrant was issued. He eventually served five years in prison.

Then, there's Jerry Hall. Almost a year after the murder, Hall contacted law enforcement to say Michael stayed with him on July 2. Michael left the house around 10:00 p.m. and returned at midnight drenched in sweat and wearing different clothes. Michael was acting "nervous and strange" while boasting that he traveled a long way on his bike. "Long enough to get to my dad's house," Hall recounted Michael saying.

Hall then said that, on the morning Rolland was discovered, Michael received a call around 8:00 a.m. about the murder. Michael's response was very matter-of-fact. More like, "Oh, they found him already?" Michael then started crying, paced around, and announced he was going to Clinton to pick up his brother.

It was no surprise that Hall had pending charges at the time he came forward with this new information. When he did not get a better deal for "turning" on Michael, he pled guilty to distributing and manufacturing meth.

Later on, in 2010, a woman named Robin Stokes told an associate Michael was with her the night of the murder. Stokes said she lived with him for a year and a half. She kicked him out in early 2007 when she discovered he was operating a meth lab in the backyard.

Stokes said one night Michael had shown up late with blood on his shirt. Michael explained he got into a fight with another patron at Sassy Reds, a run-down strip club on the northern end of town and only a few blocks from Robin's house.

Michael was always complaining about money, Stokes would recall. He was irritated that his mother couldn't give him any money because she was broke, and she was broke because Rolland dragged his feet on selling the family house. Michael was testy about his dad cutting him off, despite being a lawyer and having more money than any one person needed.

But the night of July 2 was different. Stokes said Michael felt like a different person, "a darker person. There was something sinister with the way he was talking about his situation."

The next day, at Michael's request, Stokes threw his clothes away in a dumpster. After she did so, she heard about the homicide on the local news. By then, Michael was long gone. Stokes said, upon her inspection of the clothes, they smelled like paint. She thought nothing of connecting the two until later.

Stokes had no legal problems and no pending charges. She was the only person who came forward not listed as a "known associate" with any criminal record. Yet none of her concerns were investigated further. Law enforcement would argue the nearly three years it took Stokes to come forward made it impossible to corroborate anything she said.

***

The week after the murder, the Missouri Department of Corrections called Detective Duren to report a conversation where Michael was talking to his incarcerated wife. Michael mentioned a gun used in the commission of a crime. The DOC had only a portion of the call—they picked up on the suspicious chatter late—but Michael mentioned leaving a weapon at a property near Greenfield.

The Dade County assessor reported Alberta owned property there but recently transferred title to Al and Sherry Rose. Duren wanted consent from the Roses not because he needed it—a search warrant would be easy to obtain—but because he wanted to talk to Al Rose himself.

# OBSESSIONS

As the children grew older and started moving out (or had to be thrown out), more rooms in the family home became space for Rolland's book collection. Further, as the money accumulated from Rolland's practice and an expanding portfolio of rental property, he decided a home should befit his success and serve as a monument to his abilities.

Rolland got wind of a land sale on a twenty-acre tract north of town. He bought the property in 1976 but didn't complete the construction of the palatial mansion until 1990.

At the time of its construction, it was ornate and grand. It sat at the top of a glistening hill tucked away among the woods. There was no traffic, but you were only a few minutes away from town. It was a bit of paradise that a comfortable lifestyle could afford.

Rolland put the house's title in Alberta's name only. Legally, this made little sense. Given Rolland contributed all the money to build and maintain the house, it was his house no matter what the title said. He didn't have any creditors at that time. If anything, Alberta would run up credit card bills and need to be bailed out. Having the house in her name made it more susceptible to debt collection.

Faith speculated later that this was Rolland's way of making Alberta feel as though she contributed to the family. Rolland would call it "her" house as a way of boosting his wife's self-esteem. What Rolland didn't think through was, if things ever soured in the marriage, she would really think of it as her house. In fact, this would become her obsession.

When the family moved to the mansion, Rolland's first decision was to place his books in the upper part of the house. The mansion had no basement but plenty of guest rooms. Alberta envisioned space for kids to come back and visit; Rolland envisioned more storage.

Yet it took only a few years for the weight of the tomes to cause damage to the structure. In a letter Rolland wrote to novelist Jonathan Franzen some years later, he said the best way to measure the effectiveness of a third-floor library was by the "presence of cracks in the first-floor kitchen ceiling."

There was simply no way the house—as built—would support the growing collection. Rolland's solution was to build a library that would. After dropping a half million dollars into construction of the house itself, he spent another $200,000 to add a three-story library in the back. The library measured thirty-two-by-thirty-five feet, with wood-paneled alcoves jutting out from the exterior walls toward the center on both floors of the room. Rolland's library also had a feature he knew wasn't matched by any other collector.

"My library, by the way, is the only one in the world guarded by a pack of wolves."

That novelty aside, Rolland was well aware of the library's lasting impact. "I spent $200,000 to lose about $300,000 of value onto the house," Rolland later joked. "Who the heck would want a room like that in their house?"

As his collection grew, and it grew at a clip the collector estimated cost him $50,000 per year, Rolland's methods for securing signatures also required rethinking. He began questioning his approach to mailing multiple copies of books to authors. He sent poet Maya Angelou over a dozen copies of one of her collections to sign. She only returned three, with a note saying she thought that was enough.

With Anthony Burgess, Rolland sent a box full of first-edition copies of *A Clockwork Orange* with some lesser works for the author to sign. (Rolland was very clear about what constituted a first edition of the author's seminal work: The US first edition was "untidily excised," which therefore "mutilated" the book. "It was a salesman's copy for soliciting bookshop orders," Rolland bemoaned in an essay about the writer.)

None of the books were ever returned. Rolland, knowing a signed copy of the writer's work would be worth up to $3,000, wrote four follow-up letters. No response was received.

Using a connection at a posh London bookstore, Rolland snagged an invitation to an exclusive mixer where Burgess would be in attendance. With a few gin and tonics in his system, he approached Burgess and mentioned he sent the author's reps a package with books to sign. Burgess simply suggested he signed them and "the return package must be tied up in customs."

Yet Burgess, in his autobiography, specially referenced how collectors would send him books to sign. The author said he would discard the book but "keep the postage for personal use."

In his essay about the folly of capturing Burgess's inscription, Rolland rejects the idea it is rude to speak ill of the dead. "I love to speak ill of the dead and my favorite topic is Anthony Burgess." The author's biggest sin: "He is too much like me."

Rolland found traveling to book signings and getting his boxes of first-edition books autographed not only ensured success, but would help form a personal connection with the author.

He told essayist Nicholas Basbanes he had the ambition to make the authors he admired "a part" of himself. "I want to get as close to the writer as possible where I can become a part of their biography."

Rolland traveled to places like San Francisco, Chicago, New York, and Washington, DC, ten days out of every month. He would subscribe to the major newspapers from those cities to find out which authors would be at which locations and at what times. He would call his travel agent to make arrangements when a reading was announced.

Rolland recognized the true relationship he had to develop was with the events coordinator of a bookstore, who would let collectors seeking signatures know about issues that might arise with each author. Some writers would only sign hardcover books. One author refused to sign uncorrected proof copies. "Those are not books," they would sniff. But the coordinator often convinced the writer otherwise on Rolland's behalf.

Rolland compared this to the situation as a lawyer where it is better to be liked by the clerk than the judge, as the events coordinator—as opposed to the owner of the shop—was the gatekeeper to the authors themselves and had their own unique grapevine detailing what logistical challenges might come up.

Noting the start time of the reading, Rolland would arrive early to "renew my friendship with the book people and breathe the spirit of the shop." He would remark that a "pseudo proprietary" interest would work its way into his brain and remind him of Addison's. He would straighten books and pick up candy wrappers on the floor. "I might re-position paperback titles by the author of the evening in full display near the cash register." People would come up to him and ask to approve an out-of-town check or help locate a paperback copy of their favorite author. Sometimes he would oblige their requests.

Once, at a reading, a customer thought he must be the author. "Will you sign my book now," she demanded, "so I won't have to sit through the reading."

Rolland laughed at the mix-up, but the woman persisted. "I looked for a moment at the pen she was hazardously poking at my chin, and then, as a lover of books, I did the only proper thing: I signed it."

Rolland wrote essays spelling out basic rules of etiquette for interacting with the author: "1. Be respectful of the writer's time. Do not ask questions that are stupid, intrusive into the personal likes or require long answers. 2. Do not offer advice on any matter, even if it is in my area of expertise, unless asked. 3. Do not ask the writer to critique anything written by me. My essays are rather good but my attempts at fiction are not. If I want Madison Smartt Bell's help, I should enroll in his creative writing class."

Some writers were more than happy to sign whatever Rolland brought in. When he presented Michael Chabon a stack of his *New Yorker* short stories, the events coordinator reacted with a frown and told the author that he didn't have to sign those.

"I'm Rolland Comstock," the collector said to the writer, who was there to sign copies of his then-new book *The Mysteries of Pittsburgh*.

Chabon said, "Of course I will sign whatever he wants. He wrote the first fan letter I ever received."

Another favorite haunt of Rolland's was the DC bookstore Chapters. It was at a signing for Richard Russo's *Nobody's Fool* where David Streitfeld, a writer for *The Washington Post*, met Rolland and decided to do a profile. In the article, Streitfeld described the hybrid wolves with their shining coats and yellow eyes as giving the estate a bit of a "Grimm fairy tale feel."

This article led to other profiles from *The Times*, *The New Yorker*, and the Associated Press as well as appearances on C-SPAN and National Public Radio. Rolland even made his second appearance in the *National Enquirer* in a profile of strange obsessives in an article titled "Collector Maniacs Make a Killing!"

Rolland became a premier celebrity among book collectors for several years. Authors' managers would seek him out. He would get invited to private receptions and be allowed to talk with an author in advance. At the time of these profiles, Rolland could confidently say that his collection was nearly fifty thousand pieces.

Even Drury College offered him a class to teach on book collecting as a part of their Library Arts curriculum. While not well attended, the class allowed Rolland to dig into the mechanics of his hobby, as well as share some of his more treasured anecdotes.

Before he died, Rolland became particularly interested in Jonathan Franzen. Like Rolland, Franzen was a Missouri native raised in the St. Louis suburb of Webster Groves.

Rolland conducted exhaustive research over a controversy on what was defined as a "first edition" version of Franzen's *The Corrections*. Rolland noted there was a debate forming among book collectors regarding Franzen's controversial decision to reject Oprah Winfrey's coveted Book Club inclusion.

As Rolland noted in his essay "Corrections to '*The Corrections*,'" the Franzen novel was initially published with an inverse page, and several hundred copies had this error. "Franzen's eye fell on page 430 as he skimmed through a publisher copy," Rolland wrote as he recalled a correspondence he had with the author. "It didn't look right. Something was wrong. Pages 430 and 431 were transposed." The true first edition, Rolland argued, contained the "O" sticker and the mixed-up pages.

Rolland shopped his copy to publications, but it was so obsessive that some thought it was too much even for the obsessives who read their journals.

What did Franzen himself think of being one of Rolland's "writers"? In correspondence to the collector, he said it was an honor "to know some of my books are in the library annex of yours, and happy to think that I'm a tiny piece of your biography."

Rolland admitted the irony that he'd turned away from writing and academics to pursue the law and now, once he made a small fortune practicing law, he could afford to be a writer. "H. L. Mencken was once asked what type of writing paid the best. His answer was 'ransom notes.'"

Rolland didn't need to write ransom notes to make money, but still wished he had more time to write or at least could be hired to be a full-time college professor.

The pursuit, nonetheless, kept Rolland entertained and notorious. In the *Rural Missouri* profile, Rolland was asked what he would do if he ever ran out of space in the library. Would he build another wing? He looked around and answered in a hushed voice.

"I wouldn't want to say without checking to see if the room is bugged. If my wife were to hear I am almost running out of room right now, I think she'd murder me tonight!"

# IN-LAWS AND OUTLAWS

Al Rose didn't look like anyone's idea of a lawyer. He had a bushy beard and wore long hair in a ponytail sometimes. When he wasn't in court, he would wear short-sleeved button downs that showed off his chest hair. But he was a good lawyer. Scarily good.

Rose started working for Rolland in 1984, fresh out of law school. While he did his job and got results for their clients, Al would talk about things around the office that made others uneasy. He would travel to Texas and Arizona for survivalist training, he would say. Preparing for race wars, he would add with a laugh while no one could tell whether he was kidding.

Al traded guns. People who rode motorcycles and looked pretty rough even for the motorcycle-riding crowd would sometimes come in with guns. They would disappear into Al's office, then would leave with either a bag filled with cash or with nondescript boxes. Usually, hanging back when the office closed at 4:30 p.m. and that's when the rough biker types would start showing up.

One night, during tax season, Faith went back to her office to pick up some files. No one heard her come in, and she walked by the conference room to see Al and his buddies examining semi-automatic weapons splayed out over the table. Faith stood there in shock. Al saw her, quietly got up, and shut the door without saying a word.

There was a Springfield Police Department substation around the corner from the office, and Al would remark how nervous this made him. "With all the gear I've got in here," he would add as a reminder.

Faith told Rolland the activities going on in the office made her and the staff nervous. Rolland seemed unmoved by his daughter's plea. Al was weird, Rolland thought, but smart people could be strange. He dismissed it as an overreaction. If Al had guns in the office, so what? He wasn't shooting at anyone.

Al knew Faith was ratting him out and responded. She would show up and find office equipment missing from her desk. Her computer unplugged. Important files deleted. She had to install a deadbolt. When the deadbolt got removed by bolt cutters one night, Faith simply moved out and rented another office a few blocks away.

In depositions over Rolland's death, Faith said the argument over Al was the only serious rift she ever had with her father.

Faith was now gone and no longer overseeing Rolland's day-to-day work. He was already out and about traveling for his book collection. Faith also helped Becky in managing Rolland's real estate holdings property. With Faith gone and Becky on maternity leave, Al convinced Rolland to put one of his buddies in charge of managing the rentals.

When Becky returned, Al refused to let her resume being in charge of finances. Without Faith around, Becky felt she had to approach her boss about her own apprehension.

Rolland, loathing confrontation at work much like his hands-off approach to fathering, was reluctant. This behavior seemed worse than what Faith told him, he observed, but Al was still bringing in money. Al wouldn't do anything to screw up a perfectly good situation. Rolland decided things would work themselves out.

In the meantime, Al developed a relationship with Sherry. She had taken over Faith's job as receptionist some years earlier. Sherry was just Rose's type: blonde hair and blue eyes.

Al and Sherry married, and Rolland's new son-in-law waited for the keys to the Comstock kingdom. But they never came.

There are, at a minimum, two stories of the breakup. The first one: Al demanded to be a named partner. In addition to being family, he was the only lawyer who bothered to show up and bill hours. The law firm would go downhill if not for him. Rolland refused, arguing the only reason anyone came to the law firm was because of his reputation as one of the best probate lawyers in the state. Regardless, the refusal to treat Al as an equal was when he and Sherry both left.

The other side goes something like this: Rolland started checking the firm's bank statements. He found several large transfers, tens of thousands of dollars, that could not be accounted for. The same thing happened with the rental properties. When it came to money, Rolland finally decided on confrontation.

Al denied being the recipient of these transfers, but he could not explain how the money went missing. Rolland told Al he could quit, or Rolland would turn in the evidence he had to the police as well as the Missouri Bar. Al chose to leave. Sherry went along with her new hubby. Rolland never turned over the information he found so the allegations were never substantiated.

No matter which version is believed, Rolland's relationship with Sherry never recovered. They would still talk, and Sherry was still invited to family functions with an implicit understanding Mr. Rose could stay home.

A week after Al and Sherry left, someone stole Rolland's Chevy Blazer from the firm's parking lot. Everyone in the office knew Rolland would leave his keys in the ignition. Police found it a few blocks from the law firm. It had been set on fire and destroyed. Rolland left nothing of value in it. Since theft wasn't a motive, revenge seemed likely.

Despite an investigation, the police could not conclude who stole the car and set it ablaze. Whoever had done this crime was careful to leave no trace of evidence behind.

For the next ten years, Al and Rolland maintained a professional relationship. They would chat in court. When Alberta and Rolland went through their divorce, Sherry was sympathetic that her mother had been duped by a lying husband.

***

Detective Duren called the Rose Law Firm and got Al on the phone. He agreed to talk. Yes, he was at the office now with no pending appointments until the afternoon. Rose's office was on the north side of town in a drab office complex across from a shiny new Walmart Supercenter.

Duren began by noting he was curious about how Detective Wade described Rose and Sherry on the morning Rolland was found dead. They were at the pool having a drink, almost like they were celebrating, Wade had written. Al was quick to point out the police did visit him and his wife on the day before a holiday, and it wasn't too odd to be enjoying a cocktail given the slow pace of business that week.

Even though they knew Rolland was dead.

Duren shifted to asking how Rose found out about the murder so early in the day.

"Oh, I was at court that morning, and one of the clerks told me he had been found dead. I felt bad. Rolland and I had cases against each other, and he was nothing but nice to me when we talked."

"What do you know about what happened to him. How he died?" Duren read back Wade's notes that made a point Al specifically knew Rolland had been murdered, his head "shotgunned" off.

"I am almost certain I heard it from a bailiff," Rose kept talking. "You know, law enforcement guys like to talk about what they know."

Even though Al just said he'd learned about the murder from a clerk, Duren let the discrepancy pass. "Do you have any thoughts about who might have killed him?"

"I think the family is always a suspect at first. I know Alberta is screaming at me saying law enforcement is going to drive her to an early grave."

"How so?" Duren asked.

"She's had a lot of health issues. The last few years were pretty stressful with her and Rolland. I worry the stress of this will kill her."

"Do you think she would have killed him?"

"Oh, I doubt Alberta would give up the money she was going to get from the divorce settlement for the thrill of killing someone."

An odd choice of words.

"Our detectives said Alberta told them she always had a gun on her. Do you know why Alberta felt the need?"

"Well, Rolland made a lot of threats. But he was a lot of talk. I saw the guns at Christmas, and I was worried they were so old that they might blow up her on if she tried to use one. I know all about guns and I know about how to shoot them. I told her to buy a gun, and she could go shoot it at our property in Dade County."

Duren could have used Al's reference to the property to simply ask for permission for the search. But Al was giving him some decent information, so he decided to keep talking.

"Have you talked to Alberta about the case?"

"I've told her she shouldn't talk to the police. That she needs to get a lawyer and have the police talk to the lawyer. I've given her a few suggestions, but I don't know if she's done anything with it."

Duren asked about how they communicated. Alberta told Wade and Weatherford she didn't have a cell phone, Duren repeated to Rose.

"I think she has a TracFone. She doesn't want to get a plan." Duren took a note. The detectives thought Alberta was lying about not having a cell phone—she seemed evasive when she answered the question—and they were checking with local providers. She did have a landline, and detectives were already seeking records of calls that went in and out for the weeks leading up to the murder.

Later in the week, when the records for the landlines were retrieved, they revealed Alberta had taken a call from her nephew Kevin Thomure on the day of the murder. It was the only call made to or from her landline that day.

When detectives questioned Thomure, he became defensive. He said he never called her, and the records were a mistake. The detectives assured him there were no errors. Even after several minutes of questioning, he simply denied making the phone call and said it was ridiculous anyone would consider Alberta a suspect.

No one in law enforcement ever asked Thomure about whether he knew Rolland Comstock or his whereabouts on the second or third of July.

This TracFone was a new detail. Cops called them "burner phones" because they didn't leave any record of who was called.

Duren also brought a photo of the black Coach bag and asked Al if he had seen it.

"Doesn't look like anything I've seen. But I see that wolf pendant. Alberta likes her wolves."

"You think this is Alberta's bag, then?"

"Hard to say. Just noticed the pendant. Rolland likes wolves, too."

"What about Michael?" Duren asked. "Have you talked to him in the past few weeks?"

"He's very nervous. Mike knows having a criminal background will always make him a suspect in these sorts of things. No matter what."

"What about you?" Duren said with his eyes fixed directly with Rose's steely glaze. "Some might say you didn't like your father-in-law."

He was trying to find something, anything that might rattle Rose. But Duren didn't seem to have any tricks that could throw Rose off.

"I know Rolland and I had a rough history. But I got along with the old guy. We got along well." Pause. "Regardless of what people say."

Didn't change his tone. Didn't shift his sizable body weight. Rose kept going.

"It wasn't just business that got between us, you know. He molested my boy."

"Pardon me?"

"My son. When he was a teenager. Rolland had him over to the house and plied him with alcohol, and I was told something sexual happened. That was very upsetting to Sherry."

"Did you report this to anyone?"

"No, no. My boy is tough. I dealt with Rolland. That's why the business ended. I made him a lot of money, and I took that away."

This was a story Rose never told anyone, or at least no one could recall it. Rose told Wade the day after the murder that he quit the firm because Rolland was "stealing money" from clients. Becky and Faith would maintain consistently that Al was the one stealing money from Rolland's firm.

Rose kept going. "I wouldn't say Rolland was gay. I think he was bisexual. Either way, doesn't matter to me. Except when it came to my kid. I told him I would leave him on his own, but I wouldn't tell anyone about what happened. And I didn't. Until now. I do think Alberta knew that he had a history of molesting kids."

Duren would make a note to find something...anything about this claim.

"Who might have been motivated to kill Rolland?" Duren asked, seemingly forgetting he already asked the question at the beginning of their conversation.

"What do you know about Velma Brown?"

Duren wrote the name down. Didn't ring a bell even though Wade noted the name during the interview with Alberta. "Who's Velma Brown?"

"It was an estate where Rolland wrote himself in as a beneficiary. He was planning on getting about two and a half million dollars. It's sort of a long story, but her family sued Rolland over it. Ended up settling with a neighbor boy named Billy Lowell. Billy was pretty mad at Rolland about that."

"How long ago was that?" Duren asked.

"In the early '90s. Estate is still open. Rolland still owed money to Alberta from it."

The sheriff's department contacted him, and Lowell said it was a strange situation to be in as a young boy but never thought anything negative toward Rolland Comstock. Had almost forgotten about the Velma Brown situation entirely. All he got from his old neighbor were a couple of books.

It was strange that Al would have considered such an incidental person to be a suspect. Perhaps that was the point: Give the sheriff's department an absurd lead to follow.

"Anyone else?"

Al shook his head. "I told the lady detective I thought Faith and Becky would get some money under Rolland's trust."

Duren realized he was covering tilled ground. Time to get to the topic of the moment. "You mentioned there's a piece of property where Alberta shot her gun. Property you own. Can you give us permission to check it out?"

"Sure, no problem. But Alberta moved a travel trailer there. It's hers, and I cannot consent to letting you search that." Duren pulled out a form that was pre-written but added a line about not being able to search the trailer. Al signed. He even gave Duren directions.

Duren left the office without asking about the keys or the FedEx envelope or where Rose was on the night of July 2.

***

The property was at the end of a dirt road outside the county seat of Greenfield. The gate was unlocked. Duren took a few other deputies with him. It was late in the day, and he needed some help searching the acreage before dusk. Per custom, they contacted the Dade County sheriff's department to let them know they would be in the county. A few local deputies swung by as well, for lack of anything else to do. Too hot to commit any crimes, they joked.

The deputies waded around five feet of brush with metal detectors finding nothing in particular. They covered every bit of the property. There was no gun nor any signs a gun was buried there. There was no sign anyone had been target practicing. They looked in the trees to see if any bullets were embedded in the bark from target practice. Nothing indicated anyone had been in the area for some time.

There was a trailer at the northern edge of the property looking like it had been dragged through sewage and then bashed with a baseball bat. Duren couldn't figure out what anyone would do with a trailer in such horrible shape. If there was a gun on the property, it would be in there.

Even though Al couldn't consent to a search of that structure, the door appeared pried from the frame. The deputies justified going into the building to check for threats.

The trailer was ransacked. Drawers were opened and emptied. Contents and papers were all over the floor. There was no sign of a gun. No bullets. No shell casings. Figuratively and literally, the forty acres in Dade County was a dead end.

***

Almost a week after the murder, the Highway Patrol returned the ballistic report and concluded Rolland was shot with a .38 Colt Cobra.

That was the gun old Judge Burrell had given to Alberta many years ago that she said was stolen.

The gun had a history, as it turns out, revealed after detectives pulled a report from August of 2001. Rolland called the sheriff's office to report a robbery. He noted that jewelry and a handgun were taken from the family home. Law enforcement responded to the scene and took a statement from Rolland, who said his son Mike had been asked to leave the house because he was "out of control" and his eight-year-old daughter, Ashley, was present.

Michael needed money to leave town. When Rolland suggested they talk privately, Michael ran up to the master bedroom. Rolland followed, but Michael had run back downstairs with the gun and personal items. Then, he stole Stephen's car and sped away.

"He was high from anger and not from dope" was how Rolland ended his statement. Alberta also gave information to the police about the type of gun: a .38 Colt Cobra.

Deputies located the vehicle and pulled Michael over. They drew their weapons, ordering the driver to remove anything he had on him. It took a while for him to comply, so much so that the report notes the officers muttered to themselves about whether they should fire on the car.

Michael removed a black item from his waistband and tossed it out an open door. Complying with screamed demands, he exited the car with his hands up. As he was pinned to the ground, Michael said that "my fucking dad won't prosecute me!"

Sure enough, the Comstocks—including Steve, whose vehicle was stolen—pressed no charges. This was still not enough for Rolland to cut Michael off. For a time, anyway.

***

The black Coach bag found in Rolland's library was tested for fingerprints and dusted for follicles. Notably, Rolland's fingerprint was not found on the bag. Neither were Alberta's.

As far as the items in the bag, only Alberta's prints were found on them as well as those of one of her lawyers. David Adair represented her in one of the many post-divorce lawsuits between her and Rolland. Adair requested permission from the court to withdraw as Alberta's lawyer...on July 2, 2007. Law enforcement were quick to note Adair was never a suspect as he would have no motive.

It was concluded the bag belonged to Alberta. It seemed to everyone it was too big of a coincidence that the briefcase belonging to the ex-wife was sitting around a murder scene.

The withdrawal's timing might help establish something about Alberta's mindset at the time. July 2 was also the same day the real estate listing on the mansion expired. Many witnesses noted Alberta had no money because Rolland couldn't (or wouldn't) sell the house. Maybe money was running low, and things were getting desperate. Her lawyers who were fighting her ex-husband were quitting. The real estate sat in purgatory.

In terms of evidence, what Duren had was a briefcase and a gas station attendant who saw a truck that looked like Alberta's. There were bullets shot from a gun that the ex-wife once had but now could not find.

Duren needed more. Todd Myers, the lanky and bespectacled senior prosecutor assigned to the case who won a fair amount of first-degree murder cases in a young career, agreed.

The television stations weren't talking much about Rolland's homosexuality. The library and the wolves were interesting enough to keep most reporters from digging for more lurid details. But such salacious matters would get mentioned by a criminal defense lawyer and be off-putting to the God-fearing Greene County citizenry comprising the jury pool.

Such matters weren't relevant. Despite the rumors, there was no proof this murderer was an amorous stranger from the internet. Almost without fail, people were killed by someone they knew. In most of those cases, it was almost always a relative. Money was usually as good a reason for anyone to become homicidal. Rodman was out of the picture. Stephen and Faith had good relationships with their dad. Alberta, Sherry, and Michael did not. But nothing tied Sherry to the crime scene. It would still be months before Michael's DNA was tested.

If Alberta committed the murder, it would have been due to the accumulation of three years of anger. She found out her husband of nearly four decades was gay. The divorce was ugly, but even when it was over, the legal fights continued, mainly over the house. The house became a symbol in her mind of the failed marriage. When the listing expired and nothing happened, she became determined. She would confront him in person.

Maybe she wanted money from the old man. Maybe she wanted to scare him. Maybe she thought killing him would make the legal problems go away and she would get the house. She gets in her little red truck and drives toward Missouri with her gun. A gun she told Weatherford and Wade she never went anywhere without it until it was stolen by her brother while she was in the hospital. But, even though she never went anywhere without this gun, she didn't report it stolen. Or maybe she just put it in the trailer in the middle of nowhere after some target practice and didn't think about it until later, as would be a story told by other witnesses later.

Either way, Alberta stops at the gun store on the Oklahoma border. She has a panicky conversation with the owner at closing time saying she needs a cheap .38 for target practice. She drives off and heads toward Missouri an hour and a half before Rolland is shot dead.

But was she doing this to create a story that she was buying a replacement gun that would not be used in the murder? Or did she buy a gun impulsively because she knew she would have to get rid of her gun—the Judge Burrell gun—after what happened that night?

Not long after that, Alberta stops and fuels up at the gas station in front of Walmart. The clerk sees the truck but doesn't see the driver. The driver didn't come in to pay. There is no evidence of any credit card associated with Alberta being used. Maybe she used a gift card that couldn't be traced.

She keeps going. Maybe, along the way, she talks to Michael on her TracFone. The phone that leaves no records. She knew Michael was out of money, too. Both of them were broke because of Rolland, their common enemy.

Maybe they would both go over to his house and lay it out for Rolland. If you won't sell this place, give us some cash. You've got several hundred dollars just in that coffee can. Don't lie and say you don't have any more stashed away somewhere.

Maybe they meet up as Alberta drives along the western end of town and they go together. Or maybe he meets her there. Neighbors interviewed by the sheriff's department said they saw a white truck with a flat bed in front of Rolland's house the day of the murder but could not recall the precise time. The truck that looked a whole lot like a Jerry's Appliances and Repairs truck.

Either way, Alberta is careful. Though Rolland is nearly deaf, the wolves will alert him to someone coming up the driveway. But they will know her vehicle.

She lifts the chain off the gate with her shirt so as to leave no prints.

The sliding door to the kitchen is always unlocked. Alberta walks in. She finds Rolland in that library that sucked up all their money. The library that took all of Rolland's time and affection, when he wasn't talking to little boys from Mexico online.

He's caught off guard. She's screaming about what a horrible person he is. About how he dragged his feet on selling the house. *Her* house! Alberta puts the Coach attaché down and pulls out something. The gun.

Rolland knows this situation is different than their previous arguments. She's never shown up to the house before. In all the years she had that gun, he never saw her holding it. Now she is waving it at him.

In her ranting and raving and threatening, she forgets the briefcase. She just thinks about how she has no money. How she lives in this little house. How he lives in this big house, a house he had because she had given up her life to raise a family.

How could he do this to her, she wails. Her life was ruined. She needed needs money now. Rolland, knowing there is danger in Alberta's voice, tries to usher her out of the library. Out of the house. He goes away for a second as she's yelling and finds a copy of *Lord of the Flies.* Maybe it was already out because Rolland was thinking about selling it. He holds it out as he moves toward her, promising her that she can sell it and make plenty of money. "It's the most valuable thing I have," he croaks.

He gets her into the kitchen. She wants the money, the cash in the coffee can or the envelope. Whatever it is. Where is it?

Rolland puts the book down on the kitchen table. He is pleading with her, trying to tell her he has a contract on a house near Faith's and is going to sign it first thing in the morning. He doesn't want this house anymore. She can have it.

The wolves stand at attention. They are used to seeing these people yelling and fighting.

He repeats he doesn't want the house, in case she doesn't hear him. She cannot hear him. Her thoughts are at full volume. Everything turns red. She loses any concept of herself or what is going on.

Before she realizes it, the gun is aimed at Rolland and the trigger is squeezed. She physically reacts to the kick of the gun. A bullet whizzes by him. She squeezes again. Another shot grazes his chin. She lowers the gun, wanting to shoot him in the chest but hitting his stomach. He screams, but his breath is taken away. She snaps back to it. Panicked, she knows what she has done and what she cannot undo. He stumbles. Maybe he lands in the chair at the table. Maybe he drops to his knees on the floor. She shoots him in the back of the neck. Grazes the neck. Then she shoots him again. This shot knocks him to the ground.

After she catches her breath, panic starts to seep in a bit. Alberta would have realized what she had done. Would she have taken the money? Would her thoughts have been that clear?

Maybe Michael was there, in the background, or maybe outside because the wolves would not trust him, pacing and smoking a cigarette he throws on the ground. Rolland described him as a "sociopath," and a sociopath would be able to think clearly despite all the blood and mayhem. He would know they shouldn't leave the scene empty-handed. He knew exactly where the money was. He knows Rolland's ring will be easy to sell. Michael would maneuver around the blood already pooling and grab the cash. He could pluck the ring right off the old man's finger.

Alberta would give Michael the gun. Maybe he throws it in the lake. Maybe he disposes it on his way back to wherever he is staying. Just throws it in a random dumpster where no one will think to look.

They would leave as quickly as they came. The whole thing takes ten minutes. Maybe fifteen. Alberta would be able to race back to Fairland before anyone realized she was gone. This time she would take I-44 back to the state line. The only reason she'd taken Highway 60 was to visit the gun shop.

She barely gets out of town and starts having car trouble. Who knows what it is. She panics. Michael can't help because he's off getting rid of the gun. Al would be more reliable. She might not have even told him why she was in town or what she had done. Would he ask?

The truck makes it to the Halltown exit. There's a gas station with a big parking lot. No one will notice a truck on the edge of the property. Alberta leaves it there, and her son-in-law will help make arrangements to get the vehicle towed back to Oklahoma.

Al drives her back home. Maybe they don't even talk about what happens. Al could have simply assumed Alberta was in some sort of pinch without asking any questions.

Once he drops her off, there will be so many thoughts swirling around their minds that Al forgets to give Alberta her keys. He assures her the keys can be overnighted, perhaps. Just in time to pick up the vehicle from the auto shop once it's towed down to Oklahoma. Once the Rhoten boys can pick it up.

Alberta would be in the house alone. Alone with what she did. She ended it by killing the man who was ruining her life. The question was whether she could live with herself.

Then there was the question of intention. When did she know she would be a murderer? When she found out the house listing didn't expire? When her lawyers told her she needed the money to keep fighting Rolland in court and they were quitting? As she drove to Springfield to confront him? Or was it the moment right before Rolland was shot? The answer would mean the difference between first-degree premeditated murder or a murder of passion.

It was a good theory, but it was nothing anyone could prove and certainly nothing that would lead to any charges for anyone involved.

# SCENES FROM A MARRIAGE

"It was not that she simply hated him," Rolland's personal lawyer, Bob Stilling, told investigators about Alberta's motives. "She quite literally wanted to ruin him." Bob practiced law for thirty years and said it was "the nastiest divorce he had ever seen."

"Well, the divorce wasn't all that nasty. It's everything that followed."

While the constant traveling to satisfy Rolland's book obsession makes for a fun story, it also made for a lousy marriage. Alberta married Rolland for the money, which she got. But there was also a sense of prestige with being a lawyer's wife. Membership to the country club. Volunteering for the Junior League. Going to important parties with the important people of Springfield. This was not unambitious for a woman from Dade County. Most lawyers would have afforded this life to a spouse. Alberta hadn't hitched herself to just any lawyer.

Rolland took her to plenty of parties. There was a group of solo practitioners who, due to their inability to throw firm-wide soirees, would get together and get properly sloshed around the holidays. Lawyers who hung out their own shingle often did so because they could not get along with anyone else. Or didn't want to get along with anyone else.

They were often weird. Their spouses were weird. The whole vibe of the get-togethers was weird.

Alberta recalled one Christmas party where a notorious drunkard lawyer convinced Rolland to help him kill a goose wandering the property. That would be dinner, the stumbling dope proclaimed. There Rolland was, drunk himself, with a hatchet chasing after some petrified bird before a group of horrified attendees. He never caught up with it, and the incident was largely absorbed by everyone's inebriation. Save Alberta, who found it embarrassing.

There were benefits. Alberta went on some trips. She admitted these were pretty elegant and fanciful. Rolland was particularly fond of going to London for the Christmas holiday and always brought her along. These people knew how to dress for a party, with gowns and tuxedos. This was a world far removed even from the higher echelon of the biggest town in the Ozark Mountains. But these were Rolland's "book" people. They talked about things they wrote. Or collected. Or read. Alberta knew her place at these events. Smile and nod. Laugh on occasion when the response demanded it. Even if she did talk, she would have nothing to say. What did she have in common with a bunch of snooty book collectors? Plus, some of them just seemed flat-out fruity to her.

In the end, Alberta had to understand something about herself: She liked the money. She wanted the money. But she was just as content in a bingo hall with her sister, Carmel.

Alberta visited Oklahoma often. First, it was monthly. Then, she started going once a week. She and Carmel were inseparable. They talked on the phone all the time. One relative, during the murder investigation, said Carmel was the "mastermind" between the two of them. If Carmel had an idea, Alberta would go through with it. After Alberta came back from a visit, she was usually armed with some new and wild conceit.

Not that Rolland, always with his nose in a book, paid attention to anything Alberta said. Always hiding in his "book room." If he wasn't clacking away at his typewriter with his desperate, yet flowery, pleas to get attention with men of real talent, Rolland was jabbering with some collector or a bookstore owner about some author he recently met, or some unpublished short story he just *had* to get the writer to sign.

The phone in Rolland's library was a separate line, preventing eavesdropping should someone pick up another receiver. It didn't matter. He spoke in a stentorian manner that carried throughout the house. Most nights, as Alberta huddled with a newspaper and a drink, she could make out almost all the conversations.

There were also late-night calls. Occasionally, Alberta crept to the door for a listen, but Rolland was very good at keeping his voice down when the circumstance demanded it.

Marriage benefitted Rolland, too, if only for appearances' sake. In a town like Springfield, being single always raised questions. Even if someone didn't think you were gay, they would think *something* must be wrong with you. Having a spouse erased doubt from people's minds. Clients sitting down in Rolland's office—he never used a conference room—faced an Olan Mills portrait displayed prominently on his desk. Clients knew this was a respectable family man, like they were. They saw that photograph and nodded.

People still talked. Springfield was provincial, even with its big-city pretensions. Becky's brother, a Springfield police officer, told her when she started working for Rolland that everyone knew he was a "fag." His beat included Commercial Street and its skid-row assortment of homeless shelters, soup kitchens, and gay bars. Springfield's prolific gay bar scene was permitted to continue because it was easy to identify who frequented it. It was a form of segregation.

In Springfield, a handful of well-connected families ran things. They picked who ran for office and which zoning rules benefited which businesses. This was a town where nationally known brands, like O'Reilly Auto Parts and Bass Pro Shops, started out as family operations.

Those families remained interested in their hometown more than on national domination. Even when those very companies did, in fact, become household names, their leaders still had a desire to be seen as local leaders.

The people who ran the town had gay kids, too. But they were part of a protected class. They could have a "black-tie coalition," as they called it, because the family money backed them up. It was easy to be gay when your relatives made six-figure donations to the art museum or the regional theater.

While Rolland was a Springfield native, he was a north-side guy with no pedigree like some of the richer kids who attended Drury College with him. Even though Central High School was literally across the street from the college, few kids ever could cross the hierarchical barriers as Rolland had.

Lacking the protection of the rulers of the town, Rolland couldn't be himself the way some others could.

As Becky's brother correctly noted, Rolland liked the Oz on Commercial Street. It wasn't just because it was close to his office, but because it lacked a certain type of pretension he had seen with gay settings in larger cities. It was mainly men, though some butch women hung out there because it was a safe place.

He would later confide to Becky the sex wasn't even important to him. There was a "comradery" in the gay community that felt good to him.

Becky wondered if every boss talked to their employees about these things.

Rolland was perfectly fine with the gay bar on skid row. People would see his car outside. What else would he be doing there? Lawyers were as viciously gossipy as the average sewing circle. Rolland was not just the eccentric lawyer with the book collection, but "funny" as well. Lawyers talked to their wives, wives would talk to their friends, and word got back to Alberta.

Alberta put on a brave face when people would ask why Rolland would be at such a place. She was tending to a home that didn't require as much as it once had. With kids leaving, she found herself with less and less to do. Among the few friends she had, Alberta knew people spoke of her marriage with pity, if they discussed it at all. A stray, direct comment would get through from time to time, but Alberta always believed most people in her circle thought the marriage was a sham. Some of these same women warned her before the marriage.

Without kids and without a casino short of a two-hour drive, Alberta studied to become a real estate agent. She passed the test, printed business cards, and had signs made up. But she never landed a client. She never showed a house and never joined a real estate agency. Faith got to leave high school early during her senior year to answer the phones for Mom's venture. It never rang. But Faith still got a nice salary from Rolland all the same and had plenty of time to work on the crossword puzzle.

While Alberta seemed interested in real estate, Rolland never trusted her with what had become a sizable real estate holding throughout the city. One of the ways he was able to seize so much property was by requiring his clients to sign over a mortgage on their property to ensure payment of legal bills. If the client ended up in arrearage, Rolland would foreclose on the deed of trust and then bid on the property himself at the courthouse steps.

Once the foreclosure was done, Rolland would turn the properties into rental opportunities. Becky moonlighted by collecting rental checks and ensuring maintenance was performed. Nothing too expensive, she would be reminded. Becky and Jack always got the work done on time and well within Rolland's tight budget.

Faith would keep the books and pay the bills. It was a nice system with enough checks and balances from the two people in his world Rolland trusted the most. He would never trust Alberta with his money, after all, and her desire to work in real estate herself was ignored when it came to Rolland's burgeoning slumlord empire.

Without much to do, and without many houses to show, Alberta concluded perhaps she could teach herself to be psychic. She bought tarot cards and studied the ability to look into the future. Besides entertaining her children's friends with bad premonitions, there wasn't much medium business for Alberta, either.

Failing to grasp anyone else's future, Alberta thought about her own and what she could do with "her" house. She heard from a friend that a breeder had come across a litter of wolf-hybrids and was unsure if there was a market for a potentially dangerous creature. Seems a German Shepherd out in the mountains found herself loose and in an amorous mood when a wolf came across her. Luckily for her, the wolf was in the mood for love and less interested in lunch or protecting his territory.

Alberta was always interested in wolves. She collected figurines and wore shirts with those piercing, beautiful eyes. She thought they were pretty and mysterious. Having spent time in the tribal areas of Oklahoma, she thought of the wolf as spiritual.

She begged Rolland to adopt the whole litter. He found the idea insane. But he also saw it would make Alberta happy and give her something to do. Who knows, it might be another interesting quirk to have a pack of semi-wolves roaming around the house. There was something outrageous to the whole idea that Rolland thought played into his image.

They adopted the mother and the puppies. The breeder cautioned that the wolf half of the puppies were in desperate need of a den mother. It was a package deal. They could never be separated. At first, the notion of these extremely feral creatures roaming around a house, even a big house with lots of acreage, was a problem. Furniture was destroyed. Floors were so scratched they appeared dug up. Territory had to be marked, so the rugs reeked of urine and the joists began to sag from excessive wetness.

But the inside of the house was just the tip of the iceberg. The wolves would use the roof of Rolland's Cadillac as a perch. Within a week, the vinyl top was ripped to shreds, and wolf-shaped dents marked the car from bumper to bumper.

For the neighbors, who began to notice pets going missing, they took alarm at these animals that were allowed to roam free in the yard next door. Certainly, having wild animals at a private residence was illegal.

The sheriff would be called, but deputies would say they weren't the agency to handle the matter. All complaints about these mangled, malicious mutts were transferred to the Missouri Department of Conservation. They sent out agents to investigate whether the Comstocks were breaking the law that clearly stated wolves, as well as any other animals defined as "exotic," could not be kept by private individuals without a litany of paperwork submitted to, and ultimately approved by, state bureaucrats.

This was a clear-cut case, according to the lawyers for the state. Now, this was where Rolland got more involved. Instead of merely being pets, the wolves became Rolland's cause. Like any area of the law he touched, he devoured statutes, regulations, and cases.

"Keeper of dangerous wild animals must register animals—exceptions and penalties" was the title of the law. It seemed clear no person was supposed to keep a wolf (or a "cheetah, jaguarundi, hyena, or Canada lynx," among other creatures specified) without registering said creature with local law enforcement.

"But not wolf-hybrids," Rolland observed in red letters and extra yellow highlighting ink. Another statute Rolland photocopied noted that failing to register a wolf was "a misdemeanor" and could result in a sentence of up to a year in county jail.

"No indication as to what *class* of misdemeanor," Rolland noted. Another note suggested he could argue the regulation as insufficient because it lacked such a classification.

But Rolland obviously knew he was on shaky legal ground. Also, in the "wolf file" was an article by Dr. F. T. Satalowich, noted public health veterinarian, who said, "[The Missouri Department of Conservation's] policy on hybrid wolves is as follows: If it looks like a wolf, regardless of the percent of the wolf in the cross, it is considered a wolf. Therefore, at this time, all hybrid wolves can and must be permitted. In the near future, they will be considered to be illegal in Missouri."

"Could 'grandfather' argument be made if we had permit before 'hybrids' became illegal," Rolland's notes wondered. While there's little elaboration about how that phrase is used, the legal understanding of "grandfather" would mean that, if the law was changed to list hybrids, Rolland and Alberta would be in the clear, because they had the dogs before the law changed.

After letters with threats of lawsuits crisscrossed various lawyer desks, the eggheads in Jefferson City relented and dropped their investigation. Rolland decided to go ahead and add fencing that went three feet deep into the ground so no animals could dig under the fence. Neighborhood dogs had less of a chance of getting slaughtered, so aggrieved neighbors dwindled.

Rolland, having fought on behalf of the pack against the tyrannical forces of government, became more attached to the dogs—wolves. Whatever they were, they started treating Rolland as their pack leader. More so after the mother passed away.

"I've even lost the wolves to that husband of mine," Alberta complained.

The inattention. The endless trips out of town. Not even for business, but for a hobby that was costing them money. The loneliness of the big house on top of a hill with an iron-cast fence everywhere you looked. Alberta felt like a prisoner of her own affluence, a woman tortured by a life she once coveted.

The book trips were one thing. But then Rolland started taking weeklong sojourns to Mexico. At first, he said he was going to a book collectors' conference. Some author invited him, Rolland boasted. Whatever, Alberta thought. Just another reason to leave her behind.

After returning from one of these trips in late 2004, Rolland conspicuously left out his luggage. Lying out in the open, in their marital bedroom, as Alberta dramatically emphasized in court filings later, was a matchbook for a gay resort.

Her stomach sank. Her skin became cold. Alberta sat on the bed waiting for him to come out. When he did, wearing the bare necessities and thus more vulnerable, she thought, Alberta revealed her discovery.

"Is this what I think it is?" she asked. He denied it, saying it was just a regular hotel. She screamed. She cried. Alberta pointed out it was clearly advertised for "gay clientele." She accused him of ruining her life. The last thirty-eight years were a lie. A joke! He finally admitted that, yes, he went to a resort for gay men. But he did not consider himself to be a gay man. Rolland just liked the comradery of the community, as he told Becky time and time again.

Alberta could not believe what she was hearing. "You go to a gay resort but don't think you're gay?"

Rolland protested that it was complicated. He would later be more forthcoming in conversations about his sexuality. He liked women and men. Although he still rejected the "bisexual" term because it was never about sex in Rolland's mind. The physicality of relationships was merely symbolic, as he saw it. Such nuances were lost on everyone else.

Alberta wanted him out of the house. She demanded a divorce. Rolland tried to beg her off, but he had no heart for it. The marriage wasn't even worth salvaging considering what he just revealed. She wanted him to sleep downstairs until he could move out. It was her house, after all. Legally, that's what the deed said.

Rolland began doing what he did best: arguing until his opponent went into submission. He couldn't possibly sleep in another bed due to his ailments. His joints. His back. It would kill him. Rolland begged. Pleaded. She relented. Alberta would stay in the guest bedroom, the one room she prohibited from being filled with books. The room was designated for whenever Carmel, Stephen, or Michael needed a place to stay.

Over the next few days, Rolland simply paid her $10,000 to go somewhere else. She rented a drab and faceless corporate apartment on the far south end of town. The second Alberta left, she regretted it. The mansion became a reminder of her anger for him. She would get that from him if it was the last thing she did.

**Rolland's wolf hybrids enjoying their favorite chew toys—Rolland's car. Photo courtesy of the Rolland Comstock Estate.**

The Springfield Leader & Pres

SPRINGFIELD, MISSOURI, FRIDAY AFTERNOON, DECEMBER 7, 1984

**Top Dog**

Butch the bulldog shows his attorney, Rolland Comstock, around the grounds of his house — a $55,000 brick structure at 2538 N. Campbell Ave. Butch's master, the late William W. Morrison, left his pet the house, its furnishings, a car, a van and a $20,000 savings certificate, all valued at $98,500.

**Butch enjoys dog's life with $98,500 estate**

By Barbara Clauser

See DOG, Page 8A

**School d ends IBM**

Officials halt firm's

By Leo Mullen

**Police par quiets ille**

**Rolland and his prized client, a French Bulldog named Butch. Photo courtesy of the *Springfield News & Leader*.**

**Rolland in the front yard of his home. Photo courtesy of the Rolland Comstock Estate.**

**Rolland and his prized library.**
**Photo Courtesy of Missouri State Library**

**Rolland as a young lawyer/lawmaker. Photo courtesy of the Rolland Comstock Estate.**

**Rolland's pitch to voters of North Springfield. Photo courtesy of the Rolland Comstock Estate.**

**Rolland and another view of his palatial book collection.
Photo courtesy of the Rolland Comstock Estate.**

—News and Leader Staff Photo

Sixteen-year-old Rolland Comstock, who is just now discovering the troubles a "small businessman" encounters when he strikes out on his own, stands above among his books at the shop he operates at Pacific and Robberson.

★ ★ ★

**Rolland and his exploits as a teenage bookstore owner.
Photo courtesy of the *Springfield News & Leader*.**

# A HAM SANDWICH

There was the theory about what happened to Rolland Comstock. Proving it required much more.

Around July 17, Detective Duren traveled to Fairland specifically to talk with Alberta about the new information investigators received. About the truck at the gas station. About the TracFone. About the briefcase. They also had a freshly signed search warrant allowing them to remove computers, clothes, and shoes and get a swab of her saliva.

At first, Alberta had no trouble handing over clothes and shoes. They took the cigarette butts. They even took the FedEx envelope. But, according to the narrative he produced, Duren did not ask any follow-up questions about the keys initially seen in the FedEx package. Keys to what?

After swabbing to obtain her DNA, Duren showed her a photo. "We found this in Rolland's den. Is this your briefcase?"

"Yes, that's mine."

"We're aware," Duren revealed. "It has documents that belong to you. Why would this be in Rolland's den, ma'am?"

She regarded the photo. "We, I, left it for him."

"You left it for him? When was this?"

"It was a little under a month ago, I think. I think it was the last week of June. That's when I was in Springfield last."

"Did you see Rolland then? Did you talk?"

"No. No, we didn't. I left it out at the gate."

"You said 'we' earlier," Duren noted. "Was someone with you?"

"Yes, my sister Carmel was with me. We went to Springfield to look at the house and to see Stephen. I don't know if I've told you this, told the people that were here last, but Rolland left the house in terrible shape. He never kept it up. The real estate agent complained about it. The way it looked. Rolland would say…"

She caught herself. Alberta knew better than to wind herself up about the house again. "I left the bag at the gate. I didn't go in."

"You left this at the gate," Duren repeated back. "Why did you do that?"

She looked at the photo again and then looked toward her kitchen. "There were documents. Important documents I thought he would need."

"We've looked at the documents that were in the bag. What did you think was so important that you needed to get to him?"

Alberta put her hand to her head. "I don't really remember. I thought he would need something in there."

Later, Duren would ask Becky and Faith about this assertion. Both agreed Alberta would have done nothing to help Rolland at this point in their relationship. Secondly, if she had, Rolland would have crowed about it to either one of them or Bob Stillings. Stillings would also fail to recall Rolland mentioning anything about this bag. Rolland would have thought it was so funny and outrageous that he would have shared it with at least one of them.

Most importantly, there wasn't anything in the bag Rolland needed. The real estate documents were all copies. As far as the estate planning documents of Alberta's, there was no reason Rolland would consider them "important." It is possible Rolland could have taken documents out, but nothing had been retrieved, and again, the three confidantes knew nothing of any documents he may have discovered.

"Did you talk to Rolland about—"

"I'm sorry, Detective," Alberta interrupted. "I realize I need to make a call."

"But Mrs. Comstock, we're having a conversation here," Duren protested. He had Mirandized her again, but it was also her house. She was not being held in custody, and he couldn't necessarily stop her. Not with the little evidence he had.

Duren heard a muffled conversation, then some high-pitched yelling. He tried to walk up to the door to get a better bead on the conversation, but the door burst open just as he started to stand.

"I have been advised by counsel to not speak to you unless he is here to assist me with questions."

"That's certainly your right, ma'am," Duren conceded. "Is your lawyer here in town? Could we go to his off—"

"He is in Springfield. If you need anything from me further, please call him." She handed Duren a business card. Tim Richardson—Attorney.

This must have been the lawyer Rose said he was trying to get Alberta to talk to just a few days earlier.

But he was not well known as a criminal defense lawyer, Duren would later learn. He handled issues for small businesses in the area. Contracts. Real estate disputes.

Maybe there was some grand strategy. Or maybe Alberta was acting out of panic and just hired the first person Al suggested. Either way, she had a right to a lawyer and was going to exercise it.

Simply saying she had a lawyer wasn't enough to keep Duren from continuing to ask her questions. The US Supreme Court said a lawyer literally must be there in person to keep an interrogator from speaking to a suspect.

Alberta stayed resolved in her assertion. She never answered a question from law enforcement again. She would now have other people to speak for her.

On his way out of town, Duren stopped at the Firing Range and talked to Mike Friend. He discussed Alberta's handling of a gun. It wasn't terrible. For a woman, Friend added. Alberta had taken her permit classes there and was pretty bad, Friend remembered. He recommended continuing to practice. He then remembered she said she had been going somewhere in Missouri to target practice while she was getting her gun permit. "Green something" was all Friend could recall.

"Greenfield?" Duren asked. He usually tried to avoid prompting people being questioned but hoped they could cut to the chase.

"Yeah, said it was her son-in-law's place, but she had a cabin or trailer or something. Said she liked target practicing with potatoes." Later in the conversation, Friend said Richardson had been down there the day before to speak with him about the case.

***

Carmel was on the investigators' list. Detective Weatherford went back to Fairland separate from Duren to knock on the door of every house in Alberta's neighborhood, to see if they noticed anything strange or unusual on July 2. Or if they had seen Alberta coming and going.

Alberta kept largely to herself since moving to Fairland in 2005. At first, she lived with Carmel. But then, Carmel's daughter, who lived across the street, moved away. When Alberta got her settlement money from Rolland, she bought the house. The only person in the neighborhood who spoke to Alberta with any frequency was her sister.

Other neighbors knew they were related but knew little else. No one recalled talking to Carmel, either. Both women stayed in their homes or were away. Did they remember anything about the house or about Alberta from the second or third of July? Not a neighbor could recall whether they had seen her or her sister or the truck on either one of those days. The house had no garage, only a carport visible from the street. People remembered seeing cop cars in front of the house on the night of the murder, but that was it.

Carmel stood outside waiting for the police. She looked like her sister. Shorter. She welcomed them in but then said she had been told by Alberta's lawyer not to talk to the police. About anything. They tried.

She resisted. The Greene County Sheriff's Office left learning nothing about what Carmel knew or didn't know.

Yet three years later, in a deposition taken in a civil case, Carmel appeared under subpoena and had an explanation for everything. Every theory developed by Duren had a neat, convenient explanation.

"Do you know where your sister, Alberta, was on July 2 of 2007?"

"Yes, I do. She was at home. Across the street. That's where she lives."

"Right, of course. How do you know that?"

"We talked that day on the phone. A couple of times. She was upset about the real estate listing. It just expired, and she very much wanted to get the divorce past her."

"Was that on a landline? Cell phone?"

"I don't remember. She called me. I don't remember seeing the caller ID."

"Did you see her that day?"

"Yes," Carmel offered. "I saw her between 8:00 and 8:30."

"Was that in the morning?"

"No, that was p.m. At night." Rolland's neighbor, Mac Mathis, heard gunshots shortly after 8:00 p.m. This was the time the sheriff's department zeroed in on when Rolland was fatally shot. Carmel could precisely state where Alberta was at the time when Rolland was being murdered.

"You saw her?"

"Yes, I was at her house between 8:00 p.m. and 8:30 p.m. Then I left and came back at 10:00 p.m."

That would have been how long it took—more or less even with car trouble—for Alberta to drive back to Oklahoma. Again, the precise time Alberta would have to have her whereabouts accounted for.

"Why did you go back?"

"I was worried about her. She was upset. About Rolland. About the house."

"How long did you stay then?"

"About ten minutes. She was in bed. She was trying to sleep. Very tired. Very upset."

"So, you are saying you talked to Alberta Comstock during the day on the second of July of 2007 between 8:00 p.m. and 8:30, as well as right after 10:00 p.m. Is that correct?"

"I didn't talk to her when I saw her at 10:00 p.m., no. She was asleep. I walked in and saw her sprawled out on her bed. I didn't want to wake her, so I stood there to make sure she was okay. Then I left."

This story was so convenient, so easy. Carmel was providing an alibi for her sister and trying to put together details explaining anything away while being careful not to contradict whatever Alberta said previously, since she might not remember precisely what was said back in the summer of 2007.

"Do you know the last time Alberta was in Springfield or was at her ex-husband's house?"

"I believe it was in June. We were there. Yes."

"You were there with her. Did you go to Rolland's house?"

"I didn't go into Rolland's house. We drove by. She wanted to see the house. See what condition it was in. She also wanted to see Stephen, and he lives just down the road."

"Uh-huh. Do you recall anything about what happened when you drove by Rolland's house?"

"She also wanted to drop off some books. She had some books of Rolland's that she had taken when she was moving furniture out of the house."

Books, not "important documents" as Alberta said.

"But you all didn't go in?" Carmel was asked. "You just drove by?"

"No, Alberta went in. Yes, she had the books in a black bag, and she went into the house to drop them off. She said Rolland wasn't there."

Alberta told investigators she left the bag at the gate. Upon this admission, Duren sent the bag to be tested for dirt. Grass. Anything that would indicate it had been outside for any determinable amount of time. That test came back negative. This was shared with Alberta's attorney. Now, there's this story. Carmel was insistent. The bag wasn't left outside.

"She left her bag in the house?"

"Yes, at the bar, and we drove off and she realizes she left some other documents in the bag. Documents that belonged to her."

Not documents Rolland would find important, as Alberta said before asserting her right to have an attorney present. Documents that, in fact, were of no use to Rolland.

"When did she figure this out? That she left the bag? That she had left documents in the bag?"

"We were on I-44 just outside of town. We were turning off of Highway 13 and heading west. That's when she noticed she didn't have the bag."

This interchange was not even five minutes away from Rolland's house.

"You didn't think to go back for these documents? That would have been ten minutes round trip to go back and get this bag."

"She thought she might be back. She thought she could get it later. No big deal."

Carmel was asked about the books. About the documents. She didn't seem to have an answer for any of those questions, had no idea what was in the bag. Seemingly Alberta never mentioned this on the drive to Springfield or on the way back to Oklahoma.

"Do you know if Alberta has a gun?"

"Yes, she had a gun that you could hold in your hand. I think she said it was a .38."

"When was the last time you saw her with that gun?" she was asked. At this point, anyone familiar with the case knew Alberta said she had it with her all the time until it was allegedly stolen while she was in the hospital.

Her brother took it. But he said that was not the case.

Maybe her doped-out neighbors. They knew the doors weren't locked. The scared woman who needed a gun but didn't lock her doors.

"It was in May of 2007. It was at the trailer."

"The trailer in Greenfield?"

"Yes, she took it up there to target practice and she left it there."

"Do you know why Alberta left the gun at the trailer?"

"I don't know. I don't think she remembers leaving it there."

Alberta seemed to have lost everything relevant to the murder investigation.

"Mrs. Comstock told us she went everywhere with that gun. That she's scared. Why would she have left it there for all of this time without getting it?"

A pause. Carmel's eyes shifted. "Well, I don't know. By the time I remembered what happened with it, Rolland had already been shot. I said we should go up and get it..."

"Get the gun?"

"Yes, we should go up and get it, but her lawyer told us that was a bad idea. 'Don't go up there because the cops have already been up there' is what he said."

"You didn't go up there after Alberta talked to her lawyer?"

"Oh, no, we ended up going."

"When was this?"

"The week after we heard the police left."

"When was this?" Duren's report said he spoke to Al Rose on July 17 and got permission to search the property. Duren and some other deputies went that afternoon. Which meant, according to Carmel, Alberta went back to the property in late July.

"That must have been right. We went to the trailer and saw that the door had been pried open and there was no gun inside. We figured the police must have taken it when they were there."

To believe Carmel was to believe she saw Alberta at the very moment law enforcement knew Rolland had been killed. Also, Alberta wanted to help Rolland by bringing back his prize books. To believe that would mean believing she chose to leave the bag there instead of backtracking a few minutes to retrieve it. Plus, she would have left a gun in a trailer in the middle of nowhere for two months.

It filled too many gaps. But it didn't fill them perfectly. Because there were significant discrepancies.

Back to July of 2007, and as far as the criminal investigation was concerned, Carmel wouldn't talk. Alberta wouldn't talk. Michael wasn't cooperating and was hopping around from place to place. Law enforcement was keeping tabs on him, but he was out of money. Had nowhere to go and relied on the good graces of people like Sammie Johnson and Robin Stokes. People who would sell him out, or were hoping to sell him out, to help with their pending criminal charges.

However, prosecutors believed there was enough to get a search warrant and obtain physical evidence from Michael. The prosecutor, Todd Myers, wrote up everything he had about the case so far, including the statements law enforcement had taken from Michael's associates. None of this was good enough to arrest anyone. But it did give the State of Missouri probable cause to get more information. A judge would have to determine if the warrant justified execution.

The warrant had to be carefully written and executed quickly. Michael was living with someone in Northwest Springfield, a sketchy part of town. This would be an iffy proposition, as Michael had no place where all his clothes or all his shoes would be. He could have left them at any number of places. Or tossed them, as Robin Stokes had done. This was not necessarily about getting physical evidence, but about getting proof that Michael was at the scene. The clothes might reveal DNA that matched DNA found at the scene. Which meant also getting Michael's mouth swabbed so saliva could be collected and checked against. The shoes might match prints left at the scene.

So far, the only matches law enforcement found were from Alberta's fingerprints on documents in the briefcase. Everything else belonged to Rolland. There were no other footprints other than Rolland's found on the floor of the kitchen and foyer. The ones where he stomped the ticks to their splattering death. In fact, the coroner noted the sole of Rolland's shoe was also covered in the skin of dead ticks.

Law enforcement followed Michael and knocked on the door of the house where he was staying. The deputies showed him the search warrant. He nodded and let them into the house to collect a random assortment of his clothes and shoes. He asked when he could get them back. Couldn't say, was the response. The deputies also noted they needed to swab his mouth. He nodded again and opened wide.

DNA test results would not be released until July 2008 when the sheriff confirmed Michael Comstock had been at the scene of the murder.

Why did it take almost a year to reveal this information? Publicly available data in 2010 revealed the average time between submitting a DNA test and receiving a test result in Missouri was around eight months.

That explained almost two-thirds of the delay.

With the one-year anniversary of the murder approaching, reporters worked on stories to mark the grim milestone of a prominent lawyer being shot in his home. They called the sheriff's department, who could not comment on an "open case." The reporters scoffed. Their stories would describe the case as "cold."

The press release announcing the DNA results gave the press fodder. At least results were still coming in and the case was still active.

But that's all that happened. As Faith's calls stopped being answered, and Becky was the administrator of Rolland's estate, she asked Becky to start calling. After Duren explained to her there wasn't enough evidence to arrest anyone, Becky persisted. Her calls weren't returned, either.

Duren took a promotion, relieving him of his lead detective position. Weatherford was named as his replacement. He didn't have much to work with. Weatherford took the calls from the two women. He wanted to be patient. They were close to the victim. They were victims themselves, although there were only so many times a person could be told there was no new information.

Becky talked to Faith nonstop about what they knew. Or didn't know. They would morosely chat well into the night. But she had other things on her mind. Rolland was her only boss. Rolland's last associate left in February 2007. He found a solo practitioner to share the office. At least the lawyer would pay rent and be responsible for his own salary.

When Rolland died, the Law Offices of Rolland Comstock had no attorney, only Becky. Under the Missouri Rules of Professional Conduct, lawyers were supposed to have a succession plan in place where another lawyer would help wind up the practice. Someone would reach out to clients to let them know what happened, finish up cases, and shepherd them to new lawyers.

This was important for a law firm handling estate planning since a client might have come in twenty years ago to have a last will and testament drafted up. There might be little activity on that file until the client died. It was important the family knew where to go to find estate planning documents when the time came.

If the lawyer had no succession plan, as Rolland did not, the Missouri Supreme Court was supposed to step in and assign a lawyer to do this work. But no one called the high court. Becky knew every client of Rolland's. Perhaps she knew them better than he had, particularly toward the end when she would conduct meetings with them.

Becky called and wrote to the clients. This was literally no different than what she had been doing for close to three years anyway. It was routine stuff for a paralegal. But being a paralegal usually meant there was some sort of legal supervision.

The public administrator was eager to figure out what was going on, especially with the several hundred estates Rolland handled. Carolyn Little, the Democrat who had been in the role since 1980, said they would go wherever Becky went. Becky knew the files and knew what paperwork had to be done.

The public administrator staff decided on a lawyer who they felt should hire Becky. But that lawyer called Becky and was very curt, with seemingly little empathy for her situation. The staff kept pushing. Becky wasn't sure.

She wasn't sure of anything anymore.

The days were hard for Becky. She sat there in the office and wrote her letters to clients of yesteryear. Clients would call and talk about their case or about the letter they got. Those conversations would always lead to talking about Rolland and what happened. She would go down to the public administrator's office, and all they wanted to talk about was the murder and their theories. Everyone treated it like a television show. The only bright spots were when she talked to lawyers who wanted to hire her. They flattered her and talked up her reputation. She was happy that people were eager to give her a place to land.

None of them would match the relationship she had with the guy who gave her a chance out of secretarial school and treated her like a surrogate daughter. She had to go through the ups and downs of Velma Brown, Alberta, and developing dirty photos. Now she had to deal with this. Most of the time, Becky tuned out Rolland's personal problems. They were just things that rich people fought over, she thought. *I will never have to worry about that*, she reasoned. Rolland's drama just became another line on her job description.

Now, there were no more early-morning phone calls or trips out to the strange house with the spooky wolves. She remembered transcribing his vibrant and creative missives. They seemed altogether different from what other lawyers sent to the firm. Rolland's words were alive and funny, written by a brilliant mind. She learned so much from him and believed there would never be another person like this in her life.

Rolland was now just another estate to deal with. But the absence was thick. Finding him. Seeing him like that. Seeing the blood. It kept her up at night. A teetotaling Baptist, she thought a cocktail might help her sleep. She tried it a few times. It didn't work. No, she would just have to work through it. Cry through it. Talk to God, see what He would do. Even that wasn't clear.

Becky asked about the criminal investigation. Her daughter Ashley took horse riding lessons from the same farm where Deputy Sheriff Jim Arnott's daughter rode. She would talk to him then. He gave her a pat line about the ongoing investigation. "Looks promising," he would say.

But there was nothing promising. Physical evidence simply was not developing. What law enforcement found was circumstantial. Most of what they had pointed to someone who wasn't a hardened criminal. Alberta Comstock had no record. Not even a speeding ticket.

But no one is a murderer until they murder someone. Was she so unbelievably lucky that she left no physical trace in the house? Well, other than the briefcase.

Or drove four hours round trip without being IDed? Other than the clerk who swore she saw her fueling up. Or the broken-down truck as she tried to flee.

But even that evidence had problems. See, no one actually saw Alberta. Not specifically. That Walmart gas station clerk, upon being interviewed again, thought maybe she had seen the truck on the third of July. Timecards said she wasn't working then? Oh, then it was definitely the second. Other than seeing the smiley face as the driver pumped gas, no one had seen the driver. No one could place Alberta in Missouri on the night of the murder.

There was no weapon. No idea where it might be. A murder case without a weapon was daunting. Not impossible. But people figuratively, if not literally, expect a smoking gun. The gun that matched the bullets that were shot and the trigger that would have at least one fingerprint on it. That's what convicted defendants.

An arrest warrant was discussed but all knew what a judge would say: "Not enough probable cause. Go get more evidence and then we will talk." But there was no evidence. If there wasn't enough evidence to issue an arrest warrant, there wouldn't be enough evidence to actually get a conviction.

The state had to prove their case beyond a reasonable doubt. Myers had to convince the entirety of a jury of twelve people there was no question Alberta shot Rolland. Seemed like there were still lots of questions.

Which meant there wasn't any certainty as to whether they would simply seek criminal charges against just Alberta. There was an argument to be made, based on the eyewitness reports at Baumer's Food Mart, the FedEx envelope, and Michael's DNA, that others aided and abetted her in getting out of Springfield or with the disposal of the weapon.

Or that, in fact, someone else might have killed Rolland.

The fact someone else might be involved with the crime, or someone else was at the scene, would open up an argument by even a barely competent criminal defense lawyer that there was in fact reasonable doubt. The worry was that all this effort—the investigation and subsequent prosecution—would lead to an acquittal.

If it even went to trial, securing an indictment would lead to an arrest and start the process of a criminal conviction. If there was enough evidence to place Alberta at the scene, she might enter into a plea agreement. An old lady wouldn't want to spend the rest of her life in prison. She might agree to a reduced sentence. She might reveal facts leading to other convictions in exchange for a reduction in her sentence. A plea deal meant she would tell a judge she was guilty. That, in of itself, would be a victory and would close a case and bring some relief to the victims' family and loved ones.

It wasn't ideal. Nothing about the case was, though.

A judge might not issue an arrest warrant. A grand jury might.

Grand juries are common at the federal court level and frequently used in many states, but not used often in Missouri. In most Missouri felony cases, as had already been discussed, a judge must sign off on an arrest warrant that lays out the charges against the defendant. Then they are arraigned. Then the prosecutor has up to six months to hold a preliminary hearing where the judge decides if there is probable cause that a crime, any crime, was committed and the matter can be "bound over" for a trial. The preliminary hearing is informal and usually gets waived by the defendant. In a preliminary hearing, a defendant does get to confront their accusers. They get to be represented by an attorney. The proceeding is public.

Grand juries do not work that way. A selected panel of citizens hear evidence on several cases. There is no judge. The jury decides if probable cause exists to issue a bill of indictment. Like a preliminary hearing, they can issue an indictment on any crime involving any party for which evidence is presented. Under this process, the preliminary hearing is skipped altogether, and the matter proceeds to trial.

In a grand jury, the defendant is not there. They are not notified of the action. They cannot be represented by a lawyer. The grand jury process is entirely secret. In fact, under Missouri law, it is a misdemeanor to even talk about your involvement with the grand jury.

The twelve Greene County citizens sat in the jury chairs as Myers presented evidence on a number of cases. Then he got to the Rolland Comstock murder. He talked about the autopsy, the bullet tests, the fingerprints in the briefcase, the documents in the briefcase, the witnesses who saw Alberta's truck at the gas station in Monett earlier in the night as well as those who saw the truck at the gas station going back to Oklahoma. Weatherford testified. Duren came back to testify. So did Becky. She talked about discovering Rolland and about the contentious relationship he had with Alberta. Faith also testified to what she knew. The medical examiner explained how Rolland died, what each bullet wound might mean.

In the end, the grand jury members were left in the courtroom as the prosecutor exited. A marshal would alert Myers when a decision had been made or if there were any questions. After an hour, he was summoned and the grand jury announced there did not appear to be probable cause to indict anyone associated with the murder.

You can indict a ham sandwich, as the old saying goes, but you could not indict anyone for the murder of Rolland Comstock. This decision by the grand jury did not foreclose on other proceedings. But it made clear to the sheriff and prosecutor what they had so far was not enough.

Now, Myers and Weatherford could not tell anyone what the grand jury had done or, in this case, had not done. But it was clear nothing happened because no one was arrested. Things got even more quiet, and Faith got even more frustrated with the pace of the investigation.

For the time being, it seemed the whole thing was over. Whether it had anything to do with the lack of evidence or mistakes made in the investigation itself, the trail went cold.

Becky was convinced there was something more nefarious at foot. One day, as she worked through an older file, a deputy knocked on the office door. He was returning the computers removed right after the murder. Everything on the computer had been downloaded, and the sheriff's staff was going through everything they found.

Becky told the deputy to put the computers in the back. The computers were old; Becky would be surprised if she could sell them. Since she was named the executor under Rolland's will, she was stuck with trying to off-load all the office furniture and equipment. Who would want fifteen-year-old computers that could barely send emails?

As she helped the deputy with opening doors, Becky asked him if he'd heard anything new. Not that he was aware. Were they closer to making an arrest? He couldn't say. Was there anything on the computers that was helpful? He ignored the question as he placed the devices on the ground. The deputy's demeanor changed—Becky sensed there was something cold coming from this conversation. But when they finished and he was about to leave, the deputy had to have his peace.

"I've been talking to people who have looked at what's on this computer. It's disgusting. It involves kids, you know? Kids. That's the kind of guy you worked for. That's the kind of guy he was."

Becky was shocked. Her jaw agape as the deputy left. She never heard more than that about this awful allegation. There was no way of confirming what he told her. It wasn't as though they were going to release a bunch of incriminating information about Rolland now that he was dead. But Becky never knew Rolland to be this way. Had never seen or done anything that would suggest it.

She assumed a lot of the macho cops in the sheriff's department had a problem with anyone who was gay. Becky also knew from experience that churches like Baptists and Assemblies of God strongly suggested homosexuality and pedophilia were linked. Just about every employee on the force belonged to one of those churches. Heck, you could say that about everyone who lived in Greene County.

One could not be too loose in supporting the gay lifestyle because that is what it represented, preachers would say from their pulpit. It was a slippery slope that led to further deviance. It was Sodom and Gomorrah. The Romans and the Greeks fell because they tolerated homosexuality.

Becky knew that because she heard that. Maybe at one point, she believed it. But knowing Rolland turned her around. She knew his inherent goodness. She wanted to run after the deputy to tell him he was wrong. Ignorant. Prejudiced.

As she sat down shaking from the experience, Becky also knew anything she told this guy wouldn't matter. Maybe it wasn't just dirty pictures they found on the hard drive. Maybe what Al Rose said to Detectives Wade and Duren wafted to other people in the investigation and, despite there being no evidence of the son-in-law's claims, it got stuck in the morass surrounding the investigation.

That meant there were other people in law enforcement who'd made their mind up about Rolland. That, if he wasn't a kiddie fiddler, he was just an old gay guy. Who cared if he got shot? If it was his old lady, well it made sense she would be mad. Not like she was going on a killing spree. She found out her husband was a queen, got pissed about it, and snapped.

This would be what kept Becky up for many nights afterward. This was the point when it would occur to her the murder would never be solved, because there were people in the sheriff's office who didn't care if it got solved or not. They all but told her that. When she couldn't sleep, she would go to her backyard and call Faith to talk. Faith couldn't sleep, either.

Becky accepted a job with a new Springfield firm. It was the same firm where the associate who fled Rolland's practice back in February had moved. It was fancier than where Becky had worked, but she liked the associate, and he promised to do his best to give her a flexible place to work. As promised, the public administrator and its four hundred files came along.

This new law firm opened the promise that some form of justice might happen. There was a chance for resolution when everything so far seemed so frustratingly circumstantial.

# VELMA BROWN

Alberta hired Bob Wiley, a well-respected country lawyer from the small town of Crane about an hour southwest of Springfield. She wanted a lawyer who wasn't from Springfield, under the belief such a lawyer would be more likely to take her case against a well-known "city lawyer."

Wiley wasn't as old as he looked. Short in stature and wrinkled, he had what could only be described as a "hillbilly" way about him. His voice was soft but tinged with a mixture of Southern and flat Midwestern affect. His mouth would gape between words, giving the appearance of watching his mind try to process something. Only in his late-fifties, his face was worn in stature, like it was molded from the flint in the hills.

Alberta had money, but the retainer went quickly as she spent endless amounts of billable time on the phone with Wiley or his staff bemoaning the wicked nature of Rolland's homosexuality. While the details of the divorce were a little unusual—custody of a wolf pack wasn't a typical demand—there was nothing outwardly unusual about the parties' feelings toward each other. Ending a marriage was painful and full of all sorts of emotions, Wiley knew.

Her primary demand was more routine: She wanted maintenance, which is what Missouri law calls payments to keep up a divorced spouse's lifestyle. Some places call it alimony.

Alberta also wanted the house. Wiley tried to talk her out of this demand. It's a big house that would never work for just one person. Plus, it's got that library. What would you possibly do with such a monstrosity? What Wiley knew was that Rolland, being the well-regarded book obsessive he was, would never replicate the setup of that library anywhere else and almost certainly would never part with the house.

Surely a lawyer who had been in practice for over forty years would have plenty of money lying around to buy out a soon-to-be ex. Even living extravagantly wouldn't matter. A solo practitioner who could tie their shoelaces was routinely worth high six figures. The way Alberta represented his income, this should be no problem. At the very least, Alberta said there was no mortgage on the house. There would be some equity that would allow Rolland to get a loan and pay her off.

Alberta questioned the advice about giving up on the house. Rolland would be horrified if the nature of his sexuality became public, she believed. He would settle to avoid such an outcome.

Of course, clients with dollar signs in their eyes usually overrepresented the value of their spouse, remembering the feasts while forgetting the famine that almost always comes with the practice of law. Or any business, really. Getting IRS records and bank statements to back up a spouse's assertions of wealth were simply the routine in any contested litigation.

Alberta also mentioned how Rolland was withholding her inheritance from the estate of Velma Brown. There was something very fishy about how Rolland handled this estate, Alberta told her lawyer. In fact, this became one of the more acrimonious points between husband and wife up to the murder.

***

Velma was like many of Rolland's clients. A north-sider, she lived modestly but had a nice nest egg providing a comfortable living thanks to the passing of her husband, Claud. They had no children.

Velma was setting up an investment account with Claud's life insurance proceeds when her account manager suggested she talk to the lawyer across Court Street about estate planning. The bank had no formal arrangement with Rolland but heard many impressive stories about his abilities from their mutual clients.

This was in 1989. Rolland made a lot of money being across the street from that bank. Little old ladies like Velma were always needing legal help with their money, and the bank–law firm combo became an unofficial one-stop shop.

At first, Becky sat down with Velma and did the intake. They discussed Velma's family. There was a niece named Vicki Hayward who lived in Kansas City, but Velma had not seen her for many years, not since Vicki's weddings a few decades back. Velma wasn't sure what to do. Vicki was her kin, her dead brother's daughter, after all. But they weren't close. Why should this neglectful niece from the big city get any of her money? If not her, then who?

Becky finished up the meeting and brought the information to the boss's office. He sat there and read over the "Assets" and "Income" and "Information on Beneficiaries." Rolland's instincts noted ambivalence about the family, even without getting context from Becky. It had been a while since there was a walk-in with seven figures in the bank and no real familial connections to speak of. Rolland's wheels spun, and a plan was formulated.

The next day, Rodman and Sherry showed up to Velma's modest home to clean and do yard work. They would do this once a week, every week, until the old lady passed away. When Rodman would fail to show, Stephen or Michael could usually be counted on to lend a hand. Sherry stopped showing up altogether, but Faith, already working, did her part. Velma could not believe how nice her house looked, how tidy the yard appeared, and how pleasant the children were.

The children would report intelligence to Rolland to help him understand Velma's interests. There was a bookcase, and there was always a book on the nightstand or coffee table. What books? Rolland asked. Once he knew, Rolland would seek out a signed copy from the author and deliver it as a gift. Velma was, again, bowled over from kindness.

Months passed, and Rolland called Velma into the office. The old lady was sold on the Comstock family. She couldn't get over how delightful Rolland's children had been. Rolland wondered if she was actually talking about his children but kept that to himself. They talked some more about books and about the authors he met. Velma was starstruck.

Rolland prepared several documents for her trust. It's always tricky for a layperson to deal with trusts. Drafting and signing a trust isn't enough. A trust is like a shed. You can build the shed, but if you don't put anything in it, everything gets wet. Likewise, any assets left out of a trust when you die goes through probate. Since the whole point of a trust is that it survives the person who created it, and therefore is designed to avoid probate, Rolland simply offered to be a limited power of attorney. He would have access to the assets and income, and then he could place them in the trust for her. Sounds sneaky, but it's common and more often than not leads to making the process easier for the client.

But then there's the trust itself. There were thirty-some-odd pages of legal verbiage printed out. Rolland left the beneficiaries blank. Velma still didn't know what to do. Rolland began by talking about how he picked up on some concerns from Velma about the niece. About her failure to be a part of Velma's life. Perhaps, Rolland argued, there was a church or charity that might benefit from the money.

Rolland, using the information his children gathered from talking to Velma, knew she was not a churchgoer. She had no pet causes. She could think of no one deserving of her money. Not even friends. The only people who seemed to care for her were Rolland's family.

Her lawyer solemnly nodded and let the sentiment hang in the air. Velma started to cry. "Perhaps you could leave some things to my children? To thank them for the work they've done and the company they've provided." As he offered this, Rolland got up from his desk and walked over to his client, handing her a tissue. He placed his hand on her shoulder.

Velma did her best to compose her emotions. This was unlike her to be so open about her unhappiness. She felt like she could tell her lawyer anything! At this moment, Velma felt she owed everything to this man. "I could do that? If that's okay, I think that would be best."

"Yes, that would be all right," Rolland assured her. "That would be wonderful of you to do. Let me get to work, and I will get that portion completed."

A few days later, Ms. Brown came back to the law firm to sign the paperwork. She barely noticed her entire estate would be going to the Comstock family trust with specific earmarks for the three boys. Under the last will and testament, commonly known as a pour-over will that moved any non-trust assets to the trust after death, the Comstock family trust—with Alberta as the trustee—would be the secondary beneficiary that would receive the money if Velma ended up revoking her existing trust.

Which Rolland would ensure would never happen because the children would continue going over to the house and helping out, as long as it would take.

While Rolland didn't technically receive any inheritance, believing this omission was enough to avoid any allegation of impropriety, he would be named as trustee and personal representative of her estate if anything had to go to probate court.

Rolland's omission was just a formality . He was the person unofficially in charge of the Comstock family trust and would have access to any and all funds no matter what Velma's trust said.

Rolland would continue to send her gifts. During that time, she would amend her estate plan to leave specific items to others. Little neighbor boy Billy Lowell got her books. Some neighbor women would get some knickknacks. Nothing Rolland cared much about. Her taste in novels was trashy, and Rolland had no use for them. They weren't even first editions.

The last time Velma updated her trust was two months before she died. One of the changes she made was to ensure she was buried in silk underwear.

Almost immediately upon her death, Rolland filed Velma's last will and testament with the Greene County Probate Court. His old friend, Judge Burrell, would oversee the estate and certainly wouldn't blink an eye when it came to the question of whether Rolland ethically should have named himself personal representative for the estate. Common enough when a person dies with no close family and no friends; just have the lawyer do it.

Filing the last will and testament was a matter of caution. Rolland knew all of Velma's assets were in the trust because he put them there himself. But a will can be filed only within a year of death. If he didn't file the will and some asset was discovered a year after her death, it would go to Velma's heir-at-law.

But to probate a will meant giving notice to relatives who might have reason to challenge it. Velma's niece, Vicki, would be notified.

At first, she thought nothing of it. She knew very little about her aunt. But as the weeks went on, Vicki became curious about this person who was the named executor. She figured out he was a lawyer. Why was he handling her affairs? Why was his family's trust mentioned in the will, as the probate clerk informed her over the phone?

Vicki contacted a law firm in Kansas City, which looked into the matter and learned quickly their new client was left out of the trust and the family of her lawyer was going to get everything. This seemed like a clear-cut case for a will contest, they thought.

A will can be contested under Missouri law in a variety of ways. The most common is to say the person did not have the requisite capacity to understand the will. A will often says you are "of sound mind and body" when it is executed. Although that can be tough to prove. A person can have some sort of cognitive illness like dementia or probable

Alzheimer's and still have moments—days, even—when they are lucid and aware of what they are doing. Someone has to be virtually brain dead when they sign a will for the law to say they had neither a sound mind nor a sound body.

There's also a matter of undue influence. Does the person receiving the benefit have a confidential relationship with the person leaving the gift? If that person were a lawyer, it is assumed the client placed a high level of trust in the person representing them, and the lawyer would have an easier time exerting influence over their client. In almost every circumstance, unless the lawyer is writing estate planning documents for a spouse or parent, there is a confidential relationship that makes a will contest easier to prove.

The lawsuit was filed. Rolland was not surprised. In fact, he was preparing for a potential challenge all along. He encouraged Velma to see her doctor almost immediately after every amendment to her estate planning, reminding her the examination needed to include a cognitive update. Every one of her tests would show Velma was indeed competent and had her full capacities when she executed these documents. The medical records would be subject to discovery in the lawsuit and the doctor would be deposed. Rolland, thanks to the limited power of attorney Velma had given him, already knew what those records said.

That should be easy to defeat the niece's contention that Velma, whom she hadn't spoken to in decades, was out to lunch, mentally speaking.

The hard part would be proving Velma's lawyer wasn't just manipulating his client. Rolland knew how it looked because that's what it was.

Rolland also knew that simply being a lawyer didn't prevent you from establishing a close relationship with someone, even a client. Joining a profession shouldn't disqualify you from receiving an inheritance. Over a few short years, Rolland had become like family to Velma. Same for the Comstock kids. The law called such relationships "familial" or "filial." If someone was like a family, then there would be no undue influence. Thus, the will contest would fail.

But Rolland couldn't take a chance with his kids, who were wild cards in the plan.

For his family, who received the bulk of Velma's inheritance, Rolland had to go with someone who could really fight. The kids were named defendants, which meant they had to be active participants in the lawsuit. That meant answering discovery questions. That meant sitting for depositions.

Issues of alcohol and drug use could come out during the discovery process. The sons could be coached to avoid it, but people can overshare during depositions. They forget the only point of a deposition is for the opposing party to get answers to their questions on the record. People feel like they have to tell the whole story. It had the potential to be a disaster. For, as much control Rolland wanted to have over his family with the money he gave them, the less he was able to control anything.

No, he needed not just good lawyers but exceptional ones. Even if probate wasn't their focus. Rolland hired Tom Strong, better known for personal injury and medical malpractice, to represent the members of the family in their capacity as heirs of the estate. Strong was smart and worked endlessly. People would report getting voicemails from him as early as 4:30 in the morning. Strong's work ethic was just one of many tactics in his endless psychological warfare against insurance attorneys.

The lawsuit was filed in June 1993, with a trial setting in January 1994. Judge Don Bonaker, the lawyer who'd shared an office with Rolland when they first started practicing in the early '60s, was assigned the case.

Strong decided stipulating to almost every fact at issue would help narrow down the issues and minimize what could be discoverable. Since Rolland had the medical documents, Strong didn't even wait for discovery. He just presented them to the plaintiff's lawyers, shaving months off the pretrial process. They were useless to the plaintiff because they showed Velma was very much of sound mind and body.

The one thing Rolland could not get around, despite his effort to provide Strong with a tutorial on the intricacies of the probate code, was a change in how—and who—would run the estate while the litigation commenced. It was common for the plaintiff in a will contest to seek removal of the executor while litigation was ongoing.

Judge Burrell knew Rolland should not be allowed to have access to funds of the estate or make any decisions involving the estate while a will contest was happening in a different court. Burrell granted the motion right away, appointing another Springfield attorney, Cliff Brown, to serve as the executor while the lawsuit was going on.

With a new executor in place, discovery commenced. Strong focused on building up the idea that Rolland's family had "become" Velma's family. In regard to questions of sobriety, the boys would not lie about it. They would admit they had weaknesses like any other person. Strong would make sure each son would be well-coached on all possible questions.

When the time came, Rodman, Stephen, and Michael did an excellent job of glowingly recalling their relationship with Velma. The legitimate feelings they had for her. I mean, our dad was already rich. Why would we need to exploit a little old lady for her money? Oh, did they have run-ins with the law? From time to time. But we were young.

Perfect performances. Rodman's ex-wife, Sue Ann, on the other hand, was a disaster. She and Rodman divorced in 1993, yet she was deemed a relevant party by the plaintiff's lawyers since she would have direct knowledge of the events involving Rodman's relationship with Velma. They were married while Rodman was doing all this work and had been to Velma's house with him. Strong filed a motion to block her from testifying, but the plaintiffs reminded the court Sue Ann was volunteering to be deposed. Anyone could volunteer to come in and do a deposition. Strong had a rare loss in court.

Sue Ann spilled her guts. During her sworn testimony, she said Rodman freely discussed his dad's scheme to "take care of" Velma. Rodman, or any of the Comstocks for that matter, didn't much care for the old lady; they did what their father told them to do. Does Rodman do drugs? From time to time. Did he drink? Nonstop, she offered. Rodman was always in need of money because being an alcoholic was expensive. Rolland was paying him to go over to Velma's house, so it wasn't like Rodman was doing it over some "filial" relationship.

Sue Ann also helpfully gave endless examples of how Rodman was a liar whose credibility should always be questioned.

Rolland was inconsolable. Even though his son had no control over what his ex-wife would say, Rolland blamed Rodman for being unable to control her. Rodman was beyond redemption if he couldn't even bother to dangle part of his share of the take in front of a vengeful ex-wife to get her to play ball, Rolland thought. Never mind that would be witness tampering. Rolland knew how to deal with this stuff even if his no-good son did not.

If they were to survive the lawsuit and see one red cent of Velma's money, Rolland would do everything he could to make sure Rodman got as little as possible. The Comstock family would shun Rodman for good. No more allowance. No more invitation to family events. If he couldn't help his family during this trying time, what good was he?

Rolland sat down with Strong and discussed options. Tom believed the testimony was so bad that an offer to settle the case for a significant amount should be made. Rolland hated the idea of parting with any of this money he spent so much time trying to procure. But Rolland also knew the testimony would be enough to sink their entire case and something must be done.

In the end, Vicki Hayward, the niece who Velma complained to Rolland never called or visited, ended up with a six-figure settlement. But this would be less than half of what was left in the trust, as well as the $50,000 in assets that had somehow been left out of the trust, and would be subject to the probate court's oversight. The document also made clear Rolland denied any and all wrongdoing, standard language in a settlement document.

Meanwhile, back in the probate court, Rolland was reestablished as personal representative of Velma's estate, relieving Cliff of his obligations. Yet here is a moment where the impossible intricacies of probate law and the meanings of certain words can have a big impact.

Under the last will and testament of Velma Brown, the personal representative served under an "independent administration." This means the court's role in oversight is minimal. Usually, the executor can do whatever is needed without seeking an order from the court. When an executor is named during litigation, that changes to "supervised administration," and this means the court plays a more active role. Under this type of estate, every decision must be approved by the judge.

Later on, Rolland would claim he did not know the estate remained under supervised administration when he was reappointed. That, had he known, he would have conducted himself differently as its executor. Or maybe it was an oversight at the time. But those two words, "supervised" vs. "independent," made a big difference in how the divorce between Rolland and Alberta played out. In turn, many believe the acrimony caused by the estate led to a heightened sense of anger with Alberta, and that helped lead to violence.

Under the terms of Velma's trust, Alberta and each of Rolland's boys got equal shares. Rodman was paid first, with a check affixed to a note disowning him and to beg off future communication with the family. With Michael and Stephen, Rolland would dole out money whenever they could prove they were clean and trying to make respectable people of themselves. Again, Rolland was acting under the assumption he never had to get court permission to remove money from the estate. He was an independent administrator, after all.

Alberta's share was treated much the same way as Rolland handled all the household's money. As alienating and inattentive as Rolland was, he lavished his wife with whatever she asked for. Even when estates weren't closing as quickly as they should—lawyers only got paid toward the end of an estate, and that might require months if not years of work before getting to that point—Rolland cut corners and dipped into a retainer account to help with household demands. Or he would outright take money from an estate before the court authorized the lawyer to do so. Rolland always paid this money back. No harm done.

Rolland saw Velma's estate as available when he needed it. If Alberta complained about wanting a new set of clothes or the wolf puppies needing kibble, he would make a withdrawal. One might ask why Rolland didn't go through the formality of closing the estate and putting the money into the family trust as directed. Sometimes getting to the closing paperwork took more effort because there were simply too many other fires to put out. It was sloppy bookkeeping, but again, who would complain?

Not Judge Burrell, who knew Rolland would get the paperwork filed eventually. But he wouldn't be there forever. In fact, he was only there a few more years longer.

***

Alberta recounted the story to her divorce lawyer simply as another complaint on how Rolland was depriving her of money for which she was entitled. Wiley did think it was strange an estate that commenced in the early '90s was still open. Most estates take less than a year to complete. But the Velma Brown Estate was ten years and counting. Surely, the probate court would force Rolland to wrap things up.

The estate would not be subject to the divorce proceedings, as it was subject to another court's jurisdiction. By now, Judge Burrell passed away. In 1997, the Missouri legislature created a probate commissioner for Greene County that would relieve elected judges from the onslaught of work probate cases required. The elected judges appointed Carol Aiken, who was more skeptical of Rolland than Judge Burrell. But the Velma Brown matter never really became an issue for the first few years she was there.

Wiley thought maybe he should get involved as Alberta's lawyer in that case and free up that money. He explained to Alberta this would require additional fees to the divorce. Alberta sighed but knew fighting Rolland was going to be expensive.

All that remained from the Velma Brown Estate was $20,000, for which Alberta was entitled. It wasn't a lot, but it would be consequential to all involved.

# THE KING ARRIVES

Faith tapped her finger against the cigarette carton as she pondered a thought. "Beck, you remember the O. J. Simpson trial, right?"

Becky, half listening to the question, raised an eyebrow. She was at work, had a pile of annual settlements to draft, and didn't have time. This new firm was far more demanding about getting work done during the workday rather than when it fit Becky's schedule. *I miss Rolland*, Becky thought every morning as she pulled into work.

"Yeah, I mean it was a pretty big deal."

"Right, right. You know how he didn't have to go to jail, but the dad sued him and got a money judgment."

It had been fourteen years since the "Trial of the Century," so this random thought was taxing Becky's memory. "Whose dad sued who? O. J.'s dad?"

"No…no. The guy who was killed. The kid. His dad sued O. J. in civil court and got a big judgment out of it."

Faith paused, as she wasn't sure what to think of her thoughts. "What if I sued Alberta for killing Dad? I mean, for a money judgment."

The sun began to rise over the AT&T tower along the horizon to the east, and a light started to emerge in Becky's office. This didn't sound like a bad idea at all.

"I mean, why not?"

The probate filings would have to wait.

Becky got off the phone and googled "O. J. Simpson Civil Case." She refreshed herself on the details. Having been acquitted in the criminal case, O. J. was sued by the families of Nicole Brown and Ron Goldman for wrongful death, a civil tort. They received a judgment from a jury for $33.5 million after finding him liable. Not guilty but liable. Guilt was for the criminal courts.

She stared at that number for a minute. Another day that reminded her she should have gone to law school. Rolland always said she would be pretty good at the details needed in the profession. Instead of helping lawyers make money, she could be making money herself.

But Becky reminded herself no amount of money could make you feel better about losing a child. Or a parent. Although it might make the person responsible suffer.

Rolland never did any work like "wrongful death," so Becky had no idea how it worked. At least she worked with lawyers who were into that business. The new firm—Hosmer King & Royce—was fine. Different from working in the little square box off Commercial Street. This was atop a six-story building downtown. You had to take an elevator from the parking garage. The floor in the lobby was marble. There were six lawyers working there at the time she started, along with more than double that in staff, including an office manager. Each assistant helped two lawyers. Becky felt more like a cog than a right-hand woman.

But she didn't have a lot of options. She had to wrap up Rolland's practice. If she wanted a job, someone would take his files over. There was no building for anyone to move into. The city was already working with Faith to speed up vacating the premises so Rolland's law firm could be torn down.

The associate who worked for Rolland and left earlier in 2007 made a hard pitch to his bosses to buy the files and hire Becky. Given they coveted the public administrator work for years, Hosmer King & Royce said yes without blinking an eye.

Perhaps one of the better litigators working in Springfield was on the other side of the building from Becky's office. She walked up with trepidation to his slightly cracked door that read "MR. KING." He didn't keep the door shut to be unfriendly; he did it because he was a chain smoker, and his nasty habit drove the other partners crazy. So, he would sit in his darkened room—illuminated only by a small desk lamp—and ponder his numerous high-dollar cases as he was surrounded by wafting clouds of tobacco.

Becky knocked. "Yeah," he yelled from his desk. She peeked her head around the door and asked if he had a minute. Stuart King was deep into reading a snarky email from an opposing counsel. Most lawyers would shoot off something equally snarky and show their weakness, show what rattled them. Stuart read the missive and mentally filed it for another day. He took great effort to make sure nothing rattled him.

"What's on your mind?" Stuart asked. He didn't do much work with probate. He didn't find it exciting enough. He figured if Becky and the associate were making him money, he didn't need to worry about it. Stuart didn't love the fact that an estate paid out only once a year. That was all the probate court would allow. That screwed up cash flow, and Stuart was in charge of accounts receivable for the firm. But the law was the law. Not much could be done with that.

She sank into one of the oversize chairs facing his desk. Her small frame looked comical engulfed by the rich, smoke-stained leather.

"Well, I was just talking to Faith Stocker about her dad's…about Rolland's murder."

Stuart nodded. "Uh-huh."

"I think she's interested in talking to someone about filing a lawsuit against Rolland's ex-wife. For the killing, that is."

Stuart paid his way through undergrad and law school by playing poker. If he ever talked about those days, he bragged about being the youngest person allowed into the National Championship of Poker while he was still a college student at Southwest Missouri State University. He took no pleasure in poker. He just liked the grind of it. Which is precisely how he treated being a lawyer. Just a grind. Just a series of moves and maneuvers to get the other guy's money. Or to keep the other guy from getting his client's money.

Which is to say Stuart had a very good poker face. He had steely eyes that stared ahead. Right at the person in front of him. Or right through them. He had a thin gray beard that made him look like a wolf. A nickname given to him by the staff was "Wolverine." He was quiet, which could be seen as intimidating or aloof. But he was listening.

The idea Becky introduced caused his eyebrow to arch. He leaned in over his desk. The poker face cracked.

Stuart knew the broad strokes of the story. Eccentric lawyer murdered. Family member probably did it, but the sheriff's department either botched the case or didn't care too much about it. Maybe a little of both.

There were lots of unsolved murders in Southwest Missouri. If a bunch of cops decided someone deserved what they got, or if the same cops decided it was a one-off deal where the murderer wasn't going to strike again, then there wouldn't be much effort put into the case. Stuart would say the Ozarks was a good place to get away with murder. Hillbilly justice still had some cachet around here.

"Is this *just* against the ex-wife?" Stuart asked, with an emphasis on the word "just." He remembered more about the case as his brain quickly processed the situation.

Becky laid out her theory about Alberta and Michael teaming up because they both needed money from Rolland, and they would go over to the house to "scare him." That was just a theory.

"There's not much about the son, though? Just some DNA off a cigarette."

Becky nodded, stunned Stuart was taking her crazy idea seriously. "That's right. There's not much suggesting he was there. But it seems very possible."

Stuart leaned back in his chair and looked at the sparse skyline from his office. The firm was about to move to a one-story building on the main thoroughfare of town. His view wouldn't be as nice, but Stuart would own it. He only rented the view now. Stuart knew there was value in owning property because you could borrow money when you owned property. Which meant you could buy more property. Borrow more money with the new property. Just another grind for Stuart.

Looking out at the skyline helped him think. Stuart would miss that.

"Why haven't they arrested anybody? Why do you think?"

Becky found herself, as she often did when thinking about Rolland's death, choking up. She thought about that awful deputy who said Rolland deserved what he got. "I don't think they care. I think they made mistakes and screwed up the evidence. So instead of admitting they made a mistake, the sheriff's department is just going to forget it."

Stuart gave her a knowing look. She was right, of course. But that didn't necessarily mean it could work as a civil case. If the evidence was bad in a criminal case, it would not necessarily mean it was good in a civil case, even with the burden of proof being lower.

Stuart nodded. "Look at my calendar and set up a time for her to come in. I'll talk to her about it."

"Really? Okay, yeah. I will. Is there any time I should—"

"Got a deadline right now. Just get her in sometime this week."

Becky nodded and walked out, overwhelmed by the conversation. This had been just a random thought a few minutes ago. Maybe it wasn't such a bad idea after all. Should have gone to law school.

For Stuart, finding an interesting case wasn't so much about the topic or the specific details of the case. He wanted something other lawyers turned down because they couldn't figure out the right angle. Every case should be hard. Sure, he could have made more money by focusing on medical malpractice cases or nailing insurance companies for refusing to pay out in bad faith, but any lawyer could do that. Just like the crossword and sudoku he filled out every morning, Stuart needed a puzzle to do.

In the days after talking to Becky, he searched for recent articles about the case. He reread about Michael's DNA being found at the scene. In Missouri, wrongful death suits could be brought by any person defined in a class who would be entitled to a judgment. If one kid of the person who died filed a suit, all kids share the money equally.

Of course, there were exceptions, such as if a kid was responsible for the death.

Stuart knew the popular theory was the ex-wife pulled the trigger. If the news was to be believed, law enforcement thought that as well. If the son were standing there with Mom when she shot Rolland, for whatever reason, there could be enough of a good-faith basis to name the son in the lawsuit as a co-defendant. But that wasn't obvious to Stuart based on what was public.

An Instant Message popped up on Stuart's screen saying Faith Stocker was there for an appointment and she was already seated in the "big conference room." Stuart stubbed out his cigarette, grabbed a legal pad, and headed out to the lobby.

Faith and Becky were sitting at the opposite side from the window, and Stuart could hear them laughing as he walked up. At least they still had a sense of humor about things, he thought.

Stuart had a presence walking into a room that caused Faith to stand to greet him. They shook hands, and he sat down with his eyes lingering on Becky.

"Mr. King…" Faith started.

"It's Stuart."

Stuart processed the entire case after talking with Faith. After two hours, he barely filled up a page of notes. But he knew exactly what he thought the case should look like. After all, a lawyer should sit in the first meeting and imagine what the closing argument to the jury will look like. What will cause a juror to vote for you over the other side.

He knew if law enforcement didn't bring charges against Alberta and Michael, there would be no criminal case. Perhaps law enforcement was looking at other suspects. But wouldn't they have told Faith they were considering other scenarios? It could be all the evidence went cold. Or didn't go anywhere. Or maybe Becky was right. Maybe the sheriff's office didn't care.

Faith cared. Becky, too. They certainly took a financial hit because Rolland was gone. There would be damages for the kids, at least. That was enough. While the police and prosecutors knew their standard would be to prove Alberta killed Rolland beyond all reasonable doubt, a civil jury just had to find there was a preponderance of evidence Alberta was liable for Rolland's death. In one way Stuart thought there was—if it were just a little over 50 percent likely something happened, then a jury would have to vote yes in favor of a verdict.

Faith liked Stuart. He seemed no-nonsense. Cut right to the chase. That was not how her dad operated, but estate work and litigation seemed different. Different skills, for sure.

But as he got back to his office to check what voicemails he missed, Stuart was still puzzled over how to start the petition in this lawsuit. He sat there in the dark and let his mind wander over what he'd heard. It was late in the afternoon, but the July heat still emanated from the window as he looked out at the view. Then, the solution hit him.

He pulled up an older wrongful death and changed the county and the names on the caption. "Faith Stocker v. Alberta Comstock." It was short and to the point. Two pages in length overall. Stuart also found most lawyers tried to show off their case when they filed it. Missouri required very basic pleadings—just enough to give notice to the other side as to what they were being accused of. The less the opposing party knew about the direction you wanted to head, Stuart reasoned, the better.

In paragraph five, he wrote: "On or about July 2nd, 2007, Defendant, acting alone or in conspiracy with another, shot the Decedent four (4) times with a .38 caliber weapon."

# DIRTY PICTURES

After Bob Wiley got his retainer, the divorce was filed. Rolland turned to his own Bob: Stillings, that is. Stillings had known Rolland since serving as his associate in 1978. Like most associates, he figured out Rolland didn't have much interest in sharing his earnings with a partner. Plus, Stillings preferred family law as well as criminal defense over the deliberate pace of probate.

Unlike the parade of associates who left his firm frustrated and disenchanted, Rolland ended up valuing Stillings's knowledge of things he didn't want to deal with. Plus, he had boys who were often in need of a lawyer to get them out of a bind. For all his sons' criminal matters and on all his children's divorces, Stillings was the go-to guy.

Stillings got to work. He looked at the dissolution petition and immediately knew Alberta used rose-colored glasses to look at the family's finances. She also sought the house, which Stillings knew would be a nonstarter. Rolland would never give up that house.

A lump sum of money would be the easiest way to get rid of Alberta. Offer her cash and the divorce would be done. Rolland knew everyone had a price. Velma Brown's niece had a price. Every person who threatened his clients had a price. His kids all had a price. Alberta would just need to understand the lifestyle she was afforded had been built on playing fast and loose with other people's money. She would then have her price as well.

Rolland was just unsure if he could pay that price, confiding to Stillings there wasn't much liquidity. Stillings suggested Rolland look at investments: stocks, rental houses, and cash value on life insurance policies; believing a figure north of $100,000 would be enough to get Alberta to settle the case. Maybe she would take the money and they wouldn't even need to sell the house.

Rolland had no stocks. Over time, he sold off all of it to build the library. The real estate holdings had fallen into disrepair. Much of it was uninhabitable, and Rolland spent more time dealing with the city's long lists of complaints than finding tenants. He did have a retirement policy that he could close out. There would be a penalty, but the remainder would allow him to make a respectable offer.

Bob and Rolland knew it would take a few months for those policies to get liquidated. Life insurance companies didn't make money cashing out their plans, after all. The strategy, as Bob laid out, was for Rolland to provide as much financial information to Alberta's lawyer as possible. Prove the point that Rolland was broke and didn't have very much income coming in, which meant there wasn't very much income Alberta would be entitled to for maintenance. Stillings could drag out the litigation and give Rolland enough time to rustle up the money.

Of course, Stillings needed to get paid. Rolland couldn't cheat his Bob out of a retainer. After his meeting, Rolland directed Becky to cut him a check and get on the phone in order to move some accounts payable into the accounts receivable column.

Stillings then looked at the discovery he would normally send to the opposing party in a lawsuit with similar facts, and simply asked Rolland to compile that information as a preemptive strike. Rolland had no interest in receiving anything from Alberta, other than a divorce, and her lawyer needed to be quickly dispelled of the idea that Rolland had a bunch of money lying around.

Rolland sometimes wondered if they could just do a "Catholic divorce" and simply live apart as long as Rolland could provide her an allowance. He would mention it to Alberta in their conversations, but it never got very far before things devolved into a screaming match and Rolland realizing the marriage was, in fact, irretrievably broken as Alberta alleged. The notion he could avoid a large payout was a fantasy.

Rolland asked Faith to compile years of tax filings and income statements. When she was done, the picture painted wasn't pretty. Stillings looked at the information and wasn't entirely sure how Rolland was continuing to stay afloat professionally or personally given his financial situation.

Alberta's Bob showed his client what Rolland turned in. She couldn't believe the numbers. When Alberta talked to Rolland, she would accuse him of hiding money. A quick resolution to the divorce seemed far away.

Even though Rolland persuaded Alberta to move out of the house, he would still let her come over and look over "the puppies" while he was on trips to book signings, to the gay resort in Mexico, or God knows where else.

Which, despite her simmering anger, Alberta was more than happy to do. She would get to see the wolves, but more importantly, she would have full access to the house.

Her first housesitting gig was shortly after the first of the year in 2005 while Rolland was at his condo in Mexico. Alberta summoned Al and Sherry to come over and go through Rolland's emails.

Tipped off by Stephen that Al and Sherry's car was parked at the house, Faith and Becky immediately went over to the Comstock Estate and told the three to leave. Becky, once again, would assume responsibility for taking care of the house and the dogs while Rolland was away. Rolland would never allow Alberta back into the house, he proclaimed.

Then, a few months later, Rolland planned a trip to DC for a book signing at Chapters and asked Alberta again to watch after the dogs.

The last time Rolland went to Mexico, he took a number of pictures. When he got back, knowing Becky made it a hobby to photograph her horses, Rolland asked her to print off the photos, as he did not want to take these snapshots down to the local one-hour photo shop.

Quickly, Becky understood why. Many of the photos were explicit and involved Rolland with other men. At this point, Rolland already talked to her about why he and Alberta were getting divorced. This was when he'd fed her the line about not considering himself gay and so forth.

Becky gave the photos to her boss, and he took them home while not giving them a second thought. Now, Alberta was back pilfering through Rolland's personal items. She found the photos. Rolland with the ocean behind him, a cigarette in his hand, and a smile on his face. It was the happiest she'd ever seen him.

While the matchbook was circumstantial, now she had proof. Naked men. Photos that would show everyone, all his lawyer buddies and all his clients who thought Rolland could do no wrong, that he was just a perverted deviant and a cheater.

She took the photos to her attorney. Wiley agreed she should be upset but noted this was not a surprise given what Rolland already admitted. Worse, Wiley continued in hopes of changing the subject, he reviewed the documents Stillings provided, and the numbers looked correct. But that meant Rolland had no money. Wiley was able to communicate to Alberta that Rolland made an offer: $83,000, with an additional commitment to sell the house and split the proceeds. She told her lawyer no.

She left and called Rolland, accusing him of seeking to keep the house for himself. Rolland listened and could not believe she read the same letter he approved Stillings to send out. The more he tried to explain what was being offered, the angrier she got.

After calming down a bit, Alberta countered: I want the money. I want half the house. But I also want the duplex Rolland owned.

But this was the duplex Rolland sold so he could pay her a settlement he proposed, and she rejected.

Rolland reached out to Stillings and said they should offer to split the mansion, the fishing cottages down by McDaniel Lake, and the Greenfield acreage Alberta inherited but put in Rolland's name. It was nothing but weeds and chiggers but was worth at least $40,000. Stillings agreed it might work. So, Rolland proposed the idea to Alberta first when she showed up to get some clothes, "enough to open two ladies-to-wear." He mentioned the settlement and she laughed. The property in Greenfield was rightfully hers, and the cottages were totally run-down.

Rolland tried to talk to her. Then, she fessed up to having the photos. Alberta pulled them out of an envelope and said she was prepared to tell "everyone" about what she knew.

He had been reckless with the evidence of his hidden life. Rolland knew his carelessness was subconscious sabotage. It wrecked his marriage to be sure, but he wasn't so sure it would ruin his reputation.

"You want to have a press conference," Rolland posed to Alberta. "Suits me fine. Can you set it up this afternoon? It can still make tomorrow's paper." She huffed and grabbed her things. She said that she would make him "sorry."

Alberta had to rethink her strategy. Money was running short. The retainer was running dry. Without Rolland's allowance, there wasn't much income in her bank account. The principle of punishing Rolland started to diminish. She authorized Wiley to offer that she would agree to the original deal of $83,000, but only a third of the value of the house. The catch was the sale had to happen in the next six months.

Rolland countered with $75,000…total. Every potential outcome to the divorce fell on splitting up the house. "I wish to hell it would burn down," he said as he looked at an estimate from his insurance company about the rising rate given the property's disrepair. Rolland couldn't even refinance the house to pay Alberta. Every banker he talked to said the house was worthless with the addition of the library.

Now that Wiley filed his appearance in the Velma Brown matter, court clerks started eyeing it more carefully. Rolland sought no less than eight continuances to file a settlement. Even though there was $20,000 or so left to give to Alberta, Rolland knew reporting his actions would put him in peril.

The court pushed back, threatening Rolland with citation or removal as executor. In pleadings, Rolland argued a mistake had been made in keeping the administration under the court's supervision.

When the lawsuit was over and he was restored as executor, Rolland should have returned to his original status of being in charge without as much court oversight. Commissioner Aiken was not buying it.

Legal arguments weren't working. His factual arguments were non-existent. He'd taken the money without permission. Even if he wanted to ratify the action after the fact, he needed a good reason for it. Which means, under the law, the withdrawal had to have occurred to benefit the estate. Rolland did not have a good reason for doing so. He just needed money from time to time, and he had access.

Over the years, whenever he thought about the case, he realized he needed to close it. But since Alberta was the only remaining heir, it just didn't become a priority. Rolland ignored notices from the court. Asked for continuances. Received continuances. No one thought much of it. Just another annoying case that never seemed to end. Charles Dickens wrote a whole book about such a case with *Bleak House*.

Now Alberta was an enemy, and her new lawyer was involved. His taking of Alberta's money and using it for himself was a violation of not only the probate code, but the Code of Professional Responsibility. He would be disbarred if it was reported to the Missouri Supreme Court. If Alberta didn't know that, her lawyer certainly knew. Commissioner Aiken certainly knew.

Meanwhile, Alberta screamed about pornography. Again, even after she lifted the photographs, Rolland continued letting her stay at the house when he traveled.

Rolland taped three movies from an artsy cable channel. Alberta found the tapes and accused Rolland of having a dirty movie—a dirty gay movie!—in the house. The offending title was *Ma Vie en Rose*, a 1997 Belgian comedy-drama about a boy who announces to his parents that he believes he was born a girl.

Alberta told Rolland she had given the tapes to her lawyer. "She was looking for revenge," Rolland told Bob. "The court will love that." Rolland could not believe Alberta was making such a big deal out of such a "harmless, boring" movie.

Rolland wrote to Alberta the next day saying he would stop making life insurance payments on policies for Stephen and Michael based on "her threats" and she needed to act more rationally.

The reference to the boys, her boys, made Alberta realize, perhaps for the first time since she married Rolland, that she herself had no money to take care of her children. They were just as reliant on the old man as she was.

By August 2005, an agreement was reached. Alberta would get her money. Rolland would agree to liquidate various assets and give her a cash settlement. He also agreed the house would be sold, listed for $800,000 for a minimum of two years. If either party wanted to buy the house outright, they had to put up at least 95 percent of its agreed-upon value. Both of them realized they didn't have this money, nor could they get access to the money. The house had to be sold.

The judge signed the order. Rolland had only a few months to get Alberta the money he promised. The real estate agreement was entered with the house placed on the market. All the other property owned by Rolland—the law firm, the cottages by McDaniel Lake with its four tenants—would now be his. Alberta just had to sign away her interest in those properties as well.

In any other case, this would have been the end of the matter. With the Comstocks, this is when the matter started getting ugly.

Recording the real estate documents proved curiously daunting. It took Alberta a month to sign the deeds that would take her name off the rental properties and the law firm. Then, the recorder's office refused to accept the documents because the notary stamp covered up some of the text of the document.

Upon learning this, Rolland reprinted the documents and sent them back to Alberta to sign. Who then proceeded to do nothing with them despite daily phone calls from Rolland.

Toward the end of December 2005, Rolland's first payment to Alberta of $10,000 was due. Rolland claimed he was having trouble liquidating assets and getting clients to pay their bills. Christmas was also a time when clients often would skip on sending a check to their lawyer.

Rolland said he called Alberta to alert her of the delay and thought he had it worked out. He had Becky write three checks to Alberta amounting to $45,000 right after Christmas that would take care of the initial payment and a few more payments that weren't even due. Rolland instructed Becky to set one of them aside while he moved some money between accounts. The check got sent anyway. When Rolland found out, he called Alberta and immediately blamed Becky for sending that third check from an office account rather than a personal account.

"Would you tear up the check or void it" he asked. According to Rolland, Alberta agreed to tear up that check while she waited for him to send her certified funds as he offered further assurances more money was coming.

But Alberta claimed no agreement was reached. She called her lawyer and said Rolland was trying to "screw" her and she wasn't getting her money under the terms of the settlement.

Usually, if there were a problem like this, a lawyer would call the lawyer on the other side to see what was going on. To see if there was some issue that could be worked out.

In this case, a week later, Alberta's lawyer filed a variety of paperwork with the court to have Rolland's property seized by the sheriff and sold at the courthouse steps in order to satisfy the terms of the judgment entered by the court. A copy of the paperwork was sent to Stillings at the same time it was filed with the court clerk.

Rolland and his lawyer were shocked. Rolland already sent certified funds to Alberta directly. Stillings could never recall in his entire practice a lawyer filing such a levy without extensive communication leading up to it. Lots of lawyers liked to sucker punch. Wiley wasn't one of them, and this was an expensive and time-consuming endeavor. Something most people go to great lengths to avoid.

Stillings immediately filed a motion to quash the effort to sell all of Rolland's property. Wiley received the motion and called his client. Alberta did admit to receiving all but the $15,000, which she said hadn't cleared the bank.

Instead of waiting for the cashier's check Rolland told her was coming, Alberta took the original law firm check to the bank, the one Rolland told her would have insufficient funds. It promptly bounced.

When Wiley faxed Stillings back, he said Alberta would agree to withdraw the paperwork if the total amount of money due on the judgment was received. Money Rolland anticipated he would have all of 2006 to pay. Wiley also said Alberta never received the cashier's check for the $15,000 Rolland said he sent.

Of course, there was no way to track a cashier's check. Stillings told Wiley that Rolland wouldn't send another check unless Alberta signed a sworn affidavit saying she had not received the other funds, which she agreed to do. But Rolland still would not agree to pay the entire monetary judgment, which, at this point with interest, amounted to $214,000.

Stillings had to act fast. The sheriff could commence with the liquidation of Rolland's assets and the sale of the law firm at any minute. The family court commissioner had no authority over the sheriff, so Stillings moved the action to the circuit court, where he asked the presiding Judge Miles Sweeney to cease all actions to satisfy the judgment. After a hastily convened evidentiary hearing, Judge Sweeney quashed the execution.

To avoid any kind of further problem, Rolland agreed to have the cashier's check left at the Greene County sheriff's civil process office, the division of the law enforcement agency charged with enforcing civil matters for the court, so Alberta or her lawyer could pick it up. They would have to sign it out, and thus there would be proof of receipt.

While Rolland and his lawyer believed everything was smoothed over, Alberta's Bob filed *another* round of paperwork to seize all of Rolland's assets. Rolland's Bob was apoplectic. The usually soft-spoken Stillings raged to Wiley, who insisted his understanding that the judge quashed the motion was because he had gotten certain facts wrong.

Rolland was unaware of this new filing as he called his ex-wife and told her the check was waiting for her at the courthouse. Have your lawyer get it, he said.

Stillings filed another motion to quash, noting the check was available at the sheriff's department and there was now no reason for any of Rolland's property to be seized to satisfy the judgment.

The next day, Alberta drove to Springfield and went to the courthouse. But she had no intention of picking up the check. Rather, she came there armed with the photos she found of Rolland at his Mexican hideaway.

Her first stop was the Greene County Probate Court. Dana Gray, an older, wiry, and pleasant woman, was sitting at the front of the open clerk's bullpen where people would come in to file protective orders and discuss what to do when a loved one passed away. ("Get a lawyer" is often the only response a clerk can give to that question.) Dana was sitting at a desk some distance away from the counter and got up, not recognizing the woman who walked through the door.

"Can I help you?" Gray cheerfully asked.

"You work here?" Alberta asked.

"Yes, I am a clerk," Dana answered. "How can I help you?"

Alberta produced the pictures from the black attaché bag and placed them on the counter for Dana to look at. "Do you know Rolland Comstock?"

The clerk grew a puzzled look. Dana knew Rolland. Everyone did. He was in the court all the time. Without answering, she looked down and recognized Rolland's face. Dana wasn't quite sure what she was looking at.

"I want you to look at this photo," Alberta said. "I want everyone to know what Rolland Comstock is really like. You all think he is so great. Well, he's not that great after all, is he."

Dana stood there, shocked. She told this woman she had to leave and retreated, leaving Alberta standing there satisfied she had done… something.

After going to the probate court and baffling the hell out of Dana Gray, Alberta walked across the street to the public administrator's office. She asked the receptionist to see whoever was in charge. The receptionist grabbed Mary Shearholt, the office's deputy. Crazy, but loyal, Mary knew everyone at Rolland's office well and enjoyed dishing gossip whenever Becky would come down with documents to sign.

Mary didn't recognize Alberta, though, but she did notice the black Coach bag and testified to law enforcement later that Alberta was carrying the same bag that was found in Rolland's library. Alberta produced the pictures and essentially said the same thing she said to the court clerk.

Mary looked at the photos, recognized Rolland, and crossed her arms. "I don't know who you are, ma'am, but I do not want to buy what you are selling."

Alberta crammed the photos back in her black bag and stormed out. Mary figured out what was going on. Alberta was clearly on some mission to spread something salacious about Rolland. Quick enough, Mry called Becky to let her know what she had seen and to let her know something was afoot.

Becky called the boss. He said he would be at the office right away.

Becky knew, immediately, what the photos were.

Alberta got back in her truck with the skewed smiley face license plate cover and drove home to Fairland. The check stayed at the courthouse.

When Rolland got to the office, he had to sit down with each employee to explain what was going on. He apologized for putting them through what he thought would be a very rough period for their reputations, and then said he would not be offended if they wished to quit. Of course, none of them wanted to quit because then they would be out of a job. So, they stayed and endured whatever strange things were going on.

After feeling like he put his staff at ease—he hadn't—Rolland sat at his sprawling desk in his deteriorating office and drafted a memo to Stillings on all the causes of action he had against Alberta for her activities over the past few weeks. Wrongful execution and abuse of process. Illegally accessing his computer. Her attempts to defame him. Rolland believed it was enough to negotiate a reduction in what he owed her from the divorce. Take less money and I won't sue you until the end of time, was how Rolland framed the argument.

Stillings liked the approach and wrote a letter to Wiley. Rolland would just keep the money, all the money he agreed to give Alberta in the divorce, and in exchange would agree not to sue her for improperly and illicitly filing the levy against the property and for airing all their dirty laundry. Rolland was fully prepared to file as many lawsuits as it would take to make sure Alberta never had another leg to stand on again.

Wiley's response was simple: His client would not agree to anything less than what they agreed to back in August. Wiley hadn't even bothered to refute Stilling's well-reasoned arguments.

Stillings looked over Rolland's memo again and began typing up the petition for abuse of process. After a few passes, he was satisfied with what he wrote and sent Rolland a copy. But he would not file it right away. Wiley knew there was a two-year statute of limitations on the action, and there could be a time when it might be more useful.

After a few weeks, everyone had a chance to cool off. Plus, Judge Sweeney, once again, quashed the efforts to seize the law firm and the rest of Rolland's property. It didn't hurt that Rolland wrote a nice big check to Alberta for everything he owed her. He had to liquidate all his bank accounts and take out a loan against the house now that he finally found a bank that would place any value on it for refinancing purposes. Rolland had next to no money in the bank and had to add making house payments to his long list of debts.

They would still have to sell the house. But that process was ongoing and, as Stillings kept reminding Wiley, would not happen overnight. Again, under any normal divorce proceeding, this would have been the end of any and all controversies.

The rest of the year went by quietly. Rolland was able to make some money. By September, it was time to renew the listing on the contract. There had only been a few inquiries about the Comstock house, according to the agent. Only one offer, which Alberta accepted but Rolland did not.

Rolland called Alberta and offered to buy her out—$400,000. If they couldn't settle the issue with the house in another year, Alberta would have the right, under the divorce settlement, to file a partition action. That's a lawsuit when, if two owners of a piece of property cannot agree to how the property should be managed (or one of them refuses to contribute to paying the expenses of the property), they can ask a judge to order the property sold at the courthouse steps. This would be an ugly thing, Rolland told her.

Alberta rejected it. As far as she could tell, Rolland was dragging his feet. He could have taken the one offer they'd received but chose not to. Plus, he failed to make repairs to the house to make sure it retained its value. Rolland kept it this way because he knew it would prevent the house from selling and he could keep it for himself, she insisted.

Wiley suggested to Stillings that the house be sold at private auction. Rolland immediately dismissed the idea. When Wiley communicated the rejection to his client, Alberta called Rolland. "I am going to make your day," she purred sarcastically. She said she was going to get a "mean" lawyer from Kansas City. "You know, the ones who represented the niece in the Velma Brown case." Alberta's plan was to "start the divorce over" because she had been cheated.

"All Alberta wanted out of this was revenge," Rolland moaned. "I think that wish has been granted."

"I will be seventy in a few weeks," Rolland wrote to Stillings with November 9 coming up. "Before the divorce, I was barely functioning. I badly need the probate aspect of this (the Velma Brown case) to go away. My ego, the largest thing in or on my body, is shattered.

"If I don't get the probate matter resolved quickly, I am going to find doors at court closed that have been open for years."

Pitying. Desperate. In Rolland's memo to Stillings, he sounds defeated. But never not without a plan. "I believe if pushed, she will sign the closing papers on the Brown Estate. The mention of a deposition would do the trick." Rolland believed, accurately so, that Alberta would have to admit she received the money, or at least received the benefit of the money, when Rolland illicitly took it out of the account.

If she got the money, what precisely did she have to object to? He urged Stillings to take the threat of a deposition to Wiley and see if that resolved the issue.

In March of 2006, Wiley signed up to run for circuit judge that covered three counties where he primarily practiced. That kept him pretty busy, too, until the August primary when Wiley won decidedly. In that part of the state, Democrats didn't even bother. Wiley would be a circuit judge starting January 1, 2007.

Wiley still had a few months of legal practice. After talking to his client about whether she in fact would be cowed by being deposed under oath, he filed a petition requiring Rolland to file a final settlement in his role as executor of Velma Brown's affairs and to give Alberta the remainder of the money in the estate account. Wiley figured that was answer enough.

On the same day, Rolland missed the deadline to pay the homeowners insurance demanded by the mortgage company. No insurance, no guarantee the bank would get paid if an accident befell the house. They would start the foreclosure process. Now, Rolland was just desperate to get rid of the house. He would figure out what to do with the books and the wolves later.

He wrote Alberta offering to place it on the market for $500,000 and would simply give Alberta the proceeds from the sale. He would take nothing.

Wiley noted to Stillings that Rolland refused a $650,000 cash offer in March of 2006. But now he felt $500,000 would do the trick? Why was that? Wiley asked. Instead, Wiley countered and said Alberta would buy the house from Rolland for $450,000. Stillings asked for proof that she could get a loan for the money. She couldn't get a loan. The stalemate was back.

Right before his birthday, Rolland wrote another memo to his lawyer. It was full of dark predictions about his health and his ability to continue working. "Diabetes is never shown on a death certificate as a cause of death, but it issues the invitation to whatever administers the *coup de grace*. My money is on congestive heart failure. Difficulty breathing is my most troublesome disorder. The pacemaker will need new batteries, or be replaced, in January. My body is well into showing my age and diabetic condition: skin like parchment, swelling of legs and feet below the knees, lack of blood and feeling in fingertips and toes.

"Aside from losing things in plain sight before me, I don't think I have any loss of memory or diminished mental capacity. I have no problem continuing to work at home ten hours a day if needed. I am directly in line for blackmail with Brown," he admitted. "I need that off my back so that the harm to my reputation to the court is small."

He noted the current public administrator would be retiring soon. To replace her, in 2008, a number of Republicans ran for the spot. Including Becky Frakes, who, despite being a political novice, came in second place among a very busy Republican primary field. The winner of that contest bested the Democrat by a thin margin in an unusually good year for the blue team. But the new public administrator, David Yancey, bore no hard feelings. He kept Becky and her new law firm on as his legal team for three terms. Frakes and the associate who last worked with Rolland worked for a firm where Yancey had once been the office manager.

Springfield always proved to be a very small town.

"My ego problem with selling this house is not as great as I thought. I have reconciled to selling most of the library. The library will take time and can best be done by me now instead of after my death. There are about five book dealers in the US who could handle that. The best price would be by assignment rather than outright sale to a dealer."

Rolland talked about Faith's neighborhood in Western Springfield and how a four-bedroom house with a "nice, big basement" would be great for lots of books. Just not as many as he had. He also noted there were only three wolves left, with the leader of the pack having "problems getting around." Rolland's tone suggested he was at peace. Or maybe resignation.

After a few more weeks of hassling and arguing, the parties agreed to another extension to sell the house. The listing agreement was entered into with an agreed-upon ending date: July 1, 2007.

Shortly after the turn of the 2007 New Year, Rolland wrote another memo to Stillings noting "the blackmail card has been played."

"She said, 'I can keep my law license and live in the house until I die but then [the house] would become hers." She bragged that she had new lawyers who would do what she said and would no longer be pushed around.

At this point, Bob Wiley was sworn in as circuit judge, and his son Dale took over the Comstock case. He wasn't as good as his dad, but was full of confidence and liked filing complicated paperwork with the court.

Rolland was sick of the threats from Alberta about the Brown case. He told her at that point she was no longer to talk with him directly. She slammed the phone down. But then she called back and started arguing some more.

He asked Alberta about the hearing that was set on the Brown Estate. Based on Alberta's filing from the previous year, the court ordered Rolland to file a final settlement. He prepared it, laying out all his activities. Rolland knew it would be rejected. He also knew, when Commissioner Aiken saw all the unauthorized withdrawals, she may very well file the bar complaint from the bench. A few hundred dollars here. A thousand dollars there. Rolland tried to dress them up as best he could, giving them elaborate descriptors, but everyone knew what it was.

"I don't have anything to do with that," Alberta said. Unbelievable, Rolland thought.

"Rolland, I know you think I hate you. But the truth is, after knowing you for thirty-eight years, I feel like I have some duty to you. To take care of you. That's why I want to offer you this deal. So, you don't get hurt."

"I have a big sack of coping skills," Rolland wrote his lawyer. "But after hearing Alberta say she had a duty to me, that sack is getting lighter and lighter. I'm not sure I will survive all this."

But he would play along, Rolland granted. "Because she knows where all the skeletons are buried."

# THE FIFTH

From the date that the wrongful death suit against Alberta was filed to the trial itself, nearly three years went by. Litigation is complicated. Anything involving Rolland was complicated.

Stuart King whipped out the short petition. Filing a lawsuit is usually an uneventful affair. You pay the one hundred dollar fee, and the court provides the service paperwork for law enforcement or a private process server to deliver the paperwork to the defendant. Then the thirty-day period to respond begins.

When this lawsuit was filed, reporters paid attention. Articles were written noting how unusual it was that a civil suit was filed before any criminal charges were. The sheriff was called for comment. Jim Arnott—a few weeks away from his primary election—responded.

"I am not aware that Ms. Stocker has any evidence that we do not have," Arnott said defensively. "The sheriff's department has an open case and cannot comment further."

Arnott's quote misconstrued the civil process. It was not that Faith had other evidence, she just had a lower bar to establish her case. Either way, this looked bad for law enforcement. The family of a victim went to a private attorney to get satisfaction they could not get from the criminal justice system. No one had control over Faith Stocker or her lawyer.

But if the sheriff had a publicity problem, it wouldn't change the lack of progress they made.

The publicity for the lawsuit would also be a problem for Stuart. Alberta would get phone calls from reporters about her thoughts. She didn't have any because she hadn't seen the lawsuit, she would tell them.

Alberta would now be on the lookout for someone trying to serve her. If someone came to the door, she had no obligation to answer. A sheriff's deputy trying to serve a civil lawsuit had no incentive to be creative. If they knocked and no one answered, they would just come back. Unless someone was really determined, Alberta could wait out Faith and just let her waste money on mileage.

Stuart ended up hiring a private process server and Alberta received her papers. This only stoked her anger further. She thought Faith learned some tricks from Rolland. Use the legal system to bully her. Alberta remembered a letter Faith sent talking about how much she loved her still. How they would always be mother and daughter. Now, she was being sued.

Alberta knew what this was. Faith settled all the lawsuits and now was going to use this "wrongful death or whatever" suit to get the money back. Just another screw job. Just like what Rolland did with the abuse of process case. Alberta and Rolland settled the divorce and then he filed a lawsuit to get that money back. Would this ever end? she wondered. It wouldn't until they killed her, too. She knew that.

At this point, Richardson knew this civil suit would play out like a criminal prosecution. When criminal charges looked probable, Alberta set up a meeting at Carver & Cantin. Tom Carver and Shane Cantin to be precise. This was one of the best criminal defense firms in the city and would be better suited to handling the wrongful death suit.

When they initially met with Alberta, no one knew anything about the details of the sheriff's file. Law enforcement investigations are always closed to the public and only become available to an accused person's counsel when charges are brought. What they did hear convinced Tom and Shane the reason Alberta had not been prosecuted was because the evidence was flimsy. Circumstantial.

Plus, after talking to Alberta, it became clear there were plenty of people who would probably wish an ill fate for Rolland Comstock. Other family members, parties who were snookered out of an inheritance, some random guy on a sugar daddy website. Michael seemed particularly suspect. There would be plenty of other parties where the finger could get pointed. That would create doubt in the mind of the jurors. Make it easier to get a defense verdict.

They knew Stuart King was no slouch, but he would only be as good as the facts he had to work with. Tom and Shane's plan would be to make those facts look even worse.

The defense started with a motion to dismiss for a number of reasons. None of which would be very compelling. The one motion Tim filed that Stuart knew he would have trouble with was a "motion to make more definite." The defense argued that, by pleading Alberta conspired with "unknown" others to kill Rolland Comstock, this limited his ability to conduct discovery or to call witnesses for deposition. How precisely would Faith prove anything against a person who wasn't even mentioned by name in the lawsuit?

After a number of judges at the circuit level recused themselves based on knowing Rolland, the case landed on the bench of Greene County's newest: Judge Michael Cordonnier. Appointed by Republican Governor Matt Blunt the previous year, Cordonnier was a sharp insurance defense lawyer at a previous point in his career. He was already developing a reputation as a workhorse judge who would take just about any case and move it quickly.

Stuart didn't like Cordonnier's background with insurance companies. He often was on the other side of the courtroom from lawyers like Cordonnier. But the judge did know Stuart was good and almost certainly could be trusted to recite the law when the court had a question. Mutual respect between the jurist and the counselor was built in just a short period of time. Stuart was happy with Cordonnier drawing the short straw and saw no need to try and remove him as judge. Hopefully, the other side wouldn't try either.

Cordonnier was convinced the phrase Stuart included in his lawsuit was too vague. "If you need to amend your pleadings later, you will have latitude to do so," the judge reminded him. For the time being, that line would get stricken. Stuart got it. He'd taken a chance, and the judge called it out. Best to see how the rest of the trial worked out. Now that the court ruled against the fairly pedestrian dismissal request, it was time to do written discovery.

There's a lot of things that get asked in written discovery that are routine. Who are your witnesses? What do you expect them to say? What paperwork do you have that helps prove your case? That sort of thing.

In civil law, there's a discovery process where you can request admissions. That's where a party lists off things they want to prove or disprove and asks the party to admit or deny what is written. Under Missouri law, you cannot object to requests for admissions. If you do object, it is considered non-responsive, and you can get a judge to consider the response as an affirmative. Or negative. Or whatever helps your case the most.

Stuart decided to be as direct in his questioning as possible.

"Admit you have not accounted for the location of the .38 caliber revolver to any member of law enforcement since the death of Rolland Comstock."

"Admit that, on or about July 2, 2007, you shot Rolland Comstock four times with a .38 caliber weapon."

"Admit that you caused Rolland Comstock's death."

After thirty days, Alberta answered those questions by "asserting her rights under the Fifth Amendment of the US Constitution and Article I, Section 19 of the Missouri Constitution not to answer this request."

This was her answer to every significant request Stuart sought. In a criminal case, a person can assert their right not to incriminate themselves. It's a basic tenet of American democracy that the government cannot prosecute you for a crime and demand you participate actively in your own conviction. In fact, a prosecutor can't even mention to a juror that a defendant has pleaded the Fifth. A prosecutor cannot even draw attention to the fact that they did not cooperate with the investigation, or that they didn't take the stand in their own defense.

In a civil case, there was no prohibition against any of this. A jury could be told this and infer any answer they wanted. If Alberta refused to say whether she shot Rolland Comstock, a civil jury could assume the answer to this question was "yes."

They could also just as easily infer the answer was "no," but the public didn't think that way. Anyone who's watched a movie or TV show set in a courtroom "knows" you plead the Fifth because "you're guilty of something." In a civil case, that means you are liable as well.

Stuart would also be able to point out Alberta stopped cooperating with the sheriff's investigation. He would say Faith cooperated. Becky cooperated. Steve cooperated. All of them wanted to get to the bottom of who killed Rolland. The only two who wouldn't were Alberta and her sister. Neither seemed interested in getting to the truth. The jurors should ask themselves why that was.

For Alberta's lawyers, they knew there were other reasons their client would assert her constitutional right to keep her mouth shut. For starters, Alberta freely admitted her memory was slipping, and it wasn't simply due to old age. It might be dementia caused by all of her strokes and worsening heart conditions. Might be something worse, like Alzheimer's. If Alberta told authorities one thing in 2007 and then said something entirely different in 2008, it wasn't necessarily because she changed her story. It could be that she truly did not remember the event in question at all. Maybe she didn't remember where the gun was when she was first asked. But maybe she knows where it is now. Not because she was trying to be evasive but because that's how the disease worked.

For law enforcement investigating the case, they could see these varying answers as obstruction of justice. Alberta's attempt to frustrate their investigation into the murder. Lying to the police was a crime, too, and for Alberta's lawyers that was sufficient reason for their client to plead the Fifth.

Lawyers also advise their clients to assert their Fifth Amendment rights if there is another line of questioning that would be self-incriminating. Of course, the defense lawyers allowed her to answer some of the questions and plead the Fifth on others. Which meant that such an explanation was incorrect, and technically opened Alberta up to the fact she was using her rights strategically and not as contemplated by the Constitution.

No one would know the reason she pleaded the Fifth—her lawyers were bound to not share such information—but everyone assumed the true answer to the questions would get Alberta into a lot of trouble.

Stuart also asked to depose Alberta just to hammer his point across. The Carver & Cantin office was on the sixteenth floor of the Hammons Tower, and Stuart rode the elevator up to the firm's ornate offices overlooking the leafy neighborhoods of North Springfield. Alberta was already seated in the conference room, and she looked past Stuart as he walked from the bank of the elevators.

Tom, wearing a bow tie and suit, greeted Stuart with a handshake. Stuart was wearing a short-sleeved button down and a pair of jeans. He looked like he might do some yard work later. The styles perfectly contrasted the two men.

For thirty minutes, under oath, Alberta answered every question about the gun, Rolland, and her whereabouts on July 2, 2007, by asserting her Fifth Amendment rights. It was a formality at this point and would be important to have her on the record making this assertion in the event something happened to her before trial. Stuart hoped not. It would be better to have her take the Fifth in front of the jurors.

For the time being, Judge Cordonnier set the trial for a five-day setting beginning on June 10, 2010. The date being so far out had nothing to do with the lawyers' schedule and everything to do with the sheer volume of cases in front of Greene County judges. There were simply not enough courtrooms and jury pools to accommodate every lawsuit and criminal action that demanded a trial of one's peers right away.

In the meantime, Carver sent a records request to Greene County seeking the entire criminal case file. Prosecutors quickly filed a response asking the court to declare the file closed under Missouri's Sunshine Law. It was an open investigation, and files from open investigations were not subject to a routine records request. Judge Cordonnier agreed.

The defense wanted to depose Faith next. They developed a theory that the wrongful death suit was meant to negate the settlement in the other cases. Faith and Becky agreed to give Alberta money. Now they wanted to take it away. "This was about greed and not justice" would be a primary argument.

There was a question as to whether something else was afoot. Ashley Comstock, Michael's daughter, was a beneficiary under Rolland's trust. Even though Rolland cut off Michael, he always assured the family Ashley would be provided for.

Technically, since Ashley was still under eighteen, her share would stay in the trust and be released to her later on. Faith had not provided any money to Ashley's trust. In fact, although they had no direct communication, Al and Sherry heard Stephen was asking questions about why he hadn't received money from the estate as well.

The defense thought it was possible Faith misappropriated the trust fund money. Maybe she spent it for her own benefit. When she realized she would have to pay the other beneficiaries, she decided the only way she would get the money back was to file a lawsuit against Alberta to make up the difference.

The theory was nonsense. The wrongful death suit proceeds, if any, would not go through Rolland's trust or his estate. If Faith had done something with the money, which she had not, this lawsuit was not going to magically help replenish the trust's coffer. Moreover, if Faith's handling of trust funds were really in question, the beneficiaries could ask her to account for her work. If they were unsatisfied with that answer, they could sue her. No one asked her for an accounting.

Regardless, Faith's role as trustee became a key strategy of Alberta's defense. Poor old Alberta being persecuted by her sticky-fingered daughter. Just interested in the money. Make Faith the bad guy and maybe that pulls attention away from Alberta in the juror's eyes.

The defense sent discovery to Faith asking for information about her role as trustee. Stuart would object. How was this possibly relevant to whether Alberta killed Rolland, his responses would all but say. Cordonnier, knowing discovery rules allowed people a little bit of latitude without going on fishing expeditions, limited the scope of what Alberta's lawyers could ask for. This was one time Stuart was glad an old insurance defense lawyer was the judge. Insurance lawyers hated broad discovery requests, and this was a rare time it worked in Stuart's favor.

But there were other routes to get this information. Again, if Ashley asked for Faith to account for her work as trustee, she was entailed to them. By the time the accounting was filed, however, Faith released all the money to the beneficiaries of the trust. They received every penny for which they were entitled. But Faith still had to hand over an accounting of her work. That's what Bob Stillings told her to do.

Faith might be the first to admit she focused more on her client's paperwork than on the paperwork for Rolland's trust. It was tough, she admitted under oath on a number of occasions, to really focus on Rolland's business affairs because doing so reminded her of what happened to him. Reminded her of what her mother had done to her father.

Faith had done her job and everyone got their money, but the messy appearances allowed for inferences.

By the time Faith was deposed, another lawyer was added to Alberta's team. Evelyn Mangan, a noted probate attorney herself, looked at the evidence and knew how to make Faith and her management of trust funds a liability for the plaintiff.

Stuart saw her entry of appearance. Never saw her in court. Went into his associate's office and asked about her reputation. "Nothing is ever easy with her," the associate opined.

Stuart shrugged all of that off. Lawyers have different approaches and different personalities, he thought. But he was about to find out how difficult it was going to be.

When Faith was deposed at Tom and Shane's office, Evelyn was sitting there with the biggest pile of paper Stuart had ever seen. Over the course of the day, Evelyn grilled Faith about nearly every transaction she made as trustee and did so with the precision of a bull in a china shop. Evelyn would hand her the wrong check, then spend a couple of minutes trying to find the right check. Then, Evelyn would have the wrong information in her notes and have to spend time trying to figure out what indeed Faith was looking at. It was absolutely infuriating and made the day go forever. Meanwhile, Stuart objected to nearly every question Faith was asked.

Stuart was loath to object. His rationale was, even if a question was objectionable, the jury would think you were trying to hide something. But the deposition was unlikely to ever be submitted during the trial—no jurors would see Stuart's objections—and there was nothing relevant about Faith's role as trustee to the question of murder. Evelyn would shoot back that Faith and the beneficiaries of the trust had plenty of motive to see Rolland dead and how Faith handled the trust administration absolutely was relevant.

The gist of Evelyn's questioning went toward the defense's theory that Faith was up to something. That she had taken "loans" from the trust to help pay for the building she was going to move into on Commercial Street, the building Rolland intended to move his practice into. That she would accept money meant for the trust into her own personal account.

The latter part was easy enough for Faith to explain. Her personal account and the trust account were at the same bank. Accepting paperless transactions were already set up in her account. Setting them up for the trust would cost money. Stuart thought Faith's system caused larger problems than it was avoiding—you save one hundred dollars, but it appears funds are being co-mingled. A big no-no.

More problems loomed. Stuart knew Greene County law enforcement was sitting on a ton of evidence. Interviews. Reports. There were detectives Stuart wanted to depose so he could ask questions about the work they did and who they suspected. Every time he tried to depose someone involved with the investigation, prosecutor Todd Myers would sweep in and move to quash the subpoenas.

This was bad, and Stuart knew it. If he had to handle this lawsuit like a criminal prosecution, he needed the men and women who conducted the discovery for the prosecutor. That was the cops and, so far, the prosecutor was getting the judge to keep Stuart from talking to them.

In the meantime, the defense sought and received, over Stuart's objection, a continuance of the trial to June 27, 2011. The defendant argued there was more discovery to be done. Stuart told Cordonnier any other discovery, given the lack of cooperation from Greene County, was not going to be necessary. His case was ready to go, although Stuart only made this argument to cover up his frustration with how he was being thwarted by prosecutors in building his case.

If Stuart was frustrated, law enforcement was equally so. Other than random drug addicts showing up to put the dime on Michael Comstock, no other evidence was materializing. Jim Arnott was now sheriff. The elected prosecutor, Darrell Moore, was running for what would be a losing congressional race, and his deputy Dan Patterson would soon cinch the mantle of prosecutor in the August 2010 primary. In Rolland's era, Democrats would routinely put up a fight and sometimes win. In the era of the Tea Party, the Democrats didn't have a shot in Greene County.

Myers would watch discovery requests come in. He would have them quashed. The order from the court declaring the murder investigation records closed meant that, not only would the contents of the file be held secret, but no one could talk about them either.

With a new prosecutor sworn in, there was a new approach to the civil case. Patterson urged cooperation with the wrongful death suit. Let these other lawyers have what they need. Maybe a fresh set of eyes wouldn't hurt.

That directive did not include access to physical evidence. All it did was allow all lawyers to look at the investigative reports conducted. To see what the sheriff compiled. This also meant Detectives Wade, Weatherford, and Duren would be allowed to testify. Everyone involved knew this was unprecedented, but no one had any better ideas.

Now that this roadblock was cleared, Stuart had to rethink everything he was doing. Essentially, the Comstock wrongful death suit would be an entirely different proceeding now that all this new information was available. Much of it was very helpful. Stuart saw Alberta's inconsistent statements. He could compare those to the inconsistent statements Carmel Rhoten made during her deposition in the summer of 2010. He was able to identify all the work the sheriff had, and hadn't, done. Stuart saw the interview with the Monett gas station clerk for the first time. He also saw there were multiple interviews with the clerk, and the woman clearly had a problem remembering when she was at work.

He saw, also for the first time, eyewitness reports that Alberta's truck was just outside of Springfield the day after the murder. Of the keys that were FedExed to her. Much of this helped build evidence Alberta had been in the area. The preponderance toward Alberta being held liable was starting to tilt in Stuart's direction.

But there were other signs, not so helpful. There were conflicting reports on Alberta's gunshot residue test. In separate depositions, Wade testified the results were negative while Duren testified the test was a partial positive. Stuart would have to go all the way to Jefferson City and depose the crime lab custodian just to lock it down. The test produced at the deposition revealed Alberta did have a partial positive, which Cantin would explain away because she handled the gun—the "cheap .38"—at the Firing Range the day before the test was conducted.

Rumors were also floating around the sheriff's department that the DNA test as to Michael's saliva was negative. This turned out to be untrue. More of a distraction than anything, because Michael wasn't going to be a part of the case. At least not part of Stuart's case.

As more evidence became available, Stuart still had to deal with Evelyn's accusations that Faith misappropriated funds. The defense wanted to see how much the other beneficiaries received from Rolland's trust. Stuart implored the judge to limit the information that had to be produced. Cordonnier was waffling on whether he was going to allow it. Fiduciary responsibility as a trustee was not something the judge had much experience with, Stuart knew.

There was also an issue of Rolland's secret life emerging from the defense's discovery. Whether Rolland had relationships with men who were abusive. With men who had criminal histories. There wasn't much, but the suggestion was just as damaging as any proof that could be uncovered.

Stuart knew he couldn't avoid the issue of Rolland's homosexuality. His plan was to introduce it early in his opening statement and put it out there as no big deal. Sure, it was the reason Alberta divorced him. But it should have nothing to do with whether he died.

The judge agreed and limited how much of Rolland's personal life could be discussed. Good news for the plaintiff.

Stuart wasn't simply worried about redeeming Rolland's death or bringing peace to the family. All of this would be symbolized by the verdict, and the verdict would only concern itself with money.

A hard concept for many people outside of litigation to wrap their heads around, valuing the loss of a human life, but that's what a wrongful death suit must do. What did a family lose, from an economic perspective, by Rolland's death? When someone dies young and healthy with a spouse and minor children, that can be worth a lot. The family lost the support that person could bring for years to come. There's one less person to contribute to household expenses, like the mortgage. There's one less person to help pay for kids to go to college. This hypothetical is an example of a wrongful death suit where the damages would be significant.

Rolland was an unhealthy seventy when he died. He had no spouse to support. His children were older and not as reliant as they once were. Besides, an adult child who relied on a business relationship with their father—as was Faith's case—was not as appealing as having a little tyke who had no other options. Simply put, from an actuarial perspective, Rolland's life did not have the worth it once had.

There were emotional components. The loss of a loved one leads to the loss of life events. A loss of weekly conversations and a friendly visit. Also tough since, in the wrongful death class, only two of the kids had any kind of positive relationship with Rolland. Sherry, Rodman, and Michael hadn't lost much at all in terms of emotional support from Rolland being gone. As far as Faith and Stephen, there was value to this relationship, and that was much tougher to enumerate.

Stuart pled not only actual damages, the measure of the loss of Rolland's life, but punitive damages. This was the measure of how Alberta should be punished if she were found liable. There should be some punishment for a person performing an intentional act that ended a person's life. This wasn't like she was speeding down the street and didn't see a pedestrian step off the sidewalk. What Alberta did was no accident. That would mean depriving her of money she received from the settlement with Rolland's trust and his estate.

To the degree the defense wanted to make this case about money, they were correct. But every civil case is about money. Stuart also knew the public was inundated with anti-tort rhetoric about the "greed" of trial lawyers. Business groups wanted every case to be about a hot cup of McDonald's coffee…leaving out the fact the plaintiff in that case had significant burns. Didn't matter. It was the perception. People could get outraged so easily if they were trained to do so.

Maybe a Greene County jury wouldn't care much about homosexuality, but they might care about someone wanting money that they were not "entitled." This part of the Bible Belt and its stingy, conservative juries weren't exactly a litigator's ideal audience.

But none of the parties would get close to settling as the case dragged on.

Dealing with the murder over another three-year period continued to take its toll on Faith. Whenever there was a written discovery sent by Alberta's lawyer, it made her think about what happened. Every time she had to be deposed, she would have to face her stone-faced mother. Alberta wouldn't come to every proceeding about the case, but she made sure to attend when she knew Faith would be there.

If things were bad between Alberta and Faith in the aftermath of the divorce, they were irreconcilable now. As part of the settlement over the two other cases, Alberta was allowed back in the house to collect furniture she was awarded. Faith had it set up so Alberta would get to go through and do an inventory of what she would get, and then have someone pick it up. Faith insisted on joining her. Alberta asked for some time alone. Faith would not allow it.

"You fucking bitch," Alberta snarled at her. "You're no daughter of mine."

Those were the last words Alberta spoke to Faith.

Stuart won an important procedural fight that would require Alberta to take the stand and plead the Fifth in front of the jury. He wanted to ask her questions. The defense wanted her discovery answers to be read into the record. Cordonnier said Stuart could simply go over her answers on discovery and reiterate her right to take the Fifth. The judge reminded Stuart he ran a risk by asking the defendant questions. The court would not stop her from changing her answers and crawling out from under her constitutional assertion to provide answers no one heard before.

If Alberta did that, it wouldn't be disastrous. But the lawyer was quick on his feet and liked his odds about trapping Alberta in a web of her own making. He didn't think Alberta could outsmart him. He also didn't think she would expose herself to criminal liability that late in the proceeding. If she did talk, it would be on the record and under oath with the prosecutor's office and members of the investigative team in the audience. Stuart believed he could get her in real trouble if she decided to talk.

Stuart told the judge he understood that risk. But this was not good enough for Mangan, who then filed a motion saying Alberta was not competent to testify in her own defense. Alberta's dementia was getting worse, and she would be unable to comprehend the questions she was being asked.

Stuart was incredulous at the hearing on this motion. "Judge, we've been here before and this issue did not even come up. This court ruled that all Alberta would have to do is answer 'yes' or 'no' when I asked her to say whether she still wanted to take the Fifth. The defendant doesn't need much capacity to do that," Stuart reasoned. Cordonnier agreed, and Alberta would still have to take the stand.

Shortly after this hearing, the defense lawyers sent an update to the list of expert witnesses they would call. The list now included Dean Price, a bearded, burly criminal defense attorney who would testify "as to the various reasons why a person would plead the Fifth Amendment."

Stuart filed an objection. Witnesses are supposed to testify to facts. Witnesses are not allowed to testify on the law. Jurors cannot consider questions of law, only facts. Not going to happen in a million years, and these lawyers should know better. Cordonnier agreed, and Price was stricken from the witness list.

Right before the trial, Evelyn filed a motion for continuance that said, again, Alberta was too sick to participate in her defense. That her cognitive functions were getting worse. That this would represent a manifest unfairness to have the trial start the next week. There was nothing in the motion about "new evidence," Stuart noticed.

Cordonnier set pending motions for the Friday before the trial was to begin. In regard to Alberta's illness, Stuart was customarily blunt. "If Mrs. Comstock has dementia or probable Alzheimer's or some other cognitive issues, those issues aren't going to get better if we wait. They are only going to get worse. This trial will never happen if this continuance is granted on that basis."

Cordonnier agreed. He would not move the trial again.

Alberta was at this pretrial hearing. Faith was not. Faith could simply not wait until this whole ordeal was over. She wanted a good resolution, but the process had been draining.

Al and Sherry were in the courtroom listening. They left quietly after the hearing was over and went to talk to Alberta in the hallway. Stuart huddled with Evelyn and Shane about being able to contact one another over the weekend if anything was needed.

Stuart went back to the office and began reviewing the evidence folders his staff compiled throughout the week. He would add things and take things out. Hundreds of photos and documents color-coded to make them easier to locate. Other witnesses had come in to be prepped, and some of them even signed affidavits as to what they were going to say. Just in case there were any surprises during the trial. It was part of Stuart's job to make sure the trial was as boring and predictable as possible.

Over the past three years, he memorized virtually everything being put together. It was all in his head. Stuart wrote down bullet points for his opening statement, which was simply a discussion of what he intended to show the jury over the course of three to four days. He would talk about what he knew the defense would bring up, but just enough to casually dismiss it. He had all his witnesses listed out and what he needed to get from each and every one of them. That would be put into bullet points as well.

He would also have a list of what he thought the other side would ask his witnesses. Largely based on what was already asked of them in depositions and written discovery, but Stuart also put himself in the position of the defense. What would he do to try and make this case look bad? He would quiz other lawyers in the office about the perceived weaknesses in Faith's case. None of them came up with anything Stuart hadn't thought out already.

Stuart knew the defense witnesses. Talked to all of them. He added notations to page numbers in their deposition where he found inconsistencies. Much of this would have to be done on the fly, thinking about questions he wanted. Thinking about objections he would need to make to the defense lawyer's questions of their own witnesses. It was a lot to juggle, but after doing this work for nearly thirty years, few surprises came up.

In all, this amounted to a massive, hand-written outline. What he needed the jury to hear. What he needed the jury to think about. How he wanted them to get the conclusion that was required to get a favorable verdict. Stuart sat there in the dark, with no other light on in the entire firm other than the green desk lamp in front of his computer keyboard and the traffic passing behind him. He allowed his mind to wander as he stared up at the ceiling and nicotine seeped into his lungs.

If he was correct in how the other side was going to handle things, he would be closer to winning. It would then just be a matter of who got on the jury. Could he connect with them? Would they understand what he was doing?

After reviewing his outline, Stuart could imagine it all in his head. Starting tomorrow, he just had to make sure it worked.

# 'TIL DEATH DO YOU PART

When family would visit Alberta during the period of time after the divorce and the fights over the money, she could speak of nothing but her anger at Rolland. Most of them were more than happy to listen and pile on. At Thanksgiving of 2006, when Robin Stokes joined Michael and his family, Alberta talked about her conspiracy that Rolland and Bob Stillings would try to steal the house.

Al explained Rolland would have to follow the order of the court in the divorce. Alberta then went on to outline her suspicion he might get someone to buy the house, a straw man, and then turn around and sell it back to Rolland on the cheap.

"Now he could do that," Al said. "But who would take a loss on a house just so Rolland can stick it to you?"

She then mentioned she had been watching lots of crime procedural shows. *Forensic Files. CSI.* Alberta joked she was trying to learn from the mistakes on the show so she could figure out how to get away with murder.

Alberta then told the family she had gone gun shopping and boasted of receiving her gun permit.

On the way back to Springfield, Michael remarked, "Mom with a gun. That will be exciting."

Alberta would call the real estate agent and get bad news. There's no one interested in the house. It's a mess. The worst-kept house they'd ever seen on the market.

Alberta would get off the phone with the real estate agent and call Rolland immediately. "You are doing this on purpose," she would accuse. "You are letting the house fall apart just so you cannot sell it."

This was ridiculous, Rolland would counter and do his best to calm her down. "I don't have any money, dear. If I did have money, I would be giving it all to you. In fact, I have given it all to you. These repairs and upgrades are expensive, and I cannot just wish the money to appear."

That would cause Alberta to lash out about the books and the trips. Again. Those things cost money, too. You always seem to find a way to pay for those. Same arguments. Same responses.

Rolland knew from his professional experience, in any estate where there was a house that needed work but no money, the only solution was to auction off the house. Get a good auctioneer who has a strong corral of buyers who follow him around. Sure, the commission is higher than you pay a real estate agent, but you have bidders who set the price and there's no waiting for someone to keep showing the property.

Alberta did not immediately reject this idea. She got off the phone and started thinking about it. Maybe that would be easier. Maybe getting a crowd there and having them bid against each other would be a good idea. Get it up for auction on a nice, sunny day and see what happens.

But she knew it couldn't be so easy. That Rolland would be up to something. Alberta thought about it all night. She called Rolland first thing in the morning.

"I am not going to go along with this auction idea. I know what you are going to do. You'll have your lawyer show up to bid on it, won't you. And then he can just give it back to you. That's what you want. I know it."

Rolland could hardly believe what he was hearing. Where did she come up with this? Probably Carmel. Before he could answer her, she continued.

"It's too late. I've been trying to give you something fair, Rolland. But you won't listen to me. You never listen to me. I'll let you keep your law license, but I am going to get the house. That's it."

*Click* went the phone. Rolland walked to the bar and sat for a moment. He lit up a cigarette and looked out the window. Into the woods. He heard the puppies howling outside. He knew they had to be fed, but he couldn't bring himself to get up. This was rock bottom. Barely able to bring himself to the office to make any money, now the doors to the court could be closed to him forever.

He was sick. Any one of his ailments could rob him of life at a moment's notice. He worked so hard, from being the nerdy kid of a fireman to being a state representative and a successful attorney and businessman. Now, none of those accomplishments would matter at all. He would lose everything.

He went back to the library and wrote Bob. "This is driving me nuts! I can't rest, can't think, or do very much. Office income is way down since I'm not there to make deals. In the night when I can't sleep, I sometimes wish I could have the blessing of a heart attack to make this go away."

Things did appear grim on the Velma Brown front. Dale Wiley filed objections to Rolland's proposed final settlement in January of 2007. He accused Rolland of forging Alberta's name on checks. Withholding money from her. Generally, the pleading argued, Rolland's "poor attorney work and handling of the estate" cost the beneficiaries at least six figures in distributions.

Rolland could barely handle being called a "poor attorney" by this lawyer he'd never heard of before.

By her filing these objections with the probate court on Brown, Rolland maintained Alberta was violating the judgment in the divorce order that said all issues between the parties had been resolved. This should be reason enough to throw out the objections she filed. Stillings did not think this was a terrible idea. In fact, it was a very good idea. Stillings was willing to try anything in good faith. He didn't have a whole lot of other options.

Although the divorce was between Rolland and Alberta as individuals. The objections were against Rolland as the executor of the Velma Brown Estate by Alberta as a beneficiary. The law recognized a difference. Surely this was what Wiley would argue.

One thing that seemed clear to Stillings was Rolland's actions didn't harm Alberta. The money was being used by Rolland to pay for things around the house or to buy things for Alberta. She did receive benefit from the funds Rolland removed.

So far, Stillings could not get an agreement on a deposition and thus the court withheld making any final decision until that happened. Wiley would simply never agree to a date. Stillings figured if Alberta's lawyer was stalling, that was good enough.

Rolland told him about the scheme Alberta envisioned about him buying the house at auction. Stillings had to laugh. Why would he go along with something so ridiculous? he asked. Although the story suggested something Stillings was worried about. Without Bob Wiley as a calming influence, there was no telling what Alberta would do moving forward. Stillings believed it was time to get out the abuse of process petition he had written up almost a year earlier and file it. Alberta damaged Rolland's reputation and cost him lots of money in attorney fees. It was time to do something bold and hope this new lawsuit would end the constant, expensive bickering.

Stillings laid out his plan to proceed with the abuse of process. Now was the time.

"I like this idea," Rolland said. "Every single dispute that ends in disagreement turns to blackmail. You don't think this will just make her angrier?"

It might, Stillings had to admit. But it was not as though they were getting anywhere. This needs to be the measure of offense that gets her attention.

Stillings did wonder if Rolland would be okay with the idea of staying in the house until he died and then she could own the property outright. That a possible solution would be to deed Alberta the house now and reserve Rolland a "life estate." He would, legally, be able to treat the house as his own.

Maybe a new lawsuit would get Alberta to be creative.

"I have some doubt she will go for the 'till death do we part' agreement. Besides, she hasn't kept her word on any agreement moving forward."

Anything was possible. Rolland signed the petition and Stillings had it promptly filed on January 22, 2007. In order to succeed in an abuse of process case, Rolland would have to prove Alberta made an "illegal, improper, perverted use of process, a use neither warranted nor authorized by the process; had an improper purpose for doing so; and that Rolland suffered damages as a result." The first and third elements would be easy enough to prove. Finding evidence of Alberta's intentions would be tougher. Rolland was late, after all, with paying Alberta her money.

The action sought actual damages for an unspecified amount. The suit also sought $100,000 in punitive measures against Alberta for "outrageous" and "reckless" actions against her ex-husband. The suit went further to say Alberta promised to pay certain marital debts under the divorce settlement and failed to do so. Which then meant the creditors went after Rolland and he had to pay them, contrary to their agreement and one more thing adding to Rolland's financial distress.

Alberta was served on January 31, and she sent the lawsuit to her attorney. She could not believe this. She was on the cusp of finalizing the divorce, and now Rolland was serving her with another lawsuit. From her perspective, this was more smarty-pants bullying. Rolland, being the high and mighty lawyer, using his money and the courts to frighten her.

True to Dale Wiley's form, he immediately filed notice that the lawsuit should be removed to federal court. Legally, this was almost certainly correct. One of the first things a law student learns in Civil Procedure is jurisdiction. Any dispute involving parties of different states with a controversy exceeding $75,000 can be heard by a federal court.

Most parties choose not to file matters in federal court. For starters, the standards one has to prove to succeed are higher than in state courts, at least in states like Missouri. There are more procedural hoops to jump through; more legal work that needs to be done. All of this is a fancy way of saying federal court makes disputes more expensive.

If you were to ask a law professor, Wiley made the right move. As for his client, who had no money, it was less than ideal. Alberta's settlement funds were already being chipped away by continuing legal bills.

For the federal suit, Alberta retained David Adair at a firm called Haden, Cowherd, and Bullock. They usually work for insurance companies in personal injury suits but had a good reputation in federal court.

Then, for a month and a half, nothing happened. Dale called Bob and laid out a proposal. You give Alberta an additional $100,000 from the sale of the house and dismiss the lawsuit in federal court. In exchange, Alberta will drop the objections to the Velma Brown Estate distribution.

"Also, just so it is not a surprise, should the lawsuit that had been moved to federal court continue, we will be pursuing Rule 11 sanctions for what I can say is the most frivolous lawsuit I have ever laid eyes on."

If you've heard of Rule 11 sanctions, it is probably because of *A Civil Action*. There's a whole chapter devoted to how a judge in a federal civil matter can sanction a lawyer for filing a lawsuit with an "improper purpose." The threat of filing such sanctions calls in the lawyer's motives and integrity. It's not thrown around lightly.

The letter led to lots of fighting. The fighting led to multiple motions being filed in court. At the first hearing, the judge said mediation would need to happen before the case went forward. That was another requirement of federal court. The parties would go to an office, usually a lawyer who specialized in resolving disputes outside of court, and they would sit in separate rooms as the mediator shuttled back and forth trying to settle the case. The court appointed John Holstein, a former Missouri Supreme Court judge practicing in Springfield, to serve as the mediator. He was effective in the role, often getting parties to settle their differences over the course of the day. But he was also expensive. Alberta would have to pay half his fee. More money. More problems.

The date for the mediation was set for May 14, 2007. Without warning and on the morning of, Wiley canceled. Then the parties had to get together and come up with a different date. Everyone agreed to July 11, 2007.

In April, Rolland had a decision to make. For several years, City Utilities, the municipal power supplier for Springfield and the entity Rolland challenged when he was a young lawmaker in Jefferson City, had been acquiring property south of the law firm. The utility also provided public transit in Springfield and wanted to expand a service repair shop used to maintain their bus fleet. Out of money and realizing that perhaps renting an office space to continue his practice was the most cost-effective thing to do, Rolland ended up selling his law firm with an agreement he could move out by September 2009.

It was a tough pill to swallow. While he had allowed the building to fall into disrepair over the past few years, it had been a source of pride that he, as a young lawyer not even the age of thirty, had been able to build his own firm and run it for more than four decades from the same location. But Rolland had to sell. His assets were drained. Without another lawyer holding down the fort, the financial situation for the firm wasn't getting better even if it wasn't necessarily getting worse. If there was such a thing as good news during this period, Rolland didn't have the energy to travel, not even to Mexico.

Now, his law firm would be gone as well. He didn't know what to do with his staff. He could never lose Becky. But he hoped that, when he did move, she would go back to answering the phones for him. Below her skill set, but these were desperate times. Faith knew of a building on Commercial Street that was being rehabbed—the area was going through a resurgence—and began engaging in purchasing the property when it was ready. It wouldn't be cheap, but that's the price to pay when a neighborhood becomes hip again.

She talked with Rolland about simply sharing office space with her for some nominal amount. Rolland knew that would work. Perhaps they could split the staff, he thought.

In the meantime, Faith was doing everything she could to find Rolland a place to live. She wanted him close to her and got to work on finding a house that would be suitable; something with a big basement for the books was the major requirement. There were a few houses in that neighborhood for sale in the spring. The real estate agent advised Faith to wait until summer, when people would be more eager to move.

Faith wasn't really interested in the optimal time to buy. She would help her dad in securing financing for a house. Faith knew the mansion was a powder keg: The longer Rolland lived there, the angrier Alberta would get.

The fight with Alberta wasn't the only thing on Faith's mind. She was going out to see her dad once a week, and it was clear Rolland was not in great shape. She would do her best, but it was the middle of tax season and she barely had time to check on him.

After April 15 came and went, Faith usually took some time off in the summer and could spend more time with her dad. She had an arrangement with Stephen that she would pay him to keep an eye on Rolland. Faith also knew Becky was checking in with him at least once a day.

Faith would go over to help cook meals for the week. Rolland could barely boil water, she would testify later, and needed someone to prepare something other than fast food. Worse still, Rolland would often just skip meals or forget to eat. "I got too busy to worry about such formalities," he would tell her.

Skipping meals wasn't exactly ideal for his diabetes. In addition, Rolland still smoked, and that aggravated all his other conditions. The emphysema, the polyps in his throat. He was still drinking enough that his chances of falling were enhanced.

If he forgot to eat, Rolland certainly wasn't mindful about taking his medicine or going to the doctor. Faith suspected Rolland was lying about his infrequent trips to check on his medical condition. She knew he was stubborn; where else would she have gotten her stubbornness from? But a seventy-year-old going through this much stress made the risks more significant.

Then there was his memory. By Rolland's admission, he was becoming more forgetful. While there was never any reported diagnosis, Rolland spent his entire career dealing with people who had various diagnoses of incapacity. He was recognizing it himself. Forgetting recent happenings while maintaining clear memories of things in the past. He would find himself surprised by where he was in the house, as though he forgot basic comings and goings.

Rolland and Faith enjoyed their time together, catching up on cases. Rolland would mention his concerns about Steve. Steve was in trouble again. On probation and caught with drugs, Rolland put up $5,000 to bail him out. He asked Alberta to split the costs. She responded that she needed money. Stillings said the prosecutor would agree to defer prison time only if Steve went to rehab. But Steve didn't have the money. Steve worked as best he could, but his addictions got the worst of him and he routinely found himself out of employment.

Rolland couldn't imagine his only true son rotting in jail. He asked Becky to find the money from somewhere, anywhere, to pay for the rehab treatment. She said she would do her best, but estate fees just weren't coming in.

Steve was at the house a lot. Doing odds and ends. Mowing the yard. Rolland sat down with him and explained the situation. Not in legal terms but in terms he thought his children would understand. "If I pay for this to keep you out of jail," Rolland pleaded, "then it must stick. You cannot go back to this. Not one drop of booze. Not one bit of anything. If you do, then I will cut you off. That's not just cutting you off from your allowance but that's taking you out of the trust. Do you understand that?"

Steve, initially, did not understand. He did not have a problem, he protested. The police were merely out to get him because of his record.

Rolland explained this was already decided. Stephen stood up and stormed off. The wolves snarled at the sudden movement. Rolland followed him outside the house, begging him to think about it. Steve simply screamed that he wasn't going to put up with this bullshit anymore. He got in his golf cart and sped off, leaving the gate wide open as he went due south toward the lake.

All Rolland could do was stand there for a moment. The wolves stood at attention. He could barely handle all of this. *I spoiled these children*, he thought. *I provided them with everything they could want.* But it did them no good. Faith was the only one who turned out to be good for anything.

Rolland remembered taking Steve and Mike to the courthouse when Alberta was busy. While he talked to the judge, he would hear them playing out on the marbled staircase. Mike said he even wanted to be a lawyer like his daddy when he grew up. That's why Rolland said Mike was his favorite.

But Steve was his boy and had to be saved. All Rolland could do was sigh and feel sorry for himself and the mess he made for himself.

"Stay here, pups," Rolland commanded. "I've got to get the gate." He ambled all the way down his winding driveway, feeling every step in his bones.

Becky wasn't quite sure where the money was going to come from to pay for Steve's rehab, if he in fact would agree to such an arrangement. She pressured the public administrator to send down bank statements for estates that had annual settlements due. Getting the yearly paperwork submitted to the court for approval also meant the firm could petition for their fees. Their staff was doing everything they could, they assured Becky.

A thousand dollars here, twenty-five hundred dollars there. It added up. Payroll was a roulette game. Stillings would send another bill for thousands of dollars for the past month's work. Rolland now had a mortgage on the house, and that had to be paid every month as well. Now, Becky also needed to find five figures just so Steve could get out of trouble.

In the meantime, Becky couldn't remember the last time Rolland had come into the office. It had been months. Maybe close to a year.

She called him every day. Right at 8:30 to figure out what needed to be done. He would fax his written notes, and Becky would transcribe them for filing. Established clients would come in, but Becky was the only person who could meet with them. When a new client stumbled upon the firm, they would insist on meeting Rolland. Becky could never guarantee that. So, they would go somewhere else. There were lots of lawyers in Springfield, Becky knew. Most of them bothered to show up to work from time to time.

There were documents that needed to be signed. She would go out there a few times a week. Always reluctant to be around the wolves, Becky knew she needed to check up on him. After Rolland had the come-to-Jesus moment with his son, Steve disappeared. Rolland would talk about the cases, talk about the finances.

Becky never seen him like this before. Completely disheveled. A little confused. Dispirited. Such a fascinating man reduced to a shell of himself. Only his family to blame. It totally broke her heart to see the man she admired seemingly disappear before her very eyes.

But she wasn't exclusively focused on his well-being. Becky knew the firm existed only because of him. Sure, she had a reputation as a steady right-hand, and there were plenty of lawyers who would see her filing things at court and say they could use someone like her in their office. She appreciated that, but Becky was also aware many lawyers thought, and correctly so, that she would help ensure nabbing the public administrator as a client. Probate lawyers from around the city licked their lips at the prospect of such work.

Becky wasn't going to bolt just because the chips were down. But it was clear watching Rolland stagger around and rattling off a cough as he reached for another pack of smokes that he was not going to live forever.

Things began to look up in May 2007. Stillings was convinced Alberta was on the ropes based on the fact her lawyers stopped returning phone calls and sending faxes. A lack of activity suggested there was a lack of a fight. Or maybe just a lack of money.

Steve had come to his senses and decided rehab would be good for him. Not only to stay out of jail but to get his life on track. He thought it would be good for his relationships. Steve very much wanted to be there for his dad. To help Faith take care of him in his old age. Steve tried rehab before, and it never took. That was because he wasn't serious about helping himself. Now he was, and he went to tell his dad the decision was made.

Rolland was thrilled. Becky got enough settlements approved to get some fees into the office coffers. It would pay for Steve's stint and even allow the law firm catch up with expenses. It would also help Rolland with some of his personal finances that were starting to pile up, which was good because Becky was noticing a lot of problems with the office's physical structure. She was unsure if the building could wait until 2009 when City Utilities would take over.

Steve entered into a plea agreement, and the judge sentenced him to prison but suspended execution so Steve could prove he'd get his act together.

Rolland had Becky look into some clinics in the area. Good but affordable. She found a great place near Clinton that would have a room available for Steve on July 1. Becky reserved a spot with a down payment and arrangements were made. Rolland talked to Steve and felt, for the first time in a long time, his son was serious about taking care of himself.

In the meantime, Faith found Rolland a house in the neighborhood. Faith drove Rolland to see it. He approved.

The basement could handle most of his collection, while the rest would stay at an underground storage facility until a proper venue could sell off the remaining items. Rolland thought this might generate enough revenue to help pay for the house. That meant, with the first payment coming from City Utilities for their purchase, money was looking up.

He even found Alberta calling less. But he learned it was because she'd been admitted to the hospital. She had a stroke. Or maybe a heart attack. Her health wasn't all that great, either. She drank. She smoked. She, too, was stressed out from the fighting, and it took a toll.

This was the hospitalization where she said Roy Quick, her brother, snuck into her house and stole the gun. This was the hospitalization where she wrote out a health-care directive about whether she should be resuscitated in the event the heart surgery went poorly. It was found in the briefcase left in Rolland's house. Or maybe outside the house. The briefcase that had all the important documents Alberta thought Rolland needed. Although it is unclear why he would need a copy of her health-care directive.

Or maybe it was just in there because Alberta wanted to leave Rolland some of his books she found. Then the bag got left behind as a mistake. It was so hard to keep up with the stories about that bag.

When she got out of the hospital, Alberta called Rolland to say she was unable to continue helping Michael because she had no money. He was living in some fleabag hotel in North Springfield and was so hard up he was going to be evicted even from there. He had a job, Rolland said. Or at least that's what Steve told him. He can't make an honest living? Is that what he was supposed to believe?

Alberta didn't care. Her boy needed her help, and she couldn't do it. All because Rolland was keeping the house from being sold.

Rolland could not figure this out. He just paid her six figures. Where was it going? He didn't ask. He didn't want the fight. But he believed at that moment selling the house would never solve the problem. Either Alberta or their children would always need something.

Rolland explained to her what he explained by letter only two years earlier. Michael was a thief and an addict. Giving him money would only make the problem worse. "He has killed all the love I have for him," Rolland said. "I have nothing else to give him, and I am better off without him. You would be, too."

Alberta was unhappy about that answer and asked about the house again. She said the real estate agent was having no luck. No calls. No inquiries. Nothing. This was unacceptable.

Rolland told her about the new house. He would be moving out in the summer. Alberta didn't believe him. What about your books? she asked. Any book that wouldn't fit into the basement would get sold,

Rolland said. Alberta could hardly believe he would part with any of those silly books after he obsessed about them for all those years.

What about the wolves? Can they live in this so-called house you are buying? Rolland admitted he had not come up with a plan for them. They were getting older and not feeling well. Hair was falling out. Teeth were decaying. Rolland knew how they felt.

He told Alberta about a conservatory in Colorado that took care of aging wolves. It would probably be the best place for them. Rolland hated the idea of giving them away but had to face reality. He didn't have the energy. Soon, he wouldn't have the space.

Alberta pled, hoping to use Rolland's feelings about the animals to her benefit. "Let them stay at the house. I will move in. I can live there and take care of them. If you are moving into another house, it would make sense for me to be there. Let the dogs die with some dignity."

Going on about this again. "My dear, the house is mortgaged to the hilt. I had to take out a loan in order to pay you. Now, I have to buy a house. I need the money from the sale to pay the mortgage off and pay for my new house. We cannot keep this place."

She protested. "I still have a little bit of money. I can pay off half the mortgage with my settlement."

"But where is my money going to come from? I know you think I am hiding it from you, but I am not. I am broke. Maybe things will get better, but I need to sell this house. It is an albatross around my neck." Alberta's shift in demands were causing Rolland whiplash.

Alberta caught herself. Falling for his smooth talk again. She ranted and raved. Making accusations about Rolland just wanting the house for himself. The call ended angrily. Abruptly.

Even as things seemed to be looking up for Rolland, he still had to worry about Alberta. He still had to worry about Velma Brown. But he had Stillings to help with those matters. All Rolland had to worry about was making sure there was enough money to take care of Bob's bills.

On July 2, 2007, Stillings sent Dale Wiley a fax saying he tried to call about a discovery dispute. One of those boring topics. Stillings mentioned he tried calling a few times but had not heard from him.

On the same day, David Adair, sought the court's permission to withdraw as her counsel.

Alberta was having a particularly bad Monday.

***

Alberta suggested to family members a belief that, if something happened to Rolland, all the issues involving their various disputes would go away. In fact, that is not how the law works when someone dies. In a letter to both Becky and Faith on July 16, 2007, Stillings outlined what would happen next. According to that letter, they all met at Rolland's office on July 5 to discuss how things would proceed. It was always ugly business to dig into matters of paperwork and money as a loved one had barely gone cold. It was even worse in circumstances as shocking as this. Everyone who knew him expected Rolland might not live much longer, but they never expected things to end like this.

Under the trust agreement Rolland had written up for the Comstock family, Faith would be the new trustee now that he was gone. Becky had been named as personal representative under the last will and testament.

What that meant was Faith had to deal with the real estate: the law firm as well as the rental property, and the house and its contents. Including the books. All these assets had been moved into the trust by Rolland shortly after the divorce had been finalized.

When all of that was sold, there would be four people who would get to split the proceeds equally in their capacity as beneficiaries under the trust: Becky, Faith, Steve, and Ashley (Michael's daughter). Faith would be entitled to a reasonable fee for the work she did as trustee in addition to what she would receive as a beneficiary.

Becky would be responsible for everything else. Since there was no succession plan for the law firm, she would have to sell it. Bob warned her that she needed to find a lawyer to help wind up the practice. But Becky said there was no money to hire a lawyer. He just told her to do the best she could under the circumstances.

There was also the matter of the federal lawsuit. Stillings would need to let the court know Rolland died and that an estate was being opened. Bob was very clear to Becky that the lawsuit needed to proceed to make sure Alberta didn't pull any more shenanigans involving the sale of the house, which would be pursued by the trust.

While the lawsuit would be expensive, Stillings pointed out, it potentially kept Alberta in check. Becky and Faith shot each other a look. Sure, they thought. The lawsuit really put her on the balls of her feet.

There was also Velma Brown. With Rolland gone, the threat of that situation passed. There was no need to worry about the old man's law license now, and any "blackmail card" Alberta could play was off the table. But there was a sizable claim presented in the objections filed. Alberta was essentially saying Rolland's work cost her several hundreds of thousands of dollars in money she was due.

Becky asked Bob about whether the lawsuits might go away. She wanted to know if Alberta would just give up on the Velma Brown Estate and take her money without fighting over how much additional funds she was allegedly due. Bob thought it was unlikely but would try to work something out.

Faith had the same thought in regard to the house. Alberta was opposed to an auction because she developed this conspiracy about Rolland using a straw man for the purchase. Maybe now, Alberta wouldn't worry about that and could just agree to sell it as cheaply as possible.

This was the elephant in the room. Becky, Faith, and Bob all believed Alberta killed Rolland. As time went along, it became a certainty to them. If that were the case, Bob argued, there's no reason to believe Alberta would change her positions at all. She had taken this fight to extreme measures, and there was no reason to believe Alberta would back down.

She could be arrested. What would happen then?

Almost certainly Alberta would sign a power of attorney that would put someone else in charge of her affairs. This person could be far more unreasonable.

The discussion was premature, Stillings had to remind the two. No one knew how anything was going to play out. Emotions were high. Bob was still a wreck about what happened. Rolland was the guy who taught him how to be a lawyer. It meant a lot to him that Rolland sought his advice for some of the toughest moments in his life. This was a devastating loss for all three of them.

No matter how they felt, someone was going to have to handle Rolland's affairs. Which meant they were going to have to deal with Alberta directly.

Becky would take the original last will and testament down to the probate court and file it. All the clerks wanted to know what was going on. Some of them, like Dana, were genuinely concerned with Becky. Some of them just wanted gossip. Most of them could tell she was distraught. Poor dear, they worried. Would she find a job when this was all said and done?

She had to beg them all off. She needed to work on a memorial service and needed to get back to the office.

Becky and Faith talked about what to do for Rolland. He left specific instructions that he did not want a "Christian burial." A ceremony for friends would be fine per his instructions. But there should be nothing done that would be too ornate.

They decided to do a memorial service in the old courthouse where Rolland began his practice. Clients, lawyers, and judges showed up. Many spoke about Rolland's unique character and colorful background. It was a nice tribute. Becky finished the proceedings by playing a recording of Frank Sinatra's "My Way." Unsure if Rolland liked the song, it nonetheless seemed fitting for the man they were paying tribute to.

The event was held in the rotunda of the old courthouse with two levels above it. Standing right above the proceedings and away from the crowd were Al and Sherry Rose. Everyone else was on the ground level save for them. The *Springfield News-Leader* snapped a shot of the two of them, looking down on the crowd.

On August 1, just shy of a month since the murder, neighbors heard someone screaming outside of Rolland's house. Unsure of what was going on, someone called Faith and she drove north of town to see. It was Michael. "This is my mom's house! It belongs to her!" he said according to the caller. Faith called Becky and Becky drove to meet her. By the time either arrived, Michael was gone.

Five days later, someone reported that the gate to the Comstock house had been damaged. Faith filed a police report, but there was nothing they could do. No one left any evidence.

Faith had to deal with her mother almost immediately. On the same day someone vandalized the gate, Faith wrote a letter to Alberta. She could not remember the last time the two had a conversation, she wrote. Faith determined to take no sides during the divorce but ultimately found Alberta's hostility toward Rolland unacceptable. Taking those photos around the courthouse after she'd swiped them from the house was the last straw.

The purpose of the letter was to deal with the house and furnishings, which were under Faith's control. She spoke of the shock she felt over his death. "Rolland died too young and he died too suddenly." She acknowledged Alberta's anger toward Rolland but asked her to remember the "long periods of prosperity" they enjoyed as well.

After laying out what needed to be done with the house and the personal items, Faith pledged to her mother she would not engage in any hostilities against her. "I am not angry with you," she went on. "Even though there might be conflict in our road ahead, and even though this grief and misery produces sharp conflicts and underscored differences between you and me, I will not engage in angry exchanges. Too much estrangement has already happened and great estrangement seems clear. I will remember you are my mother. I both respect and love you. I know we can emerge through this process and maintain our loving relationship." The letter was measured but sincere nonetheless.

Alberta's response to the letter was to sue Faith. She filed an action against the trust to sell the property on the courthouse steps and to split the proceeds. A partition.

Given Alberta's paranoia about conducting a private action to sell the property, the fact she would ask for a public auction made no sense. In theory, someone could bid one dollar and successfully get the property.

The mediation for the federal suit was pushed into August. It was unsuccessful. Depositions of Alberta were taken after being delayed for nearly nine months. During her questioning, Stillings asked Alberta what she thought of Rolland in the last months of his life.

Almost certainly against her lawyer's instructions, she told the truth. "I hated him. I couldn't stand to even look at him. Just the sight of him made me sick to my stomach." Even after his death, Alberta had a hard time holding back her feelings about the ex-husband. Even with her as the primary suspect in his murder.

It took a year from the date of Rolland's death to work everything out. Of fighting. Of filings. Of faxes. But the parties mediated the matter again and got everything resolved. The house got sold. Anything Rolland's estate would have been entitled to from the abuse of process case was offset by whatever Alberta thought she should be paid because Rolland screwed around on the Velma Brown matter. No one would owe anyone anything. A zero-sum game.

Steve felt like the odd man out through all of this. Having a good relationship with his father and having helped him with some of his daily activities, he was not prepared for his lack of involvement with the estate.

But he was entitled to one-fourth of his old man's stuff. So when he appeared at Stillings's office the week after Rolland's murder, he was surprised to hear the lawyer, *his* lawyer on so many matters, say that he only represented Faith and could not represent him in matters involving the trust. Stillings could only say that Steve would get the same line of communication entitled to the other beneficiaries.

What's worse, as Steve learned from Stillings not too shortly later, the rehab clinic sent a scathing letter to the probation office as a result of Steve's "absconding" from treatment. "I just found out my dad was murdered. What was I supposed to do?" Steve asked his lawyer. "Wait around for a day pass?"

Yes, Bob said, that's precisely what he should have done. There was a process, it was explained to him. No matter what was going on, he needed to make sure he followed the facility's rules on checking out. If everyone who had a family emergency just left the clinic, it would not be able to ensure a safe transition back into the "real world." In fact, the nature of why Steve left, the trauma of a loved one being murdered, made him more susceptible to relapse.

The probation office recommended Steve serve the suspended prison sentence, and the prosecutor agreed. Steve threw himself at the mercy of the court. This man just lost his father, Stillings argued. In a brutal and shocking way. He just checked in. He didn't know what to do. There's no similar situation we can compare this to, Bob argued. It is simply unjust to throw this man in prison because he'd felt the need to figure out what was going on with his father.

The court was unmoved. They made Steve serve 120 days of his four-year sentence. All of this happened within two months of Rolland's murder.

When Steve got out, he found Faith's responses regarding the trust matters insufficient. In fact, she wouldn't talk to him directly at all. "Your money is coming," she would write. That's all she would say.

But it wasn't just the money, Steve would maintain. He went by the sheriff's department in March 2009 to make a complaint about the civil contempt case. He said he and Faith got into a fight about his clothes being put in storage and how she would not release them until the trust could be closed. The deputy told him it was between him and Faith. They couldn't do much to help.

While he was there, Stephen asked to talk to the detective in charge of the murder case. He mentioned the last time he saw Alberta, she pulled into his driveway at the cottages. She just sat there in her car, with Carmel in the passenger seat, staring off into the window of Steve's apartment. He went outside to talk to her. She wouldn't acknowledge him. Wouldn't look at him. He reached down to give her a kiss on her cheek, but she recoiled.

"I had never seen her act that way," Stephen told Detective Weatherford. "She acted like a total stranger." He had only recalled it recently, he told the officer. He was trying to remember everything he could about the case in hopes it would help.

It didn't help, as it turns out. This was nearly two years after the murder. No one was doing much in terms of follow-up on any leads. Two months later, Steve got caught with methamphetamines again and would be sentenced to seven years in prison. But he had a more lenient judge and got the sentence put off while he served probation again. This time it would stick. He's been clean ever since.

All the while, Faith still had to sell the lakeside properties. While she was talking to City Utilities about the law firm property, she mentioned the lakeside cottages. Since CU also provided the water service for Springfield, they owned McDaniel Lake and were interested in buying up those properties. Great news, Faith thought, as no one else wanted them.

A few months after that contract was inked but before the deal was closed, the remaining tenants cleared out and the little stone buildings were empty. A neighbor drove by and saw something suspicious. Two trucks were parked out front. One was a Dodge and the other was a white flatbed. She approached a white male with a "City Utilites" baseball cap and red hair who was holding two screwdrivers in his hand. She asked what was going on, and he said the utility authorized them to be on the property.

The sheriff's department opened up their Comstock file and asked whether Michael's work truck matched what she had seen. It had. They showed her a picture of Michael. Asked if that was the person she talked to, the one with the red hair. It was. The sheriff's department went to City Utilities and asked if anyone had been authorized to work on the property. They had not.

No one from the sheriff's department followed up on why Michael would have been at the property.

# STOCKER V. COMSTOCK

On the morning of June 27, Stuart got to the office at about 6:15 a.m. and did what he normally did. Hit the lights, started some coffee, and made copies of the sudoku and crosswords for the other lawyers in the office who would come later and join in the daily ritual. He would be gone by the time everyone else got there, but he didn't want to be rude. Of course, Stuart filled out the puzzles from the paper itself. It was his paper, after all.

Stuart was wearing a nice suit, his opening statement suit. It wasn't nearly as sharp as what he could afford, but Stuart found local jury pools did not want a lawyer showing off their wealth.

Joyce Hull came in thirty minutes later. Joyce was quiet but diligent with her work as a trial paralegal. She would sit through all five days of the trial to keep the area around the plaintiff's table organized, to meet with witnesses in the hallway, to set up the ELMO projector that would mirror documents onto the wall, and to hit the lights when Stuart was using the projector. Joyce would make sure the client had a bottle of water. Plus, breath mints. Stuart did not want the client to have bad breath. Otherwise, Joyce's job was to be invisible.

Becky wanted to help. Stuart nixed that, knowing the jury would find it strange that a key witness was also doing paralegal work. Plus, Joyce had everything so well organized he would be able to handle things from midafternoon to the end of the day without anyone behind him when Joyce had to pick up her kids from school.

The weekend before trial, Stuart received a delivery from Alberta's lawyers: a sworn statement by their client to the discovery question, "Identify the current location of what you have described as your 'Gun—.38 Special from Judge Burrell to me.'" Originally, Alberta pled the Fifth to this question. Now, she said, "I do not know the current location of the gun."

It was a non-answer delivered on the weekend before trial. The judge warned Stuart that Alberta could change her answers if he asked her something directly. That is precisely why Stuart planned to not ask Alberta any direct questions.

If the defense tried to bring this up, Stuart knew they wouldn't get very far with it. Sure, he could try and depose Alberta one night this week. Depositions during the trial were rare but sometimes needed. Not in this case. Stuart had a plan, and this wasn't going to screw it up.

***

It took all day to pick a jury. There were only two spectacular moments. One involved a man who identified himself as the child of Judith Shepherd, Rolland's first wife. Later, Stuart asked if any potential jurors had any previous interactions with law enforcement. One man raised his hand to say he'd once been a thief until he was shot breaking and entering into a house. This prompted another potential juror to raise his hand to say he had been the guy who shot the other guy. Lots of gasps and nervous laughter in the courtroom after that exchange.

All three controversial jurors were stricken. The panel of twelve jurors and alternates were sworn in and seated. Cordonnier read them instructions to not talk about the case other than with each other, and the only facts they could consider was what was presented over the next few days. They nodded solemnly.

Cordonnier asked the plaintiff if they were ready to proceed. Stuart nodded, rose out of his chair, and addressed each juror initially by looking at them directly in the eye. He then shot his eyes to Alberta, seated in her wheelchair. Funny, Stuart thought, she didn't need a wheelchair at the hearing on Friday. Now she does, just in time to elicit sympathy from this jury of her peers.

Stuart offered the jury a good morning before jumping right into his opening statement. "So, what is this case about? This case is about Rolland Comstock, obviously. Rolland was seventy years old when he died, when he was killed. He was a man of some accomplishment. He was an attorney here in town for decades, well known, practiced primarily probate law. He was also well known in the world of book collecting, traveled the world collecting books, and had a huge collection in his home. And he was killed by gunshot on the second of July of 2007. He was shot four times with a .38 caliber class ammunition. The shot that actually killed him was a center-mass shot, shot at an angle, perforated his liver, and he bled to death primarily from blood loss from that wound."

He went on to talk about why the jury should find Alberta as the person who was responsible for Rolland's death. "Let's talk about motive. The evidence will be that Alberta Comstock and Rolland Comstock were married for thirty-eight years. And the evidence will be that marriage ended...badly. And there was an acrimonious, contentious divorce, and the acrimony and the spite continued after the divorce as well. Alberta was furious. She wanted—she was mad and she wanted revenge. And so, what was she mad about? Several things. First, these folks were married for thirty-eight years, and the evidence will be that for the last ten years or so of their marriage they really lived more as roommates. And the evidence will be Rolland Comstock, throughout his life, struggled with issues of bisexuality and, over the last few years of his life, started exercising those thoughts in some way. We're not sure how much, other than he spent time with younger gay men. That much we know. That's pretty much all we know. Alberta Comstock found out, and that was the beginning of the end of this marriage, and I think that was the beginning of the steps that led to Rolland Comstock's death."

Stuart went over the details of the divorce itself. The divorce wasn't such a big deal, but what happened afterward was unprecedented. Alberta went crazy about the house, Stuart said. She went about trying to destroy Rolland's reputation. For her, the house became a symbol of a wasted life. Convinced Rolland was conspiring to keep the house for himself, the house became what angered her. On July 2, the sales listing expired and she had to write a five-figure check to hire a bunch of lawyers to keep fighting her husband. Stuart said those two events caused her to drive to Springfield to confront her ex-husband.

There was opportunity for which they would see evidence, Stuart promised. This was where Stuart whipped out the blown-up photo of the decrepit house sitting on the hill. Surrounded by massive iron fencing. With a big gate. Stuart didn't need to describe what the picture showed. It, in itself, was a thousand words that said: "This is not a house. This is a fortress."

Alberta had access to the house, Stuart noted. "The wolves trusted her. Her briefcase is found at the scene of the crime. She bought a .38 that very day and told the owner of the gun shop she was going over to Missouri to do some target practice. Alberta points in that direction. The owner sees her driving in that direction. Toward Missouri. Toward Springfield. Toward Rolland.

"Let's talk about the means that were available to her to cause this death. She owned—and there's no question about this—and had possession of after the divorce, a .38 caliber Colt revolver. And it is that gun Faith Stocker and I believe caused Rolland's death. Rolland was shot four times. There was testing done by the state crime lab on those rounds—and the .38 caliber Colt she owned, and is now missing, was one of the guns that could have fired the rounds that killed Rolland. Now, there are other potential guns—not many, but a few—so there's no way to definitively say this round came from this gun unless you've got the gun, which law enforcement has never found. Again, Alberta and her witnesses have told multiple stories about where this gun is and why it's not available now. They are inconsistent with each other, and you will hear those stories but—and I don't know which one you will hear during this trial because I've heard several, or I've read several and they are not the same and they are inconsistent with each other."

Stuart finished by pointing out there were people who wanted to help solve the murder of Rolland Comstock and there were people who did not. Alberta started out being helpful but then stopped talking. Then, when asked significant questions about the matter, she asserted her right not to incriminate herself. "I've asked her the identity of witnesses that could tell me where she was on the second of July of 2007. Won't answer. I've asked her if she caused Rolland Comstock's death. Won't answer. I've asked her to identify her cell phone provider in July of 2007. Won't answer." By the end of this trial, Stuart concluded, the jurors would find the reason why she wouldn't answer these questions was because her answers would prove she caused Rolland's death.

With that, Stuart sat down. Cordonnier asked which lawyer would give the defense's opening statement. It wasn't a given that the defense would give their opening before the trial started. Sometimes they wait until after the plaintiff finished their case.

"That's me," Evelyn piped up. "I guess." Despite the weirdly uncertain start, the defense started sowing doubt right away.

"The Comstocks are an unhappy and dysfunctional family," Evelyn said. "There is alcoholism, there's drug abuse, there are felonies, there's a bitter, vindictive daughter who refused to tell her siblings how to claim the inheritance their father left for them when she found out about it." Evelyn never mentioned Faith by name, and the jury wouldn't figure out who she was talking about until three days later. Stuart found this odd. Never assume anything with a jury, Stuart knew.

They weren't always that way, Evelyn assured the jury. Rolland and Alberta were married for nearly four decades. Going through ups and downs like any married couple. Infidelity could ruin any marriage. But it wasn't any regular old infidelity. "She found out Rolland had a preference for young Latino men, and he had been engaging in such activities for a period of years. Alberta was devastated." The divorce, however, was no more acrimonious than any other divorce and "Judge Wiley" would be here to testify to that fact.

The statement ignored the fact that the real fights started after the divorce was finalized. Evelyn simply said Alberta was trying to collect the money Rolland owed her. Money Rolland kept delaying in getting to her. He got her some money, Evelyn conceded, but not all the money owed her and not in a timely fashion. Filing an execution to seize Rolland's assets wasn't vindictive or nasty; it was something that happened every day when someone wouldn't pay them money owed and there was no other recourse.

Even when the money was paid, Evelyn continued, that left the house. Alberta and Rolland had an agreement that he would stay in the house for two years. Evelyn left out their agreement provided the precise date Rolland was supposed to leave: July 2 of 2007.

"But he was supposed to move when the house sold. All the evidence you will hear suggests he never wanted to leave the house. They contained his books." Where would those books go? Evelyn asked rhetorically. Rolland kept the house in disrepair so it would not sell, she maintained.

It was Rolland who filed the harassing suits. "He filed an action for wrongful execution against Alberta. I don't know where he filed it. Alberta doesn't know. The attorneys who represented her don't know. He filed it."

Stuart stopped writing his notes and looked at the jurors. He wondered if they were as confused as he was. What was she talking about? We don't know where he filed the suit? It was filed in Greene County! Her lawyer moved it to federal court. Stuart saw lots of furrowed brows and furious scribbling of notes on the court-supplied pads. Evelyn was giving them lots of information but not a whole lot of context, Stuart thought. Best to let her confuse them.

Evelyn would never explain what this meant at any point during the trial. But she continued. "That action was pending at the time of his death, and it was continued by Becky Frakes, who was his longtime secretary and his personal representative. Ultimately, those two lawsuits were resolved at the same time. Faith Stocker paid $250,000: $200,000 to Alberta, $50,000 to Alberta's attorney.

"Now here's where it gets really interesting," Evelyn promised. "Those settlement documents were signed in April of 2008. The payment required was not made until August of 2008. And guess what Faith filed in the interim? This lawsuit. She filed it at the end of July. So at the moment Alberta thought she settled all of her legal issues, her daughter is representing we've settled everything, she's bringing this action."

*We are at the thrust of the defense*, Stuart thought. The wrongful death suit's sole purpose was to undo the settlement, to "steal" the money Alberta received fair and square.

Evelyn countered Alberta was cooperative with law enforcement. "She didn't appear nervous or apprehensive. Alberta spoke with detectives the day Rolland had been found. She submitted to a gunshot residue test that came out negative."

Incorrect.

That the gun taken out of her vehicle and tested? "That was not the gun that killed Rolland."

Yes, Alberta ended up taking the Fifth. Evelyn said she knew how that looked. "But it's one of the tenets of our justice system that you cannot be forced to incriminate yourself in a criminal matter. And not only can you not be forced to directly incriminate yourself, you cannot be forced to answer questions which under any set of circumstances might incriminate you. That's a very, very broad protection. Someone in Alberta's situation would have been foolish not to take the advice of counsel and assert that privilege."

But the evidence no one could account for, Evelyn said, was the gun that shot Rolland. The evidence they would hear was that the gun was left in Greenfield, but was not there anymore. "The truth is, nobody knows where that gun is. Alberta doesn't know, no one we've been able to find knows. I assure you, Alberta would like to know where that gun is."

There was no DNA recovered at the scene of the crime, Evelyn continued. There were no footprints on the grounds of the Comstock property. No fingerprints in the house. "In fact, there was nothing in the house that would suggest Alberta was there when Rolland was killed."

Evelyn reminded the jury Alberta had never been charged or arrested for the murder. "Mr. King is probably going to be telling you in his closing argument that because she has 'taken the Fifth,' you should infer her answers would have been damaging to her if she answered, and answered truthfully. You may infer that. You're not required to infer that.

"But that doesn't relieve Faith Stocker from the responsibility of proving her case. She still has to convince you it is more likely than not Alberta shot Rolland. We don't believe when you listen to the evidence you will reach that conclusion."

With that, opening statements were done. Stuart got to put on Faith's case first. She took the stand to be sworn in. Faith looked over to Alberta's wheelchair and saw her mother looking away with disgust.

Stuart's purpose with calling Faith was to establish her relationship with Rolland as a way of pointing to the economic and noneconomic damage she suffered from Rolland's death. This was a challenging part of the lawsuit, Stuart knew. But Faith described not only the business component of the relationship with her dad—referrals between their mutual clients that led to income for Faith over a quarter of a century—but also the personal relationship. About how she would visit him and cook for him. About how he would stay with her when the weather was bad. About how much she was looking forward to Rolland moving into her neighborhood, a process he was starting the day he was killed.

Faith talked about the family. How Alberta and Rolland had a good relationship for all but one year of their marriage. The last one. Before that, they never argued. Never fought. "He was very generous with her."

But the divorce was upsetting to Alberta, Faith knew. She heard it from both of them. Faith maintained she wanted to stay out of it and not take sides. When Alberta moved to her south-side apartment in late 2004, Faith would visit her. Helped her with installing a dead-bolt lock because Alberta was scared to live by herself.

But one day Alberta stopped talking altogether. Faith said she learned from Becky her mom moved to Oklahoma.

Stuart also used Faith's testimony to introduce photos of Rolland, to put a human face on the man they would be discussing. There were also photos of the library, of the house, of the gate. Faith got to talk about his passion for books. Rolland loved those wolves, Faith would say. She did not. They made her uncomfortable, and the pack never let their guard down around her.

Regardless of his murder, Faith continued, the fight over the house continued. Alberta filed her partition lawsuit. Faith said there was never even a discussion, let alone a disagreement, over the price of the house. Everyone involved with the house wanted it sold, Faith swore. In the end, the trust just paid Alberta $250,000 to resolve the entire matter, and that included proceeds from the house. That testimony was important because that was precisely what Stuart was going to ask the jury to award.

Don't let Alberta profit from killing her husband, he would say.

What was her basis for filing this suit? Stuart asked Faith. "The wrongful death suit?"

"The briefcase," she responded. There was no reason that bag should have been in Rolland's house. Alberta would not have done anything to help Rolland, Faith maintained, countering what Alberta and Carmel said to the police. That briefcase showed she was there in the house.

That's all Stuart would have for now. With direct testimony, he reserved time for redirect to ask questions after Evelyn was done with her cross-examination. Opposing counsel went through the list of people who spent time in the house and asked Faith whether they were weary of the wolves. Everyone was other than Alberta and Rolland, she replied.

Evelyn asked why it took Faith a year to get Alberta's personal property to her. It was complicated, Faith responded. Whenever she would show up to pick things up, it was without advanced warning. She would have Al and Sherry with her. She would have what appeared to be a bodyguard. Faith admitted she had to call the sheriff to defuse tension.

Evelyn dropped that line of questioning to talk about Faith's relationship with her dad. They argued, Evelyn maintained.

Not really, Faith shot back.

"Hadn't you called him a bastard?"

No times Faith could recall. "Quite a few times," Evelyn would insist.

"It got so bad that you had to leave the office," Evelyn pressed. "Because your father wouldn't share money—"

Faith cut her off. "I left because of the environment of the office." When Faith said this, she looked at Al, who was sitting in the back of the courtroom. Al would be at the trial every day, even though in late afternoon he would nod off and start snoring. The bailiff would have to wake him up.

Evelyn continued to throw doubt on Faith's relationship, to challenge how much damage she faced from the loss of her father. Cooking meals for her dad once a week. Chatting about musicals at the office. Didn't seem that big of a deal to Mangan.

Next up, Stuart called Detective Frank Duren. Prosecutor Todd Myers showed up to watch him on the stand. Stuart went through the first day of the murder investigation and the subsequent weeks. All the way up to when Michael's DNA was confirmed at the scene a year later. Stuart rested. Cantin handled cross-examination and started by focusing on the fact that only Michael and Alberta had to hand over clothes, shoes, and swabs with the spit from their mouths.

"But not Becky Frakes."

"No."

"Not Faith Stocker."

"No."

"Not Stephen Comstock?"

He had an alibi and was immediately cleared, Duren had to point out.

"Not Rodman Comstock or Glenda Joplin or any of the kids who worked in the library?"

"No," Duren repeated.

"None of their houses were searched? Or their computers seized? None of that?"

"No."

When pawn shops were searched, it was never investigated whether Faith Stocker pawned anything off during that time, was there? Duren had to admit it was not.

But there were reasons for such omissions. Duren stated law enforcement looked at people who had animosity toward the victim. People who knew the wolves, who knew the back door was unlocked, knew the chain around the gate wasn't padlocked, and knew there was a wad of cash in the kitchen. Alberta and Michael were the only people who had the characteristics of a suspect.

"Was animosity the only reason someone might be murdered?"

Duren agreed robbery is a common reason.

"To secure money," Cantin rephrased. "Someone might have known Rolland had money in the house. Maybe *thought* he had money in the house. Isn't that a good reason to suspect someone might have killed him?"

"It was possible," Duren conceded.

In fact, Cantin continued, didn't Michael also have a checkered past? Duren knew about Michael from some of his previous dealings with the law. The sheriff's office also knew about the report filed by Rolland and Alberta in 2001, when Michael stole the very gun believed to be the gun used in this murder. He had stolen his brother's car and was almost gunned down by police for failing to comply with instructions.

Stuart had a chance to ask Duren to explain that only people who might be searched or investigated were people who actually might have killed the victim. There was no point in looking at non-suspects more closely. Duren stepped down. Stuart thought the detective did a good job.

Stuart then played the video deposition of the coroner, which was simply done to establish how Rolland died.

Stuart also called Glenda Joplin, who testified she had been in the house the Thursday before the murder and didn't see the black bag despite doing a full cleaning of the entire downstairs.

Stuart asked if she was afraid of the wolves.

Yes, Glenda said.

"What was it about them that made you scared?"

"Because they were wolves!" The gallery laughed.

Becky went on the stand to relive this horrible situation again as well as to recount Alberta's attitude toward continuing litigation after Rolland died. But the day ended before the defense could ask her questions. Becky would have to go on the stand first thing in the morning. Everyone went home but the lawyers, who went back to their offices to prepare for the next day.

At around 4:00 a.m., Faith received a call on her landline. It was a man breathing heavily. He didn't say anything.

"Al," Faith said to the person on the other line. They hung up. This person would call at around the same time in the morning every day during the trial.

***

Becky wrapped up her testimony that morning. Evelyn pressed her on why she would want to continue the lawsuits after Rolland died. "I think Rolland would have wanted me to continue because he started it. He felt firmly about it."

Mangan wanted to talk about how much money Becky received from the trust. It was a lot to Becky, north of $100,000. But Alberta would get nothing if Rolland died, Evelyn pointed out. "She had nothing to gain from his death, did she?"

Becky had to point out Alberta believed all the legal wranglings would end if Rolland was no longer around. Evelyn tried to strike that as hearsay; the judge allowed it since Alberta was a party and could refute it if she so chose.

Stuart had no follow-up for Becky. Relieved to be done, she didn't even want to stay in the courtroom to watch.

Bob Stillings was the next witness. He recounted the legal fights between Rolland and Alberta after the divorce and before the murder. Evelyn spent a significant part of an afternoon trying to justify the paperwork Bob Wiley filed to seize Rolland's assets. Stuart eyed the jury. Those who didn't appear confused looked bored. More good news for the plaintiff.

Bob was followed by Mike Friend, the owner of the gun shop. He was followed by the gas store clerk who thought she saw Alberta's truck in a timeline that would match when Alberta would have been driving to Springfield. Later, on Wednesday, Stuart called Detective Weatherford to discuss his meetings with Alberta as well as his personal observations as the person currently in charge of the investigation.

On cross, Cantin pointed out to Weatherford there was no physical evidence found on the grounds of the Comstock home.

Other than DNA from Michael Comstock, Cantin mentioned. Weatherford had to agree.

In fact, Cantin pressed the witness, there was absolutely nothing—no cell phone activity or credit card payments or anyone at all—placing Alberta in the state of Missouri on July 2. Weatherford said that was correct.

Stuart wasted no time in his redirect the next morning. Sure, there was no DNA. But there wouldn't be unless there was person-to-person contact, something unlikely in the case of a shooting. Weatherford agreed.

There were *no* prints of any kind found, Stuart reminded the jury.

"All this meant was the murderer had been careful; cautious about the way they moved around the house?"

"They could have used cloth to open gates and doors. Could have used gloves when they went to the house."

Cantin said no cell phone records placed Alberta in Missouri, Stuart repeated. But there were no cell phone records to place Alberta in Oklahoma.

Yes, Weatherford said. "That was correct."

"Which means?"

"Which means she never used a cell phone. Or she used something like a TracFone that wouldn't be picked up by cell phone towers." Weatherford further confirmed Al Rose said Alberta used such a phone.

Stuart seized upon Cantin's assertions that the sheriff's department hadn't searched the house of every person who had access to the house, or for whom physical evidence was found at the scene.

For instance, Stuart said, law enforcement found fingerprints of Alberta's former lawyer in the house.

"Did you have any reason to believe Alberta's lawyer killed Rolland?"

"No," Weatherford said with a laugh. "He had no reason to do that." With that, the witness was relieved.

Alberta was also called to testify. She stood from her wheelchair and hobbled to the witness stand.

Stuart confronted her with her own answers from the deposition Bob Stillings conducted in October of 2007. Stillings asked her if she had been to the marital home since the divorce. Specifically, inside the home. Specifically, to the driveway of the home. Each time during that deposition, Alberta said she "didn't think so, no." Alberta confirmed those answers on the stand. When Stuart asked her if she agreed those answers were untruthful, she said they "weren't untruthful."

Stuart then pulled out the written discovery Alberta answered in the case, specifically her answers to the request for admissions. He placed them on the projector, and the responses hovered on the wall of the darkened courtroom. He pointed out where he asked her about who could account for her whereabouts on July 2 of 2007. July 3. July 4. "I plead the Fifth to each and every date," Stuart read back to her.

Stuart referenced the questions he asked about the gun. About the briefcase. About the last time she had been in the mansion. About her cell phone providers. Pointed out she refused to answer all of that on the grounds it might incriminate her.

"Yes, that is the advice I was given."

Evelyn took over. Started by asking about Alberta's various ailments. Alberta took a deep breath. "I have extreme heart failure. I have had two strokes. And I have been to a doctor—to a neuropsychiatrist who says I have dementia."

"Many strokes," Evelyn emphasized. Alberta said that was true. "These strokes have caused vascular dementia according to your doctors and that has caused significant memory issues."

All correct, Alberta said lucidly.

Evelyn asked if she remembered being married to Rolland, what the marriage was like. It was a happy marriage, Alberta recalled. "We traveled a lot overseas and we collected books together. We entertained a lot because he was a lawyer. And we both read continually. And we just did everything."

"You divorced him for being gay," Evelyn punctuated.

"That's right."

"But Rolland wanted you to continue living in the house, is that right?"

Alberta agreed.

"Why didn't you do that?"

"I couldn't stand to look at him. Homosexuality was wrong; immoral. Same for infidelity, which Rolland admitted to."

Evelyn continued. "Do you know where the Colt is, the Judge Burrell Colt?"

Stuart shot up. "Wait a minute. I object to this." Cordonnier asked for the jury to leave. The bailiffs shuffled them out into the hallway behind the courtroom as the lawyers waited for them to leave earshot.

"My objection is," Stuart said as he did his best to keep his voice down, "to answer that question would encourage testimony contrary to the Fifth Amendment that's been pled on this case. For example, a specific question I asked in deposition is, 'I'm going to ask you, ma'am, if you're aware today of the location of the handgun given to you by Judge Burrell,' to which the Fifth was invoked and the question wasn't answered. The same was true throughout this case, with—basically with interrogatory answers until I got a fourth supplemental interrogatory answers handed me this weekend. And that's too late to start to change it."

Evelyn argued the lateness for the supplemental answer was her fault.

"At the start of this trial on Monday," Stuart said incredulously. "This had been dealt with over and over again. Yet here we were."

Cordonnier rubbed his eyes. "This objection was sustained. It is sustained again. Just for the record, and I don't know that we have ever put this on the record, we had some considerable discussion in one or more of our pretrial conferences to the effect that perhaps the defendant would like to change her mind about pleading the Fifth on certain things—I don't know what those things are, but certain things. The court made this ruling: Number 1, I would not order her to testify as to any certain thing. So if she is asked a question on the witness stand by the plaintiff's attorney, then she is going to answer whatever she answers. I think the upshot of it is Mr. King was advised to be careful about what he asked her, and if he chose to present evidence to which she took the Fifth, the safer way to do it is by written document, which he has done. At the same time, the ruling that Ms. Comstock, the defendant's attorney, could not get up and ask her about those things to which she had taken the Fifth in the past. To do so would have allowed her to have used the Fifth Amendment not to protect her rights but to foil the plaintiff's effort at discovery. That's where we are now. She was asked about that exact thing in deposition, and she refused to answer. Filing a supplemental discovery response the first day of trial is too late, in this court's view. Now that is the end of that one. Are there other similar things we are going to confront?"

Evelyn affirmed she would be wrapping things up. With that, the jury was brought in and she continued questioning her client.

"Ms. Comstock, did you still love Rolland?"

"Yes."

"Did you wish anything bad for him?"

"No."

There were those in law enforcement who believed Stuart was such a good lawyer that he could elicit a confession of out Alberta on the stand. But, as Stuart would tell them, a *Perry Mason* moment was unlikely. As usual, Stuart was right.

Stuart had no more witnesses. The defense asked for a directed verdict arguing the plaintiff had not proven their case. Cordonnier denied this motion. The defense then called their witnesses. That included Carmel, who got to repeat her answers from the deposition taken earlier. Stuart was able to cross her and get her to admit to all her inconsistencies.

Later in the day, Evelyn called Sherry Rose to the stand to say the Comstock home was a happy one until Rolland was outed. Further, Sherry wanted to add, this lawsuit was ridiculous.

The last day of the trial was July 1, 2011. One day before the fourth anniversary of Rolland's murder. Faith was recalled to the stand by Mangan as part of the defense case. Faith had not slept the night before thinking about her testimony. She also dreaded that phone call at four in the morning. Plus, she would know by the end of the next day whether the stress and strain of this trial for the past three years would be worth it.

Evelyn went through all the perceived sins of Faith's administration of Rolland's trust.

She asked Faith about checks referencing exhibit numbers that were not on the copies Faith had in front of her. Most of Faith's time on the stand involved arguments over what checks were being asked about. Evelyn acted as though Faith's confusion was evasive. Stuart had to interject frequently simply because questions devolved into confusion over what was being presented to the witness.

That direct examination of Faith took most of the morning. Stuart knew it looked bad but also knew it was smoke and mirrors. Trust funds were placed in her business account, it was true, but immediately transferred into the trust account. She didn't use any of that money. Moreover, Faith took the money she "loaned herself," as Evelyn put it, and simply deducted that from what she was entitled as a beneficiary. In the end, no beneficiary was shorted a penny they were owed from Rolland's trust.

The whole adventure into Faith's handling of the trust was to assassinate her character, to let the jury know she was only interested in money. Faith felt sick. It seemed beyond the pale she would have to account for her actions as to anything involving the trust when this was strictly about the murder of her father. How did the fact she made shortcuts with a bank account have anything to do with whether her mother was a killer?

Faith was excused. The defense rested. Cordonnier asked if Stuart was ready for closing argument. He was, and he knew this was where he had to convince his audience.

Stuart walked to the lectern. He looked every jury in the eye one last time and thanked them for being there for his client. "This is an important matter for Faith, and she wanted me to pass onto you how much she appreciates your service."

He reminded the jury this was not a criminal case. That he was not a prosecutor. That his burden was to prove Alberta was liable for Rolland's death by "around 51 percent." Stuart also prewarned the jury that the defense would remind them Alberta absolutely had the constitutional right to not to speak to anything that might incriminate her. "But we have the absolute right to instruct you to take that into consideration. The defense, in this case, cannot ask you to ignore the fact she asserted this right."

Stuart repeated what he told them a few days before what this case would be about: "hate, revenge, and money." He also reminded them he would show the motive in this case. "Putting her best foot forward to present her attitude, Alberta testified she simply could not stand to look at him. That she hated him."

The defense tried to argue there was no financial incentive for Alberta to kill Rolland, Stuart reiterated. The only people who saw to benefit as recipients of the trust included Becky and Faith, people the Greene County Sheriff's Office had not looked at as suspects.

Nonsense, Stuart said. "Twenty-four hours before Rolland was dead this property is not listed anymore. She's envisioning this property not selling, a partition sale would be the house sold really cheap, Bob Stillings buying it, and selling it back to Rolland. That's what she told Ken Weatherford she thought was going to happen. She's not getting paid, she's going to have to write a big check to her lawyer. In her mind, Bob Stillings and Rolland were conspiring to cheat her out of this house or her share. That's the frame of mind she had on the second of July, and I believe that's the frame of mind that sent her to Springfield that day."

He reiterated the different stories about the black bag, the gun, the stories Alberta and Carmel could not keep straight. "I mean, the testimony has been Alberta had this gun with her by her nightstand every day, you know, took it with her when she went anywhere. But then it's gone for two or three months and nobody can find it. Then, all of a sudden, one day she's in a frantic rush to go to the Firing Line after hours and has to leave there with a gun. To believe Alberta and Carmel, she bought the gun and went back home to Oklahoma and went to bed. No. She wanted to replace the gun she wasn't going to have at the end of the day."

Stuart had to get to the part that always worried him: when he asked for money. Jurors might be sympathetic to your case but then would be repelled by being asked to put a dollar sign on it.

"I'm not going to provide a number to you. I leave it to you to determine what the loss of a father is worth. It's a hard thing to do. But I'm also asking in this case for aggravated circumstances damages, punitive damages or the akin to those, the wrongful death equivalent of punitive damages. The damages necessary to punish. It's a tough concept, but I am going to suggest a number, and here's why. After Rolland was killed, Alberta Comstock took $250,000. And it seems wrong to me, and I hope it seems wrong to you, for her to kill her ex-husband and then take more money in the divorce decree."

Stuart put the settlement decree on his projector and went through the points of how much money Alberta would receive from the sale of the house after Rolland died.

"I show you the settlement agreement that resolved this—all issues in April of 2008, nearly a year after Rolland was dead, and she received payment of $250,000, and that ought to come—that's the punitive damage award I'm asking you for."

Who cares if Shane and Evelyn say this was only about money? Stuart concluded. Alberta killed him, and she should not be allowed to profit from it.

"But ultimately what this case is about, and I told you this Tuesday morning and I'm telling you again, Faith Stocker is not willing to hope that somebody else tries to gain some justice for her father. She's not willing to hope that at some point the Greene County Sheriff's Office and the Greene County prosecutor's office will accomplish that. She's seeking justice for her father, and this is the only way—only legal way—she has of doing that. And I ask you give justice to her. Thank you."

Stuart sat and Cantin entered. "Folks, I'll apologize out of the gate. It's hard for me to listen to Mr. King make those arguments, because I believe entirely in Alberta's innocence. She did not shoot and kill Rolland Comstock on July 2 of 2007. She didn't do it. There's no evidence of it, that we'll get to in a minute; there's no motive of it, that we'll get to in a minute; and it did not happen. That is what this case is about. She's never once been arrested, she's never once been charged. Mr. King's best evidence is Alberta took the Fifth Amendment."

Shane noted even Becky and Faith said the marriage was a happy one until the end, until Alberta found out Rolland "was a homosexual" and she couldn't stand to look at him. She couldn't oblige his wish to stay in the house. The divorce brought up strong emotions, as all divorces do.

Shane pointed out Alberta's initial cooperation. The fact she didn't appear nervous or apprehensive when interviewed by law enforcement the night Rolland was found. Maybe the reason she took the Fifth was because she suffered strokes and was diagnosed with dementia, and she didn't want to unknowingly lie.

The sheriff's department failed to interview nearly twenty people—from Shane's estimation—about what they knew. Why didn't they take the mats out of Alberta's truck to see if there were any remnants of gunpowder or dirt from the marital house?

Wouldn't a "reasonable" explanation that the *Lord of the Flies* book was on the kitchen table—where it absolutely should not have been—was because it had been in the bag Alberta left for Rolland as it contained some of his books? After all, the book was not far away from where the bag was found. Or that maybe Rolland was planning on selling it and left it out.

Shane wondered aloud about Mike Friend's testimony that Alberta could barely shoot a gun.

He talked about how the Greene County Sheriff's Office didn't even try to find video surveillance of the gas station where Alberta allegedly stopped until months after the murder, and by then the tapes were already erased.

He also brought up someone the sheriff's department should have looked at more closely. "If anybody on that list of persons of interest committed a crime, holy cow, let's look at Michael. And I hate to do this to a family member, but it is the way it is. Michael has a long history of drug use. Michael was violent to family members in the past while under the effects of methamphetamine, the scourge of Southwest Missouri. We all know it. We all read about it. We know what it does to people. We've seen the pictures of the people who use methamphetamine. We've heard stories of how they act and the ridiculous things they do. We know Michael was asking his dad for money in the weeks leading up to his death. We know there was a good amount of cash Rolland kept in a drawer in his kitchen. We know when the investigators went back through with Becky Frakes on July 4, that cash was gone.

"We know Michael used to live in one of the rental houses, we know he was evicted by his father because he was ripping things off the house and selling them for drug money."

Shane paused. "I don't know. It's just credible another person committed this crime."

Cantin noted his belief that the only reason Michael wasn't brought as a defendant in this case was because "he had no money. Nothing to collect if he was found liable. Because this is nothing more than just a case about greed and money."

Shane ended by pointing out that it was "unfortunate" no one had been arrested for committing this crime.

Stuart reserved time to respond, and he pointed out what seemed obvious about Alberta's changing stories. "The defense of this case cannot explain away every changing version of stories regarding how the bag got there, where the gun is, so forth, by saying Alberta's got memory issues. First of all, there's not a shred of evidence that Alberta has any memory issue in 2007. Nobody said that. There's no doctor that said that, there's nobody that said that. There's no evidence of that. And second is, if Alberta has memory issues and somebody asked her a question and she can't remember, what you say is 'I don't remember.' You don't make up a completely false story. That's not evidence of a memory issue, that's evidence of a lie."

Then there was Michael, who Stuart had written the petition by leaving open the idea he might have conspired with Alberta to kill his father. "I was waiting for the defense to throw Michael Comstock under the bus on this because Michael has a drug problem. True. Is that evidence he killed his father? Becky said Michael asked for some money three or four times back in 2005. And he refused him. There's no evidence as to what Michael's reaction to that was: to anger, as to arguments, bad feelings. And there's not a shred of evidence Shane Cantin has pointed to or can point to that would indicate Michael Comstock was in the house of Rolland Comstock on the second of July of 2007. He's put nothing out there to tell you that. Michael Comstock has cooperated with law enforcement in this case. Michael Comstock hasn't refused to do so, Alberta Comstock has. Michael Comstock provided clothes, they were tested, tests were negative. There's not a shred of evidence that puts him in that house.

"There is evidence putting Alberta in the house. Fingerprints on documents, the documents themselves, an attaché bag that she told absolutely no credible story to explain. Information which became known to the public after Faith and Becky Frakes settled these other legal disputes.

"I mean because they're making a point of that. 'Well, you settled this and then you turn around and sue.'" Stuart noted the evidence of the briefcase, something that had no reason to be at the murder scene, was the reason this lawsuit was filed.

Stuart told the jury he had nothing to add other than to thank them again. He was done and he sat back down at the plaintiff's table. Stillings later wrote Stuart in an email that afternoon to say it was the most impressive argument he'd ever seen in his career.

Stuart was exhausted. Being "on" for a jury over an entire week would wear out even the most seasoned attorneys.

The jury left the courtroom a little after noon to convene. The alternate jurors were released; all of their time for nothing.

Stuart knew it would be more than an hour for them to come back. At the very least, they would want their last taxpayer-provided meal before making a decision. He urged Faith to get something to eat, but to come back to the courthouse as soon as she could. He would go to the office—he had given his lunch order to Joyce—but would be back right away. Stuart would need to be there with all the other attorneys to not only wait for the jury to come back with a decision but to answer any questions they had. More specifically, to agree or disagree with whatever the judge decided would be the answer to their questions or request for clarification.

Over the afternoon, the jury would ask for specific pieces of evidence referenced in the trial but not admitted into evidence. Nothing unusual; nothing that gave Stuart a sense of which direction they were leaning. As the deliberations went past 5:00 p.m., Stuart wondered if the court would make the jury stay into the night or simply have them come back. That Monday was a holiday—it was July 4 again—so they couldn't come back until Tuesday, and surely Cordonnier would have a full slate of other matters to deal with.

Stuart conferred with the other attorneys, and they asked how long Cordonnier intended to keep the jury there. "As long as they need" was his response.

TV journalists tweeted their dissatisfaction about the pace of deliberation between live spots from outside the courthouse. Newspaper reporters now knew any decision reached would be past their deadline and therefore not in tomorrow's paper, much to the chagrin of their editors.

The bailiff announced the jury had two questions. The lawyers assembled at their tables, and Cordonnier quickly signaled to his court reporter to get everything on the record.

"We are outside the hearing of the jury. It is 5:15 p.m., and the jury has sent two questions. They are these: If money is awarded to the plaintiff from the defendant under Instruction Number 7, who would receive the money, question mark. The second question: If money is awarded to the plaintiff from the defendant under Instruction Number 8, who would receive the money, question mark. The question appears to be signed by the jury foreman, Joseph Casey.

"The court proposes an answer to the question as follows: The court cannot answer your questions. You must be guided by the instructions given."

Was that response satisfactory to the parties? Cordonnier asked. It was, all agreed.

Stuart immediately looked over at Shane and Evelyn. He saw them shifting in their seats.

Faith leaned over to Stuart, who was deep in concentration. "That sounds like good news, doesn't it?"

Stuart didn't want to betray anything. "Could be."

At 5:27 p.m., it was announced by the bailiff that the jury reached a verdict. People stopped talking. The cameramen hustled back into the courtroom. Observers sat up straight. Everyone stirred except for Alberta, who barely moved the entire afternoon.

Stuart leaned into Faith as the jury walked in. "Whatever you do," he whispered, "don't show any emotion when the verdict is read. Just look forward. Good or bad." Stuart didn't like spectacle; it made the emotional process of a case worse than it already was. Faith's nerves were completely frayed after the hostile questioning from the morning. No matter what the jury did, she was unsure if she could utter a response.

The twelve jurors were seated and the foreman identified himself. "The bailiff has advised us that the jury has reached a verdict in this case," Cordonnier said. "Is that correct?"

"Yes, sir," the foreman said. Cordonnier asked him to hand the papers to the bailiff, who brought them to the judge. The judge read over the documents without emotion and then cleared his throat.

"Okay. The court has received the verdict, reviewed it, and it appears to be in proper form. It is signed by nine jurors. The court will read the verdict as follows:

"On the claim of plaintiff Faith Stocker for the wrongful death against defendant Alberta Comstock, we, the undersigned jurors, find in favor of plaintiff Faith Stocker. We, the undersigned jurors, assess the damages of Rolland Comstock's survivors as follows: For actual damages, none. For damages for aggravated circumstances, $125,000. The verdict appears to be signed by nine of twelve jurors."

Cordonnier asked the parties if they wanted to poll the jury, to see who signed onto the verdict and why. All said no. The jury was thanked for their time, they were discharged, and court was adjourned. It moved so fast no one had time to think about what just happened.

Faith grabbed Stuart out of his chair. "What did it mean? What happens now?"

Shane and Evelyn came over to shake hands with Stuart, as all good lawyers do when a case is hard fought and everyone involved is professional. Alberta sat in her wheelchair, silently. Evelyn moved out of the courtroom pushing her client. A reporter asked Alberta about her reaction. Evelyn put up her hand.

"Mrs. Comstock is very tired after a long trial. She will take no questions."

Faith felt like collapsing from elation. The system worked. The arguments and facts were made to twelve random people, and they agreed with her. She couldn't help but remember that tomorrow would be four years since she lost her dad.

Judge Cordonnier wished everyone a good weekend and disappeared. As Stuart talked to Faith about how to collect on the judgment or whether there would be an appeal, something struck him about what happened. Now that the jury and the judge were gone, it was something he couldn't fix. It wasn't his place to have fixed it, but he knew it would become an issue. Stuart realized too late that, despite the victory, bad news was coming.

# DAMAGES

Stuart didn't think much about the trial after it was over. He lived with the Rolland Comstock case for three years. He learned the intimate details of the death and the investigation over the past several months. It was all he had done the past week. It was so late in the afternoon on Friday when the jury left that Stuart simply went to Walmart to pick up his son Zach and cooked him dinner. He would have a few drinks, go to sleep, and pick up his two younger kids—Gracie and Reagan—from their mother's the next day.

It was hard to keep what happened out of his mind. The case was on the front page of the local paper on Sunday. Reporters called his cell phone over the weekend. It was a big win. An unlikely win. Lawyers were shocked. Everyone knew Stuart was good, but this was noteworthy.

As Stuart helmed his boat on Saturday and Sunday, his mind would drift to whatever appeals the defense could mount. He tried to think of egregious objectives that hadn't gone Evelyn or Shane's way. There weren't any. Overturning a case by jury trial was very tough. But he knew the one issue that was hanging out there. Shane and Evelyn were too good not to notice.

On Tuesday, after the long holiday weekend, Stuart returned to the office after an early-morning hearing on another case. Becky—who could not be at the trial at the end of Friday—gave him a hug. There were lots of stories told about the trial, and the break room glowed from the victory. Craig Hosmer came in at 9:30 a.m., always scoffing if anyone was still chatting and not at their desk when he got to the office. Which was everyone, soaking it in as the King held court. Stuart excused himself and followed Craig to his sun-drenched corner office.

Craig wanted to talk about the big win. But it was the verdict that was on Stuart's mind.

It is settled law in Missouri that punitive damages cannot be awarded if there are no actual damages. The idea being a party should not be punished for something that didn't—in theory—cause any real harm. Real harm was measured by the actual damages.

An additur was an option. That's a procedural request to add money to a jury verdict. If the court didn't want to try the case again, then asking for an additur was appropriate.

Cordonnier could amend the punitive damages to $124,999 and then move one dollar over to actual damages and there would be no change in what was decided at all. But additurs were often awarded in extreme situations, and Judge Cordonnier wasn't exactly a risky jurist. He was conservative and liked to do things that weren't likely to get overturned on appeal. Moreover, the same statute that said punitive damages couldn't be awarded unless actual damages were also awarded, also said punitive damages could not be awarded if actual damages "were nominal." Which wasn't defined in the law, but Stuart imagined one dollar would be considered nominal.

Stuart didn't want another trial; that was too risky. He might not get so lucky with his jury pool. Stuart knew it was judicial error to not correct the verdict, and that was a compelling argument to an appeals court. Although winning an appeal is an uphill battle. There must be some other way to fix this problem. But even Stuart was having trouble figuring that out.

Evelyn called Stuart and left him a message. Stuart called her back. He knew what she was going to say, and she indicated the jury could not award punitive damages but not actual damages. The law was clear.

Stuart didn't agree the law was so clear. Arguments were tossed around: Additur. New trial. Judicial error. He threw out every idea he had. This went back and forth for some time. But this was not a situation that was going to lead to a resolution without court involvement.

Stuart went to work on the judgment, as was the job of the victorious party. He emailed it to all of the other lawyers. There were little nitpicks here and there, but he got it filed the following Monday.

On the same day Stuart filed the judgment, Evelyn filed her motion to have the judgment tossed out. Stuart responded by saying she had the law wrong, was asking the court to do something "no Missouri court had ever done," and said her request would lead to an "absurd result."

The court wouldn't get it on the docket until mid-August. The judge signed the judgment, but it would not be final until all post-trial motions were heard, and then any party who wanted to appeal would have ten days to file their notice.

At the hearing, there was no one in the pews. No spectators. No press. No cameras. This was why lawyers often hated the media being involved with his cases. They always wanted to show the exciting parts. The crying. The yelling. But the real work of a lawyer? That was boring. Not worth sharing with an audience. Yet the boring stuff is where the rubber hit the road.

Cordonnier heard the arguments. Two weeks later, the court made its decision. Yes, the jury decided Alberta Comstock was liable in causing the death of Rolland Comstock. But they were wrong in how they allocated their award. They did not have the ability, under the law, to award punitive damages and not actual damages. The damage portion of the judgment would be vacated, but the liability would remain in place.

Stuart read the order. It didn't solve the issue of whether he should have sent the jury back to deliberate further. He called Faith to tell her the news. While appellate practice never favored the appellant, this was an exception, and they might get an outcome where the panel of judges simply said the trial judge made a mistake, and to tell Cordonnier to modify the judgment without a trial.

Or perhaps that would not be the outcome. The appellate process wouldn't be much easier even if it meant no evidence would be heard. While a Notice of Appeal had been filed to give everyone time to consider how to proceed, the Notice simply said what the grounds of an appeal would entail. But the appellate process would be much more detailed than that. Ordering transcripts and copies of court records. A brief would be written. Alberta's lawyer or lawyers would file a responsive brief. Then, Stuart would reply to the response. More than likely, there would be an oral argument. It could take more than a year, and that's if it stopped at the Court of Appeals. The losing side would always have a chance to take things to the Missouri Supreme Court. After all of that, there was a chance the trial would have to be redone. The process would start over again and could take more years out of everyone's life not to mention take more expenses.

A decision was made to not proceed.

Stuart went back into the bullpen of the law firm and sat down in Becky's office. Told her what transpired. They talked about the case from time to time when Becky was able to catch him. She didn't really understand what was going on with all the technicalities. That wasn't her department.

But she understood Alberta wouldn't have to pay a dime for what she did. "I think that stinks," she confessed. "I wish they would just arrest her. I don't pretend to know about what they can and cannot prove, but something needs to happen."

Stuart nodded. He said just keep calling Detective Weatherford. Keep calling the television stations and newspaper reporters. Tell them to keep the heat on the sheriff's department.

"Rolland deserves justice," Stuart told her. She smiled as a tear started to break down her cheek. Stuart nodded without saying another word. He knew anything else he said would be too emotional.

Becky again sat down and looked at the pile of paperwork accumulating on her desk that had assorted deadlines and demand. She thought about what Stuart said about "justice." Alberta wouldn't be paying any money and now she was making peace with the fact that the criminal case would remain cold. Maybe forever. But Stuart said something that made Becky realize there was some finality. While the monetary judgment was vacated, the judgment of liability had not. A jury of Alberta Comstock's peers said she was responsible for Rolland's death. The evidence was presented, the arguments were made, and this was the conclusion they reached. It wasn't murder: That's a criminal term and Becky had been researching the difference. There was peace and assurance to their decision, Becky thought.

Her mentor and friend was still gone. But Stuart had done something no one else could, or had, done. He helped bring justice to Rolland's death. She wondered how she could ever show her appreciation for all he did for her old boss.

She would still have memories of the quirky lawyer who taught her everything she needed to know in her career. About the books. Even the bad times seemed nostalgic. But she would take Stuart's advice and continue talking to the local media, and anyone who would listen about Rolland's case, in hopes something would thaw the investigation. Even after Alberta passed away in 2013, Becky would be on the news whenever the anniversary of the death neared and plead with anyone to continue looking for clues and suspects.

Becky never considered herself much of a crusader. But that's the plan God put in place for her, she was certain.

At that precise moment, work needed to be done and she needed something to take her mind off of things. But she would never forget.

Stuart was busy, too. He went back to his desk and plopped into his leather chair. The Comstock matter was done. As he lit up a cigarette, he had to sit back and think about everything that happened with the Comstock case. He had thrown everything he had at the litigation and fought back a ferocious defense. Whether the sheriff's department made mistakes or prejudged Rolland, they still had investigators who spent years trying to find evidence that would lead to a conviction. Stuart hadn't worked with Myers all that much but found him very capable. He knew from reputation that the prosecuting attorney won some difficult murder trials.

Even with all that, the best lawyers in the city and the forces of the Greene County Sheriff's Office were simply outfoxed by a seventy-year-old woman with dementia. An angry, forsaken ex-wife who literally got away with murder.

He stared at the ceiling as he exhaled. It was time to get back to work.

# ACKNOWLEDGMENTS

I spent years telling the story of Rolland Comstock to anyone who would listen. They would be delighted by the details of his life: the book collection, Butch the Bulldog, the wolves. People would also be fascinated by the murder trial as well as the ups and downs of the investigation. "This would make a great book," many people would say. I agreed with them but wondered who would do it. At one point, I decided it would be me. I want to start by thanking everyone who gave me the inspiration to take on this project.

A project that required a lot of phone calls and visits to libraries and courthouses. While I didn't catch the name of everyone who helped me, I do want to thank the dedicated public servants at the University of Missouri–Kansas City archives, the Greene County Circuit Clerk's office, the Springfield–Greene County public libraries, and the Missouri Historical Society. A special shout-out to Diane Woods, the court reporter who captured everything in the *Stocker v. Comstock* trial and put it together in a nice, neat transcript.

I also want to thank Faith Stocker and Becky Frakes for not only sitting down with me for interviews but also answering every pesky question I had as I wrote this book. Even more, they gave me access to Rolland's personal scrapbooks and files. There was no way this book could exist without getting a glimpse of everything Rolland saved about his life and times.

Becky and Faith weren't the only ones to sit down with me on the record. I also want to thank Stuart King, Bob Stillings, and Stephen Comstock for taking the time to recount what they remembered about Rolland as well as their experience during the criminal investigation and civil litigation. There were many others who would talk to me off the record who provided a great deal of information for this book, and I appreciate their thoughts and insights as well.

There were lots of friends and family who read through the manuscript at various points to offer suggestions and critiques. Becky did this more than anyone else. She not only read it for accuracy but also made suggestions for making it better. I also want to thank Caroline Leavitt for her review and edits.

I want to thank Tom Cull of Cull & Co. Ltd. for taking a chance in representing a novice author. In that same vein, I want to thank all the professionals at Post Hill Press for shepherding me and this book through the publishing process.

Acknowledgments would be incomplete without thanking my parents and teachers for encouraging my writing over the years as well as pushing me to challenge myself.

Finally, I cannot thank my wife, Claire, enough for enduring me and encouraging me to make this book a priority. Everyone would be lucky to have a partner like her.

# ABOUT THE AUTHOR

Photo Credit: Kim Wade

James Owen left the family farm to become a lawyer to some success. In fact, that is where he became involved with the intriguing circumstances that make up *The Wicked Among Us*. He was appointed a judge and, after that, worked in state government for a few years. James now runs the nonprofit Renew Missouri focused on clean energy advocacy. James lives in Columbia, Missouri with his wife, Claire, and their two kids, Cecile and Miles, along with an unruly dog named Rosie.